Africa by Road

Sarah Ebben '15

Africa by Road

2nd edition

Bob Swain and Paula Snyder

Bradt Publications, UK
The Globe Pequot Press Inc, USA

First published in 1991 by Bradt Publications.
This edition published in 1995 by Bradt Publications,
41 Nortoft Road, Chalfont St Peter, Bucks SL9 0LA, England.
Published in the USA by The Globe Pequot Press Inc, 6 Business Park Road,
PO Box 833, Old Saybrook, Connecticut 06475-0833.

British Library Cataloguing in Publication Data
A catalogue record for this book is available from the British Library
ISBN 1 898323 29 1

Library of Congress Cataloging-in-Publication Data
Swain, Bob
        Africa by road / Bob Swain and Paula Snyder. — 2nd ed.
        p. cm. — (Bradt guides)
        Includes bibliographical references and index.
        ISBN 1-56440-946-5
        1. Africa—Guidebooks. I. Snyder, Paula, 1954- . II. Title. III. Series.
        DT2.S9   1995
        916.04'329—dc20   95-39189
                                                            CIP

Cover photographs *Front:* White Desert, Egypt (Chris Barton)
Back: Zimbabwe (Jochen Hübene)
Photographs Hilary Bradt, Peter Cook, Nick Cotton, Nicky Dunnington-Jefferson,
Edward Paice, Geoffrey Roy, and Bob Swain
Illustrations Sarah Elder
Maps *Inside covers:* Steve Munns   *Others:* Patti Taylor

Typeset from the authors' disc by Patti Taylor, London NW10 1JR
Printed and bound in Great Britain by The Guernsey Press Co Ltd

ACKNOWLEDGEMENTS

Thanks are due to everyone who contributed to this book including the travellers who wrote with tips from their own journeys through Africa, all the embassies, tourist boards and truck companies who supplied us with information and everyone who helped with the first edition of this book (titled *Through Africa — the overlanders' guide*).

Special thanks to Philip Briggs, H Churchill, Adrian Deneys, Brendan Martin and Ian Ransom of Encounter Overland, Luc Lebeau, Christian and Gilly Lee, Joe Hanlon, Stuart Marlow, Edward Paice, Jocelyn Phillips, Jason Polley, Anthony Ream, Bernd Tesch, Val and Gavin Thomson and Wally Wilde.

Sarah Elder '95

CONTENTS

INTRODUCTION

Africa is an adventure. Africa is a thousand adventures. It is quite simply the most wonderful place in the world to travel, knowing you are still sure to discover something new.

But the main thing that makes Africa such an experience for the traveller is the difficulty of communications in much of the interior. Atrocious roads mean that the continent is not inundated with tourists (apart from in the more accessible areas).

Yet the poverty of land communications is part of the tragedy of Africa today, acting as a barrier to the development of economic independence from the West. But in the meantime, exploring the continent's tracks and roads is one of the great challenges open to modern travellers. Let us hope the experience is used by those who visit to learn and use constructively, rather than just to take and destroy.

Of course, it is perfectly possible to discover parts of Africa with a pack on your back, taking local transport from town to town — railways, buses, freight trucks, boats, canoes. But a desire to go just where you want to, and face the challenge of personally crossing desert and jungle, means an increasing number of people are now exploring Africa on their own set of wheels — everything from four-wheel drive vehicles to bicycles.

If you like the idea of exploring Africa, one of the first decisions you have to make will be your mode of transport. Your choice will be affected by many factors — your budget, the areas you want to visit and, above all, the kind of experience you are looking for.

As well as detailed information for travellers with their own vehicle — four-wheel drive, two-wheel drive, motorbike and bicycle — we have also included information on organised overland tour companies. The book has been written so that it will be a valuable source of information for tour passengers as well as independent travellers. It is very much a book to dip in and out of rather than just to read straight through.

We have aimed throughout to provide guiding principles rather than to lay down absolute 'facts'. Everything changes rapidly in Africa — currencies can be devalued by a factor of 10 overnight, surfaced roads can be washed away in flash floods and horrific tracks can be rebuilt into smooth highways. Similarly, regional conflicts come and go and will affect any travel plans in the continent.

So you should bear in mind that any specific information given here may change, although everything we have included is as up to date as possible. We have also added a variety of narrative sections to give some sense of what real journeys can be all about — the bad as well as the good. The spirit of travel in Africa is less likely to change than the specifics.

You will undoubtedly discover changes when you are in Africa. One of the most wonderful things about travelling in the place is its sheer unpredictability — it will offer a new trip every time. Our main hope is that this book will tell you you're not utterly crazy to be thinking of a trans-African trip. It is quite feasible to plan your own expedition — and guaranteed to be a lot of fun.

INTRODUCTION TO THE SECOND EDITION

Much has changed for overland travellers in Africa since this book was first published. Political unrest and violence against foreigners in Algeria, as well as the Touareg rebellion further south, have meant that the classic trans-Saharan route through Tamanrasset has been abandoned by all but the occasional convoy. For the time being Rwanda, Burundi, Sierra Leone and Liberia remain effectively off limits.

As if to compensate, political change elsewhere has opened up routes that for many years have been completely off limits. A fragile peace between Morocco and the Polisario Front in Western Sahara means it is now possible to cross into Mauritania. Further east the end of hostilities between Eritrea and Ethiopia has opened up another north-south route.

One of the biggest changes has come from the birth of democracy in South Africa. More and more overlanders — both independents and organised tours — are now heading from south to north. It is clear that South Africans are relishing their new freedom to travel in the rest of Africa from the tour companies and overland suppliers that are springing up everywhere. Although for the moment Angola remains closed to overland travel, Mozambique has opened up and offers wonderful new opportunities for travellers in southern Africa.

This second edition of *Through Africa - the overlanders' guide* (former title) reflects these changes with new sections on route planning, revised information on where to stay and what to see in individual countries, and updates of the sections to help you plan your trip. We have also expanded and revised the section on organised truck tours.

The huge number of revisions we have made because of dramatic changes in available routes is a strong reminder of how vital it is to check your information constantly, revising your plans on the road if need be. War zones, potholes, bridges down, soft sand and mudslides — nothing is certain in Africa. But then it's the fact that you can't take anything for granted, that you never really know for sure what's ahead of you, that makes overlanding in Africa so special.

We hope you enjoy your trip — from the fun of planning where to go, to the thrill of actually getting there. Don't forget to keep a diary when you go. It will be a vivid reminder of some of the best times of your life. And we would be delighted to share your experiences in future editions of this book. If you can update our information, or if you would like to contribute an interesting story from your own trip, please write to:

Africa by Road
Bradt Publications
41 Nortoft Road
Chalfont St Peter
Bucks SL9 0LA
England

Part One

Chapter One

First steps

Having made the decision to go, you will want to go *now*. Nothing else really seems to matter. But rushing off without careful planning is the biggest mistake you can make. And you must allow plenty of time. A well-spent period of preparation means you will be more likely to avoid potential disasters later.

If that does not sound like your kind of trip, then an organised expedition may be the answer to your prayers. The tour companies will do most of the planning for you, leaving you just to tie up your affairs back home, find the price of your ticket and set off to enjoy yourself — although you should still be prepared for your share of hard work on the road. See Chapter Three for details.

Everyone else, however, will be in for a great deal of spade work — on a sliding scale depending on what kind of wheels you intend to take. If you take your own vehicle you will be in for the works; if you are brave enough to cycle you will avoid much of the paperwork and mechanical preparation. Motorbikes probably fall somewhere between the two.

If you are taking your own vehicle we would recommend a planning period of about a year. You should have bought your vehicle at the very least six months before you leave. You could cut down on this timescale if you had no other commitments to worry you — like a job! Unfortunately, most of us cannot afford such a luxury. It may sound like a long time, but once you get started you will be amazed at just how much preparation is necessary and how many details you had never considered. But don't be put off. Planning the trip is great fun and can be an extremely exciting time in its own right.

All the reputable tour companies have a wealth of experience behind them. Even with that background they are not going to set off on a trip with a battered old truck bought the week before. For their own sake, they must be sure it has a fighting chance of making it through. The same applies to your own vehicle. You must allow enough time to give it a thorough mechanical check, customise it to your requirements, test it, get to know it and make any necessary changes.

Make sure you also use this period to soak up as much information as you can about Africa, its culture and people (see Chapter Ten). It will not only make your trip much more enjoyable, it will also make your planning stage feel a lot closer to your ultimate destination.

And the more you know and respect the places you plan to visit, the less likely you are to disrupt local culture by being there to experience it. Travelling carries responsibilities as well as bringing pleasure: not encouraging dependence on travellers by casually handing out gifts; respecting religious sites and artifacts; burning your rubbish wherever possible; and respecting people's dignity, particularly when taking photographs.

BUDGETING

Like it or not, money and the lack of it are likely to dominate most plans for travel in Africa. The budget you have available will determine what kind of trip you can take.

Tour buses are one of the cheapest options — but you may want more independence than they can offer. Travelling under your own steam can be relatively economic if you cycle or take a motorbike. But the costs mount once you take a vehicle. This is where the range of options really starts to open up — the sky is most definitely the limit at the top end of the scale.

But even if your aims are relatively modest, you will undoubtedly be shocked as the costs add up — most of them before you even set off. You should take all these costs into account from the start for a realistic assessment of what you can afford to do and when you can afford to do it.

Realistically you will need to budget for a total of as much as £12,000 plus £5,000 a head for a one year trip in your own four-wheel drive vehicle. Even with a bicycle the total initial investment will be over £1,000 each with the same kind of costs while away. It is possible to do things for quite a bit less — but the less you invest, the tougher your trip is likely to be. At the other extreme, you could buy a fully converted six-wheel drive Pinzgauer and be kissing goodbye to something like £60,000 before you even start.

If it all sounds ridiculously expensive, then you are beginning to get the right idea. Your priority now is to look in detail at some of the costs involved in your trip. Decide what is essential, what is merely desirable and what is just plain luxury. Then think again about how you aim to tackle the whole thing on the basis of how much money you are going to be able to raise. Only after all this can you start the main business of planning your trip.

One word of warning on raising finance. You may be thinking that sponsorship will fall into your lap as soon as you announce to the world that you are off to explore Africa. Be under no illusions; sponsorship is a tough nut to crack. Companies have been approached so many times in the past that they will want you to demonstrate exactly how they are going to get a return on their investment. Local firms are more likely to be sympathetic than nationally known names — but they are also unlikely to have as much to offer. You must ask yourself whether the massive investment of time you will need to find any sort of sponsorship is worth it.

The following are some of the major costs you will have to meet. The figures quoted are a rough guide to the extremes you will come across. Ideally, you should look at your own requirements under each of the headings and check out what these are likely to cost.

The vehicle

For most this will be the biggest single expense and the most important decision to be made. Obviously you have to budget according to what you can afford. But it really is worth investing in the most reliable and comfortable vehicle possible. It will be the centre of your life for the duration of your trip — your home, transport and lifeline. Buying wisely could well make the difference between heaven and hell on wheels.

There has been a huge increase in the popularity of four-wheel drive vehicles over the past few years. Most of these could handle a trans-African journey although some are designed more for appearance than performance. It is particularly important to remember that it will be impossible for you to buy spare parts in Africa for many of these more recent models. Land Rovers and Toyotas are the best in this respect.

The most popular vehicle for making a trans-African journey remains the Land Rover — with good reason. It is versatile, rugged, simply built and known throughout the continent. It is possible to pick up an old one for a few hundred pounds. But unless you are an expert Land Rover mechanic, the odds against a successful trip in such a vehicle are stacked heavily against you. On the other hand, a fully converted new model is going to set you back well over £20,000. If you are going to buy new and are planning to be out of the country for a long time, you should look at buying tax-free for export. You have to make sure the vehicle leaves the country within six months of purchase and will have to pay a portion of the tax if you bring it back within the first three years.

It is worth bearing in mind that the savings made by buying an old second-hand vehicle may not be as great as you imagine. Higher running costs, through increased fuel consumption and more mechanical failures, mean it can end up proving just as expensive as buying new. Look carefully at factors such as running costs and depreciation of resale value when making your final decision. If the difference is not going to be that great, the additional comfort and reliability of a new vehicle are sure to be worth the extra.

A good compromise between the two could be an old vehicle with a reconditioned engine, which you could probably pick up for around £5,000. The price of a good second-hand Land Rover (without reconditioned engine) that you are likely to be able to trust ranges from around £2,000 to £5,000. All of the contributors to this book who travelled in second-hand Land Rovers, bought vehicles within this range.

A motorbike is obviously a lot cheaper — but will only be able to carry one person. You will need to budget between £1,000 and £2,500. A bicycle is only a little cheaper — in order to get the quality you need to stand up to African conditions you will probably need to spend up to £1,000. The big savings with the two-wheel options come on radically reduced costs for preparation, equipment, paperwork and fuel.

Vehicle preparation

Depending on the level of reliability and comfort you want or need, the extra costs can range from a few hundred pounds for extra fuel tanks and minor modifications through to many thousands for a full professional conversion job. The choice very much depends on your circumstances. But you should bear in mind that the more you do yourself, the cheaper it will be and the better you will get to know your own vehicle.

Equipment

It is amazing how all of those 'essential' bits and pieces can mount up. Any major items, such as a roof-top tent, will need to be budgeted separately. But if you are starting from scratch, you will need to put aside at least £1,000 to cover the rest. Once again, the total will be less for travellers on two wheels — if only because you cannot carry anything like the same amount.

Spares and tools

If you already have a good set of tools, fine. If not then you are going to have to invest in some. If this is the case, then you are probably not a mechanic anyway, so it will be best to stick to the basics. Nevertheless, you will need to allow up to £250 to cover them.

As far as spare parts are concerned, they can prove an excellent investment. Spares are universally difficult to come by in Africa and can be very expensive. You should therefore carry as many as you can — being careful not to overload your vehicle as a result. However, carrying the right kind of spares can be a good investment. You can often swap lighter items like gaskets for things you really need — like springs. It is also sometimes possible to sell unused spares at the end of the trip for a reasonable price (don't expect to make a fortune — but it can be worthwhile).

Health

Not something to skimp on. Putting together a comprehensive medical kit could cost £200-250. A full set of vaccinations plus malaria tablets for your trip could cost well over £100 if you get your jabs at one of the specialist clinics. You can save a lot by getting as many vaccinations as possible from your GP. It's always best to check out what's available on the NHS before you start. As far as health insurance is concerned, you obviously get what you pay for. But at the very least you will be looking at several hundred pounds each.

Documentation — before you leave

This is a major expense — and one that comes as a big shock to most. Top of the list for those with any form of motorised transport comes the *Carnet de Passage* (see paperwork section later in this chapter for details). If you are unable to lodge a bond equivalent to several times the value of the vehicle, you will have to take out a non-refundable insurance policy to cover you against default. In addition you will have to pay a deposit of £250 to the issuing authority and then pay for the carnet itself (£57.50 for 10 pages or £67.50 for 25 in 1995). In many cases, you won't get a great deal of change out of £1,000 for a reasonable four-wheel drive vehicle, although you may be able to cut this back with a more modest valuation.

Germany is a particularly good country to find second-hand vehicles at a reasonable price. With a greater tradition for adventurous travel than most parts of Europe, there is also a lot more help available for those planning a trip. The price of a week or so spent in Germany could well turn out to be a cost-effective step in your early planning stages.

Insurance policy costs will depend on what you feel you need. Some form of personal insurance is essential — although on shorter trips it may be possible to use elements of your household policy. Insurance from organisations and clubs tends to be cheaper. For example, one of the best buys is from the Cyclists' Touring Club — it might be worth joining just to get their insurance, even if you plan to use some other form of transport.

Comprehensive vehicle insurance is not available for Africa. Insurance for loss and damage only is available through Lloyds but is very expensive. Other documents such as an international driving licence and international registration documents are low-cost items.

Documentation — on the road

You will not be able to get many of the visas you need before leaving home as most are only valid for a relatively short period. This means regular stops in capital cities to stock up on your next batch. Visas need to be included in your budget — costing anything from £2 to £60 each. Their cost may even affect your route. For example, several people we know decided to cut out proposed routes through Gabon and Congo when they realised the visas were at the top end of the scale.

You cannot buy third party vehicle insurance to cover Africa before you set off, but it is compulsory practically everywhere. Although it is policed more actively in some countries than others, it is a good idea to be covered wherever you go. If you have an accident, the alternative could be a hefty bill which will wipe out your trip completely. Because cover is typically short-term, it will be relatively expensive — about £200 should cover a comprehensive African trip for a year, less if you miss out West Africa. (See page 16 for details of policies available.)

Certain extra charges are also sometimes levied on foreign vehicles such as road tax when you take a vehicle across the border into Tanzania. Customs will often make a small charge at borders (mostly official, some not so official). All in all, you will probably find that these 'extras' could mount up to as much as £200, though you can cut back on some of this if you have enough patience. Overtime charges for working at lunchtime or after hours are one of the most common 'extras' — though you will often not be told about this until after the work has been done.

Vehicle repairs

An unpredictable extra, this is obviously more likely to hit you with an older vehicle. If you take plenty of spares and are a reasonable mechanic, repairs need not pose a major financial burden. But if you have to rely on local parts and local labour, the total could easily mount up.

Shipping

If you are planning to ship your vehicle back at the end of the trip (or indeed start your journey by shipping one out), this can be another major expense. The lowest prices from Mombasa, Dar es Salaam or Cape Town back to Europe are all over US$1,000 for a container. But beware of all the hidden extras, these can add as much as another 50%. South African ports, for example, charge an extra US$450-$500 per container. You will be encouraged to use a shipping agent — but this does add considerably to the cost. You will always be able to deal directly with the shipping line if you persevere — the agents are often more trouble than they are worth anyway. You will also be hit by further handling charges when it comes to collecting your vehicle at the other end.

Of course, shipping a bike can be much cheaper — particularly if you share a container. It is even possible to hitch a lift by putting a bike inside a vehicle already being shipped. Air freight for motorbikes is also pretty reasonable. It is generally possible to take a bicycle as luggage on most air lines.

Remember that whatever you do at the end of the trip (unless you drive home) you will also need to find the price of the airfare to your final destination.

Personal expenses

After everything else on the list, you might justifiably wonder if you will have any money left to spend. In fact, food, accommodation and personal spending can be extremely low. US$10 a day each should easily be enough — even with the occasional extravagance in a Western-style hotel.

Selling a vehicle

On the plus side of the balance sheet, however, comes the possibility of selling your vehicle at the end of the trip. But beware — this is nowhere near as easy as it might sound. See page 17 for details.

Fuel

This is a major but incredibly variable cost. The volatility of the economies of many countries (and of the world oil market) means it can be difficult to predict the total cost with any accuracy. You can keep the amount you need to spend under control by using a newer vehicle with better fuel consumption, using lower-cost diesel rather than petrol, aiming to avoid some of the higher cost countries and stocking up with as much fuel as possible where it is cheap.

Past experience has shown that US$150 for each 1,000 miles covered should be enough in a second-hand Land Rover even if you take in some of the more expensive countries. A new diesel vehicle with good storage capacity should work out far cheaper. But remember — you cannot count on any of these prices remaining stable. Other travellers should be able to tell you the costs in countries you are about to enter, allowing you to judge when to stock up and when to run supplies down.

Fuel prices constantly change — sometimes it is possible to get a bargain, other times you might get ripped off. You should therefore never rely on any guide to fuel prices in Africa; this is why the reference sections for each country in this book only give a general indication of costs and some comparison with neighbouring countries. However, advance knowledge of the likely costs of fuel in the various countries allows you to stock up in cheaper areas. You will generally be able to get information on the latest prices from other travellers.

We stress that the specific figures below offer a rough guide only to prices of fuel in some African countries. This indication of price differentials should be of use for your initial planning and when other information is hard to come by.

Country	1994: Approximate price per litre in US$	
	Diesel	*Petrol*
Benin		30¢
Botswana	40¢	46¢
Burkina Faso		141¢
Cameroon	45¢	56¢
Central African Republic	58¢	71¢
Ethiopia		37¢
Kenya		56¢
Mali	49¢	76¢
Mauritania	38¢	73¢
Morocco	36¢	78¢
(in Western Sahara)	33¢	

Country	1994: Approximate price per litre in US$	
	Diesel	*Petrol*
Namibia	43¢	51¢
Niger	40¢	
Nigeria	6¢	8¢
Malawi	23-25¢	28¢
South Africa	41¢	56¢
Tanzania	45¢	50¢
Togo		39¢
Uganda	87¢	105¢
Zambia	67¢	
Zaïre	60¢[1]	102¢
Zimbabwe[2]	25¢	39¢

1 This is the average cost when buying a barrel, but fuel could cost a lot more depending on availability.
2 In January 1995 the government increased the tax on fuel taking the cost of a litre of diesel up to 30¢ a litre.

ROUTE PLANNING

Your route is bound to change while you are actually on the road and meet people with tips and advice born from recent experience. But you ought to have an overall plan of what you intend to achieve from an early stage, so you can sensibly plan the timing and costs of your trip.

Poring over maps in the months before you leave can be great fun. But beware — nothing is quite what it seems in Africa. That wonderful red highway cutting through the jungle may not even exist and many excellent roads are not even marked on the most recent of maps — even on the latest Michelin series (undoubtedly the best general maps of the continent).

It does no harm to start out by setting down a list of the places you would like to visit. But you will then have to confront the reality of Africa, fitting your desires in with the political and climatic factors that will do so much to shape your ultimate route.

When we wrote the first edition of this book, the western and Nile routes were both impassable because of war zones. Algeria was the only viable way through. As we write now the situation has reversed, with Algeria closed and Western Sahara and Ethiopia now open and offering two exciting new routes into Africa. The arrival of democracy in South Africa also means that there are now many more options for travellers wishing to start their journey there. It is worth keeping an eye on developments in the run-up to your departure. Specialist African business magazines can be excellent sources of information (although unfortunately there are not as many of these on the bookstalls as there used to be).

While you should certainly take note of advice, you need not necessarily treat this as the last word. The situation can change quite rapidly. Early in 1988, we were keen to drive through Guinea. What little information there was available suggested this would not be possible. But we went on to Guinea-Bissau anyway and checked things out with the Guinea Embassy there. No problems; visas were provided for an unforgettable drive through a wonderful country.

The other big consideration is climate. Africa is a vast continent with many different climatic influences and you will be hard put always to be in the right place at the right time. But planning can help, so here are a few basic guidelines. (More detailed climatic information is included in the country sections.)

● Try to cross the Sahara between October and March, when there is less danger from the heat.

● Avoid the West African rains. If you get caught in an area with poor roads and bridges you could be stuck for quite some time. The rains tend to start around May and last through the summer months. They start slightly later the further north you go.

● Central Africa has plenty of rain and mud to slow you down; this is where four-wheel drive really comes into its own. On the standard route across Zaïre, through Mobayi, Bumba, Kisangani and Beni, the easiest time to cross is in the dry season from about December to February. There is also a 'less wet' season in June/July, which is not too bad. In CAR rain barriers are set up during the rainy season to stop vehicles using and damaging the roads after heavy rains. These could cause you considerable delays.

● Hitting the wrong climate in eastern and southern areas is more likely to be a nuisance than a disaster, as the roads tend not to be so bad. Most rain in the east tends to fall between March and June and from October to December.

The incredible variations in roads and climate, combined with the unexpected, means it is a mistake to set yourself any kind of strict mileage quota. Just allow plenty of time — and then add some more! Many will, nonetheless, want some rough guidance on how long a trip is likely to take. Our experience shows an average of 80 miles a day over a complete trip can be achieved fairly comfortably.

Remember, you should always try to schedule in plenty of time for rest and actually to see the continent and meet the people. The more ground you try to cover in a short period of time, the less you will get out of your journey.

Sources of maps

The standard Michelin series of African maps (953, 954 and 955) are available in all good bookshops and provide as much information as most people find they need. But if you intend to explore certain areas in greater detail or have a particular interest in the physical geography of a region, there are a number of sources for more detailed and specialist maps. The best are:

Stanfords, 12-14 Longacre, London WC2; Tel: 0171 836 0189.
The Royal Geographical Society (maps are for study only, not for sale), 1 Kensington Gore, London SW7 2AR; Tel: 0171 589 5466.
The Travel Bookshop, 13 Blenheim Crescent, London WC2 9LP; Tel: 0171 229 5260.
The Traveller's Bookshop, 25 Cecil Court, London WC2N 4EZ; Tel: 0171 836 9132.
Institute Geographic National, 136bis Rue de Grennelle, Paris 75008.
Därr Expedition Service, Kirchheimer Strasse 2, D-8011 Heimstetten, Munich; Tel: 089 903 8015.
Map Link, 26E Mason St, Santa Barbara, CA 93101, USA. Tel: 805 965 4402.

PAPERWORK

Passports

Make sure you have plenty of spare pages. Most African countries are extremely fond of stamps and so can use up a lot of space. In Niger you will need to get your passport stamped at every town and when you enter and when you leave Niamey, as well as at the borders. Throughout the continent you will come across checkpoints where all your documents will be scrutinised and your passport stamped.

If you happen to have dual nationality you should take both passports as visas are often charged according to nationality. If you have two to choose from, you can always take the best deal!

Visas

Try to get as many as you can before leaving. But this is easier said than done, as most are only valid for a short period and so will be out of date before you arrive. Most visas are picked up as you go, from embassies in the capital cities or consulates in the larger towns. The consulates are often a better bet as the embassies can sometimes take several days to process an application — which can mean an enforced lengthy stay in an expensive city if you have several visas to get.

Generally speaking you should be able to pick up a visa in the capital of a neighbouring country — but do not count on it. For example, there is no Cameroon consulate in N'djamena, Chad — despite being only a few miles from the border. The major cities — like Dakar, Abidjan, Nairobi, Dar es Salaam and Harare — have embassies for most other African states.

Several months before you leave you should write to the embassies of countries you intend to visit, asking for information on the latest entry requirements (you can also pick up some interesting background material and tourist information from them). Some countries do not have an embassy everywhere, so you might have to write to the nearest embassy in Europe.

In the early stages of an overland trip, UK nationals have a fairly clear run on visas — they do not need one for Morocco, Tunisia, Niger or Togo. You can apply for a visa for Burkina Faso before you leave home as this is one of the few that is valid from the date you finally enter the country; this is such an eminently sensible system you may well ask yourself why other countries do not follow suit. There is no Malian Embassy in London, but you can get your visa in Brussels, Paris, Algiers or, easiest of all, from the consulate in Tamanrasset, Algeria.

A 'standard' trans-African trip to eastern or southern Africa will not require too many visas to be picked up en route — UK citizens only need them for Algeria, Mauritania, Nigeria, Cameroon, CAR and Zaïre on the most direct route. Once you stray from this route, however, you will find that more and more visas are required — particularly if you decide to tour West Africa, where all but French citizens will need a host of visas.

Specific visa requirements vary a great deal according to nationality. Most requirements for European travellers have now been harmonised — apart from special arrangements for UK travellers in most Commonwealth countries and similar arrangements for French nationals in former French colonies.

Other travellers, such as those from Australia, New Zealand and the USA will have different requirements — for example, unlike UK citizens all will need visas for Niger, and Australian and New Zealand citizens need one for Togo. If in doubt contact your own embassy for further information. Another good source in London is The Visa Shop, 1 Charing Cross Underground Arcade, London WC2 4NZ (Tel: 0171-379 0419).

Another visa bureau is Travcar, Tempo House, 15 Falcon Road, London SW11 (Tel: 0171 223 7662). This has been recommended as a good place to get Mauritanian visas — which can be very difficult to obtain. The charge is £15 plus courier fees to the Mauritanian embassy in Belgium.

Advice in books on which embassies in Africa are the best to use — the cheapest visas, the most pleasant staff, etc — tends to be even more useless than advice on the state of African roads; they are changing all the time. But whereas you take the roads as you find them, many of the bureaucratic hassles complained of by travellers are of their own making — so warnings you read may simply be the result of an inexperienced or unfriendly traveller hitting the wrong official on the wrong day. African officials are no more likely to cause you problems than any other officials — as long as you treat them with courtesy and accept that you are now living in African time and have left Western clockwork behind you.

Photographs

It is essential to take along a good stock of passport-size photographs of yourself. You will need to supply two, and sometimes more, every time you apply for a visa. They may also be needed for other documents you apply for, like photography permits.

Vaccination certificates

Yellow fever is the main vaccination certificate you are required to have for entry to most African countries. Others may require you to have certificates for cholera or meningitis if travelling from an infected area — Tanzania is one of the few remaining countries that insists on a cholera certificate for entry; this is a problem as the vaccine is not particularly effective and only lasts for six months. Check with your GP or one of the specialist health clinics for travellers (see page 21) before you go.

Letters of reference

These can come in very useful if you are up against big bureaucratic problems. A reference from a bank or other financial representative can be used to prove that you will not be stranded through lack of funds. A character reference may also be helpful if you are in a tight corner.

Insurance

Medical insurance is absolutely essential. Shop around for a good deal as prices and cover can vary substantially. Policies generally include some cover for personal belongings — but this is unlikely to include theft from a vehicle. The best deals on trips of up to 90 days are annual multi-trip policies. (See also section on *Documentation — before you leave* earlier in this chapter.)

Comprehensive vehicle insurance is less important. Lloyds offers a worldwide policy covering loss and damage — but it is extremely expensive. It is available from Campbell Irvine, 6 Bell Street, Reigate, Surrey RH2 7BG; Tel: 01737 223687 (a company experienced in meeting the insurance needs of overlanders).

Third party vehicle insurance is not available in advance for most areas — although you can extend UK insurance by green card as far as Morocco or Tunisia. After that it is both advisable and compulsory (policed to varying degrees) to buy third party insurance locally. Once you reach Niger or Mali it is possible to buy a single policy which will cover you for the whole of West Africa. Similarly, you can get another single policy covering Central CFA (see *Note* below) countries (Cameroon, Chad, CAR, Equatorial Guinea, Gabon and Congo). You will have to shop around for a short-term policy in Kenya. Third Party Insurance Certificates are available at the border in some countries, including Zimbabwe and Zambia.

Note: The CFA (Communauté Fiscalière de L'Afrique de L'Ouest) franc is the common currency of the West African Monetary Union.

Carnet

An essential and expensive document for everyone taking a vehicle (including motorbikes) across Africa. The carnet is a system that allows you temporarily to import a vehicle into a country without paying customs duty — in some cases this can be many times its actual value.

A carnet is a book containing details of yourself and your vehicle on each of three sections of every page. At entry into a country, the first section is stamped and removed and the third section (which you keep in the book) is also stamped. On leaving the country, the second section is stamped and removed and the third section is stamped again.

The idea for the customs is to collect two matching halves; if not they will claim customs duty through the issuing authority. The idea for you is to collect a complete set of entry and exit stamps — if you fail to get an exit stamp for a country where you got an entry stamp, you are likely to have a lot of explaining to do later on.

The existence of carnets is the main factor that makes selling a vehicle at the end of your journey far more difficult than you might think. When you sell, you have to get your carnet discharged by the local customs — that means some form of duty will need to be paid before the deal can go through. If you do not work this out at the time, you are likely to be hit with a hefty bill later on.

Carnets are issued by national motoring organisations (the AA or RAC in the UK); they are expensive because these authorities need to know they will be able to recover the money if a vehicle has been sold without duty being paid.

Different countries have different regulations on the issue of carnets. Unfortunately, however, you cannot just shop around on the international markets, unless you go to the trouble of re-registering your vehicle. The carnet must be issued by an authority in the country where the vehicle is registered.

In the UK you will either need to lodge a bond equivalent to several times the current value of the vehicle or take out a special insurance policy against your defaulting on the carnet. The amount of cover required is one and a half times the value of the vehicle for most countries but up to four times the value for Egypt, Nigeria and Kenya. Insurance is available from Campbell Irvine Ltd, for a carnet issued by the AA or from R L Davison & Co Ltd, for one issued by the RAC (see page 21 for details). Even if you do sell without discharging your carnet, the insurance company is still entitled to recoup the duty from you.

You should make absolutely sure your carnet has been validated for all the countries you have requested. Customs officers will check carefully to ensure their country is listed. You may as well play safe and request absolutely every country you may possibly wish to visit — the number of countries covered does not affect the cost.

Although a carnet is likely to come in useful everywhere, it is not absolutely essential in North and West Africa. If you do not have a carnet here, a *laissez-passer* will be issued when you enter the country for a small fee. You should be able to cover most of West and Southern Africa without a carnet. In central countries, a carnet is advisable; in East Africa it is essential.

International driving licence

Available from national motoring organisations on production of a current driving licence and costing a few pounds. There are, however, two different kinds, covered by two separate international conventions. Some African countries are party to one and some to the other — so in theory you will need to invest in both.

International certificate for motor vehicles

Known as a *carte gris* (grey card) wherever French is spoken — even though it is white. It costs a few pounds, but it is a vital investment. Available from motoring organisations, it provides an official looking summary of the details and serial numbers of your vehicle. You will be asked to produce it at just about every border, police check and rain barrier you reach.

Selling vehicles

As already mentioned, selling vehicles in Africa is not as easy as you might think. Many people assume it to be a relatively straightforward operation — then spend months trying to line up a deal. The whole carnet system is, after all, designed to stop people driving somewhere and selling at a large profit, without paying local sales taxes. Getting your carnet discharged when you sell is the big headache.

Nonetheless, selling your vehicle at the end of your trip is an attractive option — and it can be done. It saves you the problem of a return journey — either another overland trip or the expense of shipping your vehicle home — it gives you a welcome injection of cash just when you are likely to need it most and, best of all, local conditions generally mean there is a healthy demand. But the laws of economics dictate that it is in precisely those places where laws and regulations make selling a foreign vehicle more difficult that the demand and prices paid are at their highest. Finding your way round this can mean getting involved in some dodgy dealing — and that means you are wide open to being ripped off.

The easiest countries to sell in are those which do not require customs carnets — although there is generally some form of national customs document which must be completed when you sell. West Africa, for example, is a market well served by the European second-hand Peugeot convoys. Of course, the problem for most people planning an overland trip is that they want to go further than this.

The most popular destination for overlanders is East Africa, which also happens to be a pretty difficult place to sell. Kenya, in particular, is a bureaucratic nightmare — unless you happen to have friends in high places. The best place to sell in the east is in Arusha in Tanzania (there is a big demand for four-wheel drive vehicles for use around the game parks). But you should still watch your step.

Even if you do manage a hassle-free sale, you will often be left with a problem getting the money out of the country — unless you are able to sell for hard currency. In Zimbabwe, currency shortages mean selling for hard cash is difficult. Vehicles are worth a lot and demand is high but it is difficult to find anyone with the hard cash.

Botswana is one of the better places to try for a sale because its own currency is convertible. Demand is highest around Maun — for use in the nearby game park.

South Africa has now also become a good place to sell — with a ready market of buyers aiming to drive north. But do make sure you sell for hard currency as converting large quantities of Rand may be a problem. Another attractive alternative would be to buy a vehicle from an overlander in South Africa, travel north and then sell in Europe.

Buying and selling a vehicle in South Africa
by Adrian Deneys
Finding a car New cars in South Africa are expensive, the cheapest new car costing approximately R45,000 (Fiat Uno). A better bet would be to buy a second-hand car. A cost vs risk relationship exists; an expensive car is likely to be reliable, and a cheap car may be a headache, but not always.

For R10,000 you could buy a reasonable second-hand car that would probably get you between destinations and be able to be sold for the same price after your trip.

Buying and selling a car will be easiest in Johannesburg. For somebody selling a car after a trans-Africa trip Cape Town may seem the obvious choice, but be prepared to wait to find a buyer (or accept a bid from a dealer!) as the second-hand car market is far smaller.

All the major South African cities have second-hand car dealers. Advertisements are found in the daily newspapers, and the prices range enormously depending on the mileage, the condition, the model, and the year of the car. The *Star*, Johannesburg's largest daily paper, prints a car section on Wednesdays. Also worth buying is the *Autotrader* magazine which has a huge selection of vehicles for sale and will advertise your vehicle at no cost when you want to sell. *Autotrader* is published on Thursdays and is for sale at most supermarkets.

Common models Landrovers (1984 models) are popular as vehicles to travel through Africa, and they change hands for about R25,000-35,000, depending on condition and mileage.

A pick-up (called *bakkie* locally) is a very practical car. A mattress in the back serves as a bed, and the car has high clearance which helps on dirt roads, especially in Namibia.

VW City Golf and Toyota Corollas are the most common vehicles in South Africa and thus the easiest to buy and sell.

After purchase Once you have found a car you need to have it examined mechanically. It is well worth being a member of the AA which has a reciprocal agreement with the Automobile Association of South Africa (AASA). They will do a thorough check of the vehicle and will (probably) detect any major problems. The test takes about half a day, costs R350, and is best booked a day in advance. There are many test centres in the major cities; phone the AA (the first number in the telephone directory) to arrange a booking. (For more about the AASA see box on page 263.)

If you are convinced that the car is worth buying, either pay cash (which will give you an advantage when negotiating a price) or by bank guaranteed cheque (which cannot be cancelled). If the car is less than five years old it is prudent to establish whether a previous owner owed any money on the car (to a bank or finance company). If money is owed on the vehicle you (as the new owner) will be liable for the debt. The AA's legal department will be able to give details when conducting such a check.

Cars in good condition are sometimes sold with a road-worthy certificate (the equivalent of the British MOT certificate). If so, transferring the ownership may be done at the Traffic Department (to whom you will have to furnish an address). If you don't have a road-worthy certificate you will have to get one from a Traffic Department test centre. The test is stringent.

Selling your car Selling a car to recoup your investment can be a terrifying experience. A dealer is likely to only offer you R16,000 on a car which could easily be sold privately for R21,500.

It is best to avoid dealers (unless you need to make a quick sale), and place an advertisement in the classified section of the local newspaper. You will need an address. The best days to run an advertisement are Wednesday, Thursday, and Friday, as you can make arrangements to show any prospective buyers the car over the weekend.

Only accept bank guaranteed cheques as payment.

Documentation reference list

MEDICAL AND PERSONAL INSURANCE. Some recommended sources are as follows:

Africa Travel Centre, 4 Medway Court, Leigh Street, London WC1H 9QX; Tel: 0171 387 1211. Also has offices in USA: (800) 631 5650; Sydney: (02) 267 3048; Melbourne: (03) 670 9533; Auckland: (09) 520 2000; and Nairobi: (2) 214 099.

Campbell Irvine, 6 Bell Street, Reigate, Surrey RH2 7BG; Tel: 01737 223687. This is also the insurer for AA carnet policies.

Cyclists Touring Club, Cotterell House, 69 Meadrow, Godalming, Surrey; Tel: 01483 417217.

R L Davison, 1 Devonshire Road, London EC2M 4SY; Tel: 0171 816 9876. This is also the insurer for RAC carnet policies.

Trailfinders, 42-50 Earls Court Road, London W8 6EJ; Tel: 0171 938 3366.

The Travel Insurance Agency (Tel: 0181 446 5414) acts as an insurance broker for travel policies.

STA Travel, 117 Euston Road, London NW1; Tel: 0171 937 1733.

MOTORING DOCUMENTS. All necessary documents and a lot of helpful advice are available from national motoring organisations:

Automobile Association, (Import/Export Section), Fanum House, Basingstoke RG21 2EA; Tel: 01256 493806.

RAC, (Touring Information), RAC House, PO Box 100, South Croydon, Surrey CR2 6XW; Tel: 0181 686 2525.

VACCINATION CERTIFICATES. Available from your GP and clinics and hospitals giving vaccinations. The most comprehensive advice on health for travellers is provided by MASTA, the health information wing of the London School of Hygiene and Tropical Medicine. Their travellers' health line on 0891 224100 lets you leave details of your planned journey (calls cost around £2-3). By return of post they will send you a concise health brief covering immunisations, advice on malaria, Foreign Office advice, latest health news and a personal immunisation schedule for up to four people for £15.

Travellers' health advice and vaccinations are also available from the following specialists:

British Airways Travel Clinic and Vaccination Centre, 156 Regent Street, London W1R 7HG; Tel: 0171 439 9584 (a recorded message gives details of local clinics).

Hospital For Tropical Diseases, 4 St Pancras Way, London NW1 0PE; Tel: 0171 387 4411.

Liverpool School of Tropical Medicine, Pembroke Place, Liverpool L3 5QA; Tel: 0151 708 9393.
London School of Hygiene and Tropical Medicine, Keppel Street, London WC1E 7HT; Tel: 0171 636 8636.
Thomas Cook Vaccination Centre, 45 Berkeley Street, London W1A 1EB; Tel: 0171 499 4000.

Money

Security dictates you will want to take most of your money as travellers cheques. But it is useful to take as much hard currency in cash as you feel you can safely carry. You may wish to take advantage of changing money on the street (a decision for each individual to make — be extremely careful if you do). Some banks will not change travellers cheques and in some areas there may be no banks at all and you may have to rely on changing money with local traders. Some countries will demand payment for certain services in hard currencies.

It is worth bringing both small and large denomination notes with you. Do not under any circumstances carry US$100 bills; most banks will not accept them because of the number of fakes in circulation. Small notes are useful when you have to pay low charges in hard currency — otherwise you end up getting your change in local money. Bring a mix of currencies to take advantage of swings in exchange rates. You will also find that only certain currencies will be acceptable in some countries. The two most important currencies to carry are US dollars and French francs. The dollar is the international currency of exchange but in some banks in West Africa, particularly small towns, French francs are the only currency accepted.

Make sure you have either French francs or CFA francs (see *Note* on page 16) with you when crossing the Sahara into Niger or Mali, as you must have these to pay various charges at the border. Taking advantage of your first real African bars after the austerity of Algeria is also out unless you have francs or CFA francs to pay for your beer.

With travellers cheques make sure you carry your receipt of purchase as many banks in Africa will not change cheques without it. You are not supposed to carry it with your travellers cheques (for security), but you do not have much choice. Keep it in a separate pocket or bag, but carry it with you if you want to change money. Take a photocopy of it with you and keep this securely elsewhere.

You do not necessarily need to take all the money you are likely to need. American Express card holders can buy US$1,000 worth of travellers cheques at any of their offices with a cheque guaranteed by an Amex card. In some places you can also buy local currency with Eurocheques or Access and Visa cards. It is sometimes even possible to buy hard currency with your credit cards (shop around — different banks in the same town will have different rules).

You can also have money wired to a bank in Africa, though it can take several days. It is sensible to have someone you trust taking care of all your financial affairs back home. They should be able to help smooth the way for any transfer of funds.

Post

There is nothing better when you are on the road than a long letter from home. Make sure as many people as possible know how to contact you (unless you really do want to get away from it all).

Most major towns have a *poste restante* at the main post office. To increase your chances of actually getting the letter, ask people to address it with your surname first followed by an initial. This reduces the chance of it being misfiled.

Tales of mail going astray are legion, but our favourite is of a friend who was looking for postcards in the market at Bamako. Looking through a selection on a stall he couldn't believe his eyes; they were pictures of a traditional English wedding — and a friend of his was the groom! It turned out the pictures had been sent to him at the *poste restante* but had mysteriously disappeared.

A good and relatively safe alternative to post offices is the service offered by American Express offices (as long as the mail gets delivered to them in the first place). Anyone carrying an Amex card or travellers cheques is entitled to use the company's offices worldwide as a mailing address. This service is always free, whereas you will sometimes have to pay to collect mail from a poste restante. A booklet is available from American Express (Amex House, Edward Street, Brighton BN2 1YL; Tel: 01273 693555) giving a complete list of the addresses of its offices around the world.

PHOTOGRAPHY

Choice of equipment

This depends very much on how important photography is to you. But remember, the more equipment you take, the more you will have to carry around and the more security conscious you will have to be.

If you take photography seriously you will need a single lens reflex camera with a range of lenses — at least a standard and a telephoto zoom. Fit all lenses with a skylight filter to protect from dust.

Remember you will mostly be far from camera shops and supplies of batteries. The electronics of modern cameras are liable to play up at the least convenient moments, so it is worth considering the advantages of a manual camera — or one that operates manually as well as electronically.

Whether or not you take an SLR, it is certainly worth taking a small compact camera as well. There is a vast range of them on the market which are all fairly similar. There are many occasions when a larger camera would be intrusive but when you will get away with a compact. They are also a lot easier to carry around!

Choice of film

The sun will not always be shining and when it does you may well end up taking pictures in the shade. So take a choice of film speeds with you.

Personal preference will determine whether you choose mono, colour or transparencies. A big advantage with transparencies is the process-paid brands such as Kodachrome and Fujichrome — you can post your films directly off to the lab and have them returned to a friend back home. This is important because the keeping quality of film deteriorates sharply once it has been exposed — you should certainly not carry it around with you until you get back. As long as you post from major cities there should not be any problem with films going astray. We never lost one out of more than 100 films sent from Africa in this way and others we have spoken to have experienced a similar record.

It is a good idea to take all of your film with you as local supplies tend to be expensive and may not be the freshest of stock. If this means you will be carrying a lot then a refrigerator or cool box for storage is a good idea — but not essential. Hot conditions do not spoil film — but they do reduce its keeping qualities.

Pictures of people

Please ask permission first. Some people take a Polaroid camera so they can hand over an instant picture in return for the pictures they really want. If you promise to send pictures later, make sure you keep your word. Beware of offering money for photographs — it does nobody any favours to encourage economic dependence on tourists. A smile, a joke and friendship are far more appropriate.

Permits and regulations

A photography permit is compulsory in some countries. These are generally only available in capital cities and will normally cost a small fee. Mostly you will get by without one — but not always. Government sensitivity about cameras means you will normally be a lot safer if you do have a permit. Needless to say, military installations, police buildings, border posts, airports, trains, bridges and anything with any military significance at all are strictly off limits for photography.

Documentation and insurance

Carry a record of camera body and lens serial numbers in case they are needed for customs or insurance purposes. You may not be able to get an insurance policy covering your cameras, unless you keep them with you at all times (there are so many exclusion clauses). But do get some insurance if possible as cameras will be one of the highest risk items you will carry.

Further information

A pamphlet on expedition photography by John Douglas is available from the **Expedition Advisory Centre**, 1 Kensington Gore, London SW7 2AR; Tel: 0171 581 2057.

CLOTHES

Take as few as possible — you will not need much once you are on the road. But remember to take some warm clothing for nights in the desert and in the highlands. Something to keep the rain out is also useful. Otherwise, lightweight cotton is the general rule. Dark and patterned fabrics don't show stains and rips.

Everyone should try to be aware of local dress customs. In some Islamic countries women in particular should take care — even the tops of your arms can be regarded as provocative. As a rough guide, watch out for what local people are wearing. Their reactions to anything doubtfully revealing will soon let you know if you have crossed acceptable levels of modesty.

GIFTS

It is quite amazing just how important a small supply of cheap gifts can be — particularly for children who are desperate to help you fill your jerry cans at wells, guard your vehicle or give you directions. On the other hand, you should never hand out gifts just for the sake of it. Constant handouts can mean that the local economy comes to depend on them, and later travellers will suffer because the same will be expected of them.

There will, however, be occasions when people have greatly helped you — either in deed or in material terms. This is particularly true for overlanders, who have far more than just a backpack to consider. Generosity can be returned with a simple gift. Highly valued were news cuttings a friend regularly sent from home, but other popular ones included ballpoint pens (Bics in Africa, not Biros!). You may wish to take a few special items for people who have really helped you out. Useful gifts can also be recycled from your own supplies. Empty containers of any kind which can be used to carry water are highly sought after in many areas.

Often your friendship and the chance to swap addresses can be the most appropriate response, but don't make promises you don't intend to keep.

EMBASSIES, CONSULATES AND HIGH COMMISSIONS IN THE UK

Algerian Embassy, 54 Holland Park, London W11 3RS; Tel: 0171 221 7800

Consulate of **Benin**, Dolphin House, 16 The Broadway, Stanmore, Middlesex HA7 4DW; Tel: 0181 954 8800; Fax: 0181 954 8844

Botswana High Commission, 6 Stratford Place, London W1N 9AE; Tel: 0181 209 1484

The Honorary Consulate for **Burkina Faso**, 5 Cinnamon Row, Plantation Wharf, Battersea, London SW11 3TW; Tel: 0171 738 1800; Fax: 0171 738 2820

Embassy of the Republic of **Cameroon**, 84 Holland Park, London W11 3SB; Tel: 0171 727 0771/3; Fax: 0171 792 9353

Honorary Consulate of the Republic of **Congo**, Alliance House, 12 Caxton Street, London SW1H 0QS; Tel: 0171 222 7575; Fax: 0171 233 2087

Embassy of the Republic of **Côte d'Ivoire**, 2 Upper Belgrave Street, London SW1X 8BJ; Tel: 0171 235 6991

Embassy of the Arab Republic of **Egypt**, 26 South Street, London W1Y 8EL; Tel: 0171 499 2401; Fax: 0171 355 3568

Consulate of the State of **Eritrea**, 96 White Lion Street, London N1 9PF; Tel: 0171 713 0096; Fax: 0171 713 0161

Embassy of **Ethiopia**, 17 Prince's Gate, London SW7 1PZ; Tel: 0171 589 7212-5

Embassy of the Republic of **Gabon**, 27 Elvaston Place, London SW7 5NL; Tel: 0171 823 9986; Fax: 0171 584 0047

The Gambia High Commission, 57 Kensington Court, London W8 5DG; Tel: 0171 937 6316-8; Fax: 0171 937 9095

Office for the High Commissioner for **Ghana**, 104 Highgate Hill, London N6 5HE; Tel: 0181 342 8686; Fax: 0181 342 8566

Honorary Consulate for The Republic of **Guinea**, 22 Gilbert Street, London W1Y 1RJ; Tel: 0171 333 0044

Honorary Consulate of the Republic of **Guinea-Bissau**, 8 Palace Gate, London W8 4RP; Tel: 0171 589 5253

Kenya High Commission, 45 Portland Place, London W1; Tel: 0171 636 2371/5; Fax: 0171 323 6717

High Commission for the Kingdom of **Lesotho**, 7 Chesham Place, London SW1 8HN; Tel: 0171 235 5686; Fax: 0171 235 5023

Embassy of the Republic of **Liberia**, 2 Pembridge Place, London W2 4XB; Tel: 0171 221 1036

High Commission for the Republic of **Malawi**, 33 Grosvenor Street, London W1X 0DE; Tel: 0171 491 4172/7

Honorary Consulate of the Islamic Republic of **Mauritania**, 140 Bow Common Lane, London E3 4BH; Tel: 0181 980 4382; Fax: 0181 556 6032

Embassy of the Kingdom of **Morocco**, 49 Queen's Gate Gardens, London SW7 5NE; Tel: 0171 581 5001/4; Fax: 0171 225 3862

Embassy of the Republic of **Mozambique**, 21 Fitzroy Square, London W1P 5HJ; Tel: 0171 383 3800; Fax: 0171 383 3801

High Commission of the Republic of **Namibia**, 6 Chandos Street, London W1M 0LQ; Tel: 0171 637 6244; Fax: 0171 637 5694

High Commission for the Federal Republic of **Nigeria**, Nigeria House, 9 Northumberland Avenue, London WC2 5BX; Tel: 0171 839 1244; Fax: 0171 839 8746

Embassy of the Republic of **Senegal**, 11 Phillimore Gardens, London W8 7QG; Tel: 0171 937 0925/6

Sierra Leone High Commission, 33 Portland Place, London W1N 3AG; Tel: 0171 636 6483-6

South African High Commission, South Africa House, Trafalgar Square, London WC2N 5DP; Tel: 0171 930 4488; Fax: 0171 321 0835

Embassy of the Republic of **Sudan**, 3 Cleveland Row, London SW1A 1DD; Tel: 0171 839 8080

Kingdom of **Swaziland** High Commission, 58 Pont Street, London SW1X 0AE; Tel: 0171 581 4976-8; Fax: 0171 589 5332

High Commission for the United Republic of **Tanzania**, 43 Hertford Street, London W1; Tel: 0171 499 8951-4; Fax: 0171 491 9321

Tunisian Embassy, 29 Prince's Gate, London SW7 1QG; Tel: 0171 584 8117; Fax: 0171 225 2884

Uganda High Commission, Uganda House, 58/59 Trafalgar Square, London WC2N 5DX; Tel: 0171 839 5783; Fax: 0171 839 8925

Embassy of the Republic of **Zaïre**, 26 Chesham Place, London SW1X 8HH; Tel: 0171 235 6137; Fax: 0171 235 9048

High Commission for the Republic of **Zambia**, 2 Palace Gate, London W8 5LS; Tel: 0171 589 6655; Fax: 0171 581 1353

High Commission for the Republic of **Zimbabwe**, Zimbabwe House, 429 Strand, London WC2R 0SA; Tel: 0171 836 7755

EMBASSIES, CONSULATES AND HIGH COMMISSIONS ELSEWHERE IN EUROPE

Embassy of the Republic of **Burundi**, Square Marie Louise 46, 1040 Brussels, Belgium; Tel: + 32 230 45 35

Embassy of the **Central African Republic**, 30 rue des Perchamps, 75016 Paris, France; Tel: +33 42 24 42 56

Embassy of the Republic of **Chad**, Boulevard Lambermont 52, 1030 Brussels, Belgium; Tel: + 32 215 19 75

Embassy of the Republic of **Djibouti**, 26 rue Emile Ménier, 75116 Paris, France, Tel: + 33 47 27 49 22

Embassy of the Republic of **Equatorial Guinea**, 6 rue Alfred de Vigny, 75008 Paris, France; Tel: +33 47 66 44 33

Embassy of the Republic of **Mali**, Avenue Molière 487, 1060 Brussels, Belgium; Tel: + 32 345 74 32 and +32 345 75 89

Embassy of the Republic of **Niger**, 154 rue de Longchamp, 75116 Paris, France; Tel: + 33 45 04 80 60

Embassy of the Republic of **Rwanda**, 1 Avenue des Fleurs, Woluwe Saint Pierre, 1150 Brussels, Belgium; Tel: + 32 763 07 02/5 and + 32 763 07 21

Embassy addresses and telephone numbers in the UK are regularly updated and published by HMSO in *The London Diplomatic List* (ISBN 0-11-591746-2, price £3.95). The closest embassy in Europe is normally given for countries which have no embassy in the UK.

Chapter Two

Your vehicle and preparation

WHAT ARE THE OPTIONS?

The biggest decision you will have to make is what sort of transport to choose. All have their plus and minus points to consider. The final option of an organised tour is looked at in Chapter Three.

Four-wheel drive

This has to be the favoured option if you want the best of all worlds — and think you can afford it. Some people say travelling in a vehicle can distance you from the environment you are travelling through — the strength of the vehicle means you are safe in your own self-contained world. Our experience is that this is only true if you allow it to be. The major advantage is that you are free to go more or less anywhere you choose. Add to this the relative comfort and reliability offered and the ability to carry a fair amount of supplies and you have a winning formula. As long as you can hold down costs and not allow yourself to get trapped inside the comfort of the goldfish bowl, it can be a great way to see Africa.

Our own experience is with Land Rovers and these are still the most popular four-wheel drive vehicles in Africa. Their simple and robust design makes them ideal for the wide variety of difficult conditions. Because they are so common, it is easier to find spare parts for them than most other vehicles, and local mechanics are familiar with them.

The Range Rover does offer more comfort and is an excellent vehicle, but for use on a trans-African journey it is of fairly limited use. It does not have much in the way of storage capacity and the compensating advantages of its engine and comfortable interior have anyway been largely transferred to more modern Land Rovers.

Toyota Land Cruisers are almost as common in some parts of Africa as Land Rovers. They offer many of the advantages and are practically as well known. Also, because of their relatively low cost and previous Soviet investment in some parts of Africa, the Lada Niva has a reasonable reputation in many areas.

The Mercedes Unimog is popular among some German travellers and is indeed a wonderful vehicle. Basically a small scale and extremely powerful four-wheel drive truck, it has very high clearance. Storage space and living quarters are separate from the driving cab. You can buy them quite cheaply from auctions in Germany but the costs can really start to mount on the road — fuel consumption can be very high indeed.

At the very top of the range for a go-anywhere vehicle comes the Pinzgauer, which is available in four-wheel drive and six-wheel drive models. Supplied and customised in the UK by Overland Ltd, this is a phenomenal vehicle — at a phenomenal price.

There has been a proliferation of four-wheel drive vehicles in recent years. But beware of smaller, lightweight models which are not particularly suited to African conditions. These smaller cars are essentially meant for European roads — and would be hard put to cope with the range of African driving conditions without suffering serious damage.

Two-wheel drive

Not really suitable for more adventurous full-blooded trans-African trips but two-wheel drive vehicles can be used quite happily if you plan your route with care or fly in to areas with better roads (see below). Some do have positive advantages — either because of their comfort or their light weight — the lighter the vehicle the less power you need to get it through difficult conditions.

It is perfectly possible to drive across the Sahara and even right across Africa in a vehicle like a VW Combi — and they provide far more comfort than most four-wheel drive vehicles. But you have to time the seasons precisely, be prepared to get stuck rather more than with four-wheel drive and need to count on a lot of luck. An interesting description of a successful round the world trip is described in *Africa And Beyond* by Theresa and Jonathan Hewat (their journey took place in the early 1970s but it still makes for a good read if you can get hold of an old copy).

Some smaller two-wheel drive cars can be surprisingly good in all but the muddier sections of Central Africa. Citroen 2CVs and Renault 4s are economical on fuel and quite capable of desert crossings on main tracks, although their clearance is limited. If you don't mind the lack of space they could prove a low-cost option. We once met two Belgians who had crossed the Sahara and were travelling around West Africa in a Renault 4 — with a huge Great

Dane in the back!

There are many Europeans who keep up a constant trade in taking old Peugeots and other saloon cars in varying states of disrepair across the desert to sell in West Africa. The profit to be made in this dubious second-hand car racket is generally a lot lower than the participants expect, but it does make for a relatively cheap way to travel. Although many do get across the Sahara, many others do not — and those who make it depend to a great extent on four-wheel drive vehicles to come along and pull them out of trouble. It is wise to attempt such a crossing only in convoy.

Car hire

There is no need to drive all the way if you are short of time or do not fancy a complete trans-African trip. Much of Southern Africa and parts in the east and west are perfectly accessible by two-wheel drive vehicles that can be hired locally. If you want to get off the beaten track once you arrive, you should be able to find more substantial vehicles for hire in some of the major tourist centres. In a city like Nairobi, for example, there is no shortage of places to hire four-wheel drive vehicles such as Suzukis, Isuzu Troopers and Land Rovers, already kitted out with camping gear, cooking equipment, water containers, etc. The Africa Travel Centre in London can arrange hire in advance.

Motorbikes

Travel by motorbike can offer an excellent compromise. You keep the freedom, speed and flexibility of motorised transport but at a fraction of the cost. As well as the lower initial investment, fuel consumption will also be much lower. Of course, the sacrifice you make is in comfort and carrying capacity.

There are places where a bike can be better than a four-wheel drive vehicle. But it can have problems in reaching the more remote areas in the first place. Bikes will often find it easier to travel with other vehicles, which can carry extra fuel and water. It is generally possible to team up with other travellers in this way during the course of your journey.

Ideal bikes for Africa should have a balance of power, comfort and manoeuvrability. Unless you aim to travel on tar roads most of the time, very few people would select anything other than a good trails bike. Road bikes are simply too heavy to cope with the classic problem conditions of soft sand and mud.

One of the most popular bikes used by travellers in Africa is the Yamaha XT500. In many ways this is the two-wheel version of the

Land Rover — with a straightforward engine, which is both reliable and well-known. The 500cc engine can be rebored to 600cc if you wish.

The XT600 Ténéré and the more recent 660cc version have a larger fuel tank — though it is perfectly possible to modify the tank of the XT500. Ténérés are generally reckoned to be the best all rounders — particularly for desert travel.

Another popular choice is the Honda XL series. The main alternative to the Japanese trails bikes are BMW 800 and 1000cc touring bikes. Despite their size, their lighter steering can make them easier to ride.

Bicycle

Those thinking of driving across Africa will be amazed to learn there is an even crazier bunch planning the trip on a bicycle. If you have plenty of time and do not mind the hardship and physical effort, cycling can be the perfect way to see the continent. It certainly brings you into closer contact with both the people and the environment than most other methods.

It goes without saying you should not dream of such a trip unless you are in good health — cycling across the Sahara or through muddy forest trails can be extremely hard work. Some previous experience of long distance cycling would probably be a good idea before setting out, although Christian and Gilly Lee who contributed to this book didn't do any cycling at all before they set off on their successful trip from Victoria Station to Victoria Falls. They chose Hoo Hoo E Koo bikes (named after an American Indian tribe) designed by Gary Fisher. Other options are listed later in this chapter in the section on bicycle selection and preparation.

This is one of the hardest but also one of the most economic means of travel. The only costs you need incur are on your bike, visas and food. Even at the end of your trip, many airlines will ship your bike back for free as part of your luggage (but not all of them, so shop around).

If the idea appeals to you a good first stop would be to contact the Cyclists' Touring Club (Cotterell House, 69 Meadrow, Godalming, Surrey). Once you join the CTC, you get a wide range of services — insurance, technical advice, touring itineraries and travel information.

Sheets are published by the CTC on various aspects of travelling with a bicycle and on specific countries and areas in Africa — including West Africa, South Africa, Seychelles, Malawi, Gambia, Zambia, Zimbabwe, Algeria and Tunisia, Egypt and Sudan,

Morocco, and the Sahara. Information is also available for trans-African journeys and those planning round the world trips.

VEHICLE PREPARATION

The range of possibilities for vehicle preparation is obviously enormous — from paying someone else to do the job for you to having the fun of tackling most of it yourself.

Varying degrees of help are available. A company like Overland will provide a completely customised vehicle to your own requirements. Others will give advice and help so you can prepare your own vehicle.

Whatever choice you make it is crucial you should know your vehicle well. If you have not had a hand in getting it ready to leave, it is even more important that you should take time to become totally familiar with it before setting off. What follows is a guide to some of the more important issues to bear in mind. Everyone will have their own ideas on what are essentials and optional extras.

Baffle plate: A steel plate fitted beneath the vehicle helps protect its vulnerable underside from rocks. It can, however, make routine maintenance considerably more awkward.

Bull bars: Give some added protection. But are they really necessary?

Curtains: Well worth putting up whether or not you intend to sleep inside all the time. They provide instant shade in strong sun and dissuade prying eyes. Simple strips of fabric on curtain stretchers can fit inside the inner roof gulley of most vehicles, though some travellers are more sophisticated and fit curtain rails with proper hooks.

Electronic ignition: Helps reduce the chances of ignition problems for older petrol models.

Fuel and water tanks: If you want to avoid filling your vehicle with jerry cans, you really must consider fitting extra tanks — particularly for older models with higher fuel consumption.

Land Rovers are particularly easy to modify. You can supplement the standard long wheelbase 15 gallon rear mounted fuel tank with short wheelbase 10 gallon tanks — one under each front seat. That's a total of 35 gallons. Customised tanks are also available with even larger capacities for both fuel and water and can be fitted to most vehicles.

Plan to carry as much fuel as possible — always bearing in mind weight restrictions. Fuel and water are the two most important items you need — but they are also incredibly heavy. There is little point in being well prepared if you destroy your suspension or even break your chassis in the process.

Fuel is actually more readily available than you might think in most parts of Africa. Unless you really do aim to get right away from the normal routes you should not experience any problems. There are not many places where you will need to go more than 500 miles without supplies. On the other hand, you cannot always guarantee getting fuel when you expect to — and you may want to take full advantage of cheaper supplies when you can get them. The final judgment on how much you should carry is always likely to be something of a balancing act.

Much the same applies to water as for fuel. Make sure you carry enough — but beware of overloading. The greater your carrying capacity, the more tempting it becomes to load up to the gills. A built-in water tank can be far more convenient than a vehicle full of leaking jerry cans. The fewer items that can move around the better as far as loading is concerned. If you can do away with the need for loose fuel and water containers, so much the better.

If you do use jerry cans, however, you can get them out of the way when empty by putting them on the roof (do not do so if they are full — you should never overload your roof rack with heavy items). If you have petrol in jerry cans on the roof it spells double trouble as the sun will soon make it far too hot and consequently very dangerous.

Oil cooler: Recommended by many, ignored by others. Probably a good idea if you are likely to take full advantage of fast roads in the hottest conditions. Less useful if you are in an older vehicle.

Raised air intake: Standard on many African four-wheel drive vehicles, reducing the intake of large gulps of dust with the air. Will certainly do no harm and could end up saving your engine from damage. On the other hand, we did not fit one and did not seem to suffer for it.

Roof rack: Not absolutely essential but can be very useful — just as long as you remember not to overload it. Land Rovers in particular are not built to take heavy loads on the roof. We only used ours for a rooftop tent, second spare wheel, sandplanks and a few lightweight items. Others who carried a lot more weight experienced problems, both with a tendency to tip over on uneven roads and with structural faults — windscreens in particular have a habit of cracking up under the strain.

Seat covers: Depends on the seats you have. If they are the old plastic kind, they will be very uncomfortable in the hot sun if they are not covered. Towelling is ideal for comfort. Removable covers have the added advantage of being able to wash out the grime that will inevitably build up. Even if you do have fabric covered seats already you will appreciate washable covers — you will pick up more dust and grime than you could believe possible.

Security: It is obviously impossible to achieve 100% security. But every effort you make is well worthwhile.

Padlocks should be added to all doors and put on any items mounted outside the vehicle. Avoid any delicate mechanisms such as combination locks which will very quickly become clogged by the thick dust that will cover your vehicle once it hits the African roads. Also make sure that you buy a set of padlocks with a common key or it will take forever to find the right one.

Padlocks and hasps on all doors are a wise precaution but you should not depend upon them totally. Hasps can be forced with a jemmy so you should consider some form of internal mechanism to back them up, such as additional locks or bolts.

Windows are another problem area. Rubber surrounds in particular are a security hazard as they can easily be cut away — replace these if possible. Metal grilles on windows will help — but have the adverse effect of making you look like a security van and so worth robbing. Try to strike a balance between the two.

Some form of alarm system will undoubtedly help as it should deter a thief from continuing with a break in. But do not depend on it to safeguard your gear. The most important security system will ultimately be your own vigilance. There is a wide selection of systems available from all accessory shops.

Some overlanders take a dog with them to guard their vehicle. We even came across a Swiss ex-pat in Lomé who always travelled with one of his pet lions in his van!

Sleeping space: Many overlanders simply take a standard tent, but this does have a number of drawbacks. A rooftop tent is undoubtedly the best option as it is quick to put up, does not require much extra space, keeps you away from people and wildlife and does not present any ventilation problems. The main suppliers of rooftop tents in the UK is Brownchurch Ltd (see page 60).

A low-cost alternative is simply to add a sheet of plywood to your roof rack so you can sleep under the stars. This will be perfectly adequate in many situations but is far from offering a comprehensive solution.

Sleeping inside the vehicle will sometimes be necessary because of bad weather or lack of space to pitch a tent. Before you leave, you should think about how you would cope with this — and try to come up with something more comfortable than sleeping in the front seat or sprawled across the jerry cans.

If you plan to sleep inside the vehicle all the time, you need to come up with a system which avoids the need to move everything before you go to bed and also provides some form of ventilation. You may also consider taking along a portable tent to use when you stop somewhere for a while (the main disadvantages with pitching a tent come when you are constantly on the move).

Spare battery and split charge system: A second battery will come in extremely useful in order to run all of your electrical equipment like lights, refrigerator, fans, radio and compressor without draining your main battery. Installation of a split charge system means both batteries can be charged simultaneously. The second battery can also become a life saver if your main one gives out in the middle of nowhere.

Steering wheel cover: Standard black plastic steering wheels can become extremely hot in direct sunlight. Fit some kind of cover before you leave.

Storage: Careful planning of your storage facilities can make all the difference between comfort and a nightmare. Try to achieve a closely packed but accessible arrangement. At all costs avoid having anything loose that can be thrown about in the back. Fitted cupboards and storage space can be built by customising companies or you can do the job yourself if you feel confident enough. Remember the whole thing can easily get shaken to bits unless it has been well made.

Some kind of modular system is probably the best approach to storage. You need to be able to pull things out quickly, find what you are looking for and repack into the same space you started with. This process is generally a lot harder than it sounds. It can be very useful to split your storage space into compartments and within this pattern to store in a series of rigid sections or boxes.

Rigid plastic storage boxes are good — or metal flight cases if you can afford them. Elastic bungee cords and canvas or webbing belts are useful for lashing things down. Anything removable on your roof rack should be secured with padlocks.

Suspension: The biggest enemy for vehicles in Africa is the state of the roads. That means your suspension is more at risk than anything else. There is a great deal to be said for fitting new springs and shock absorbers all round before setting off. Some people even strengthen the chassis — certainly a good idea if you are likely to carry heavy loads.

Opinion is divided as to which springs are the best. Mechanics in Europe will tend to recommend fitting heavy duty springs for the additional strains of African roads, but African mechanics will often tell you lighter springs are more supple and less likely to break under the strain.

Towing points: Essential both for towing others out of trouble and being towed yourself. Remember to take suitable ropes and chains.

Tyres: You really should set off on such a major trip with a completely new set. Aim to fit the best you can — it will be well worth the extra expense.

Many people take a set of sand tyres as well, for the desert. But ask yourself if you really believe the extra weight and cost are worth it. If you are likely to spend an extended period in sandy conditions, you may decide in favour. If not, you can do a great deal to cope with conditions by reducing tyre pressure until you get back on firmer roads.

You will be facing a wide variety of terrain — sand, mud, laterite, rocks and metalled roads. Good quality road tyres are therefore probably the best bet. The brand you use is often a very personal choice. We use Michelin XZY and have never had any problems.

Make sure you also take spare inner tubes, tyre levers and a puncture repair kit. The only problem with tough tyres like XZYs is that they are also extremely difficult to change. Practice does, however, make things a lot easier — a few trial runs before you leave might not be a bad idea.

A good tip for prising the tyre away from the wheel rim (breaking the bead) is to place the foot of your jack on the tyre and jack the vehicle up on it. The weight of the vehicle should eventually force the tyre away from the rim. You should, of course, take care that the jack does not tip over while you are doing this.

You will probably find that initial attempts to get the tyre back onto the wheel feel like the hardest work you have ever done. But it is technique rather than brawn that wins the day. Washing-up liquid is handy as a lubricant between the tyre and metal rim.

Winch: Opinions vary as to how useful a winch will be. If you have an unlimited budget, it will do no harm, but the situations when it is likely to come in useful are normally fairly limited — in practically every situation it is easier to be towed out of trouble. A winch is really designed to be used by a vehicle to pull other objects towards it — which allows you to position your vehicle accordingly. But when it comes to self-recovery it is unlikely you will be stuck in exactly the right position to take advantage of a front-mounted system.

The main advantage of a winch is it can give you the confidence to explore further off the beaten track, away from the roads and tracks used by other vehicles. But if you plan to be as adventurous as that, it would be wise to team up with at least one other vehicle anyway.

A sensible compromise could be a good hand winch — the best is probably that made by Tirfor. Another simple winching technique is to make use of a high lift jack. If this is chained to the vehicle at one end and a winching point such as a tree trunk at the other, you can slowly pull the vehicle out of trouble. The only drawback with this technique is that you can only winch the length of the jack at a time (one metre).

EQUIPMENT

Everyone will have their own set of priorities. But when deciding what to take, you must ask yourself very carefully if you really need it — overloading is your vehicle's worst enemy. With four wheels you will be nothing like as restricted as with a motorbike or bicycle in terms of what you can carry, but when your springs start to go you will bitterly regret every extra kilo of unnecessary weight.

Here are a few of the most important items of equipment you will need to consider.

Bits and pieces: Do not forget to bring a rope to double as a washing line (you risk health problems from parasites by drying clothes on bushes or on the ground), a plastic bowl big enough to wash clothes in, and a scrubbing brush — most of the time you will be washing clothes in cold water so you will need one. Lots of plastic bags and carrier bags of various sizes come in useful all the time. A few emergency packs of toilet paper are a good idea in case you run out between the big towns, where it is generally available. Matches are available almost everywhere but it is a good idea to carry a spare box. You can buy waterproof matches at most camping shops, though the only time we used them was for entertaining children! One thing we brought which did turn out to be useful was a pocket calculator for working out fuel consumption and exchange rates. Our Swiss army knife was also constantly in use.

Compass: You may not need to use a compass as much as you think — unless you are exploring open desert. But when you do need one you must be able to trust its accuracy and be able to use it properly. Unless your compass is compensated for use in a motorised vehicle, remember that the electrics will throw it out. Stop and walk off a few paces for an accurate reading.

Cooking: See the *Food and drink* section in Chapter Four.

Fire extinguisher: Compulsory in many countries and essential for your own safety.

Hazard warning triangles: Compulsory in some countries — in the Central African Republic you are supposed to carry two.

Jerry cans: You must use metal ones for fuel; storing petrol in plastic jerry cans is dangerous as it could explode. You can use either metal or plastic for water, though make sure you can distinguish between them if you choose all metal. Also, do not store water in jerry cans that were previously used for petrol as the taste never disappears. Opaque containers for water help to avoid algae growing inside; a black container helps heat up some hot water. The number you take will depend on fuel consumption, tank capacity, route, load and how much you plan to take advantage of cheaper fuel supplies when you find them. For water, your route is the most important factor. Long stretches in the open desert will mean you need to carry substantially more.

Lighting: Fluorescent strip lighting is bright, convenient and does not put too much strain on the battery. Another popular option is a petrol lantern. Camping lights which run on small gas canisters are not such a good idea as, particularly in the desert and West Africa, replacement canisters are almost impossible to find and extremely expensive. Whatever you do, do not forget to bring a torch and spare batteries.

Machete or axe: Very useful for chopping wood and hacking through vegetation.

Portable shower: Not absolutely essential, but it can make you feel infinitely more human after a long day's drive. We have a simple plastic bottle pump action shower which holds enough water for a seven minute shower, heating water on our stove to take the chill off in cooler weather. You can also buy a solar heated shower which heats four litres in about an hour.

Radio: A good radio with plenty of short wave bands is great for picking up news both from home and on conditions in countries you may be visiting. It is a good idea to take something that is not fixed to the vehicle — both for security and portability.

Refrigerator: Particularly useful if you intend to carry a lot of film and extremely pleasant for cold drinks. Ordinary camping shops can be a good source. A fridge should ideally have its own compressor — three-way or paraffin types need careful balancing to work properly. The Engel fridge has been recommended as an efficient but expensive option.

Sandplanks: With luck and careful driving you may not need them at all, but it would be crazy to leave home without some means of getting out of soft sand. Various types of ladders and planks are available — including some made from lightweight alloys. We used aluminium alloy planks which were fine, but perforated steel or aluminium plating or sand ladders are just as good. Do not allow yourself to be talked into buying the sand ladders which you assemble from short lengths, stocked by some suppliers — getting unstuck will take you hours longer.

Seating and table: If you want a spot of comfort and can cope with the storage, then a well-built camping table and chairs do make life a lot easier, particularly for things like preparing food. They will also be much appreciated if you find yourself stuck somewhere for days while you wait for your visas to come through, or the petrol supplies to arrive. Jerry cans and storage boxes can double up — but they are not nearly so comfortable.

Shovel: An indispensable companion to the sandplanks. It may seem like hard work, but if you do not dig enough to free the vehicle properly and give yourself a flat surface to lay your sand planks on, you will only end up ploughing deeper and deeper into the sand — and that means even more digging. For sand, a long handled shovel with an angled blade is best, though in mud you want as flat an angle as possible. It is also worth considering a smaller shovel for rubbish — always burn or bury anything you are planning to leave behind, but be careful not to bury jagged cans or broken glass in game parks where animals may dig up your rubbish and injure themselves. A garden trowel is useful for toilet trips.

Sleeping bags: Your budget and personal preference will determine your choice. We invested in three-seasons bags and were glad of them in the desert and the highlands of Zaïre and East Africa. We also brought a sheet sleeping bag (a cotton duvet cover in its previous life) which we used a lot. When it really got hot at night we just lay on top of it.

Tent: A rooftop tent is strongly recommended. It may seem an expensive investment but the ease of putting it up, with no worries as to the dampness or hardness of the ground, coupled with the reduced incidence of things that creep and crawl, make life a lot more pleasant. If you do invest in one you will find yourself envied wherever you go. If you go for an ordinary ground tent make sure you bring a fly sheet unless you are only visiting desert areas. When it rains in Africa, it really rains.

VEHICLE MAINTENANCE AND REPAIR

If you are already an expert mechanic, this is unlikely to present you with too many problems; if not, you should think carefully about what will be involved. But do not worry, plenty of people make the trip with only the most rudimentary knowledge of how to fix their vehicle.

Beginners need to allow plenty of time to work on their own vehicles before setting off. That means that you will be learning how to cope at the same time as picking up on actual or potential problems. You need to develop a relationship with your vehicle as soon as possible.

Spares

Unless you are a mechanic yourself, get professional advice on a suitable set of spares to take with you. In many cases you will be able to limp along to the next big town where spares are available — but at an inflated price. In general, labour is cheap but parts are expensive — so it pays to be as well equipped as possible.

Too many heavy parts, like springs, are likely to damage your suspension. But take more lightweight spares than you think you will need — like gaskets or even a carburettor. These can be sold or exchanged for heavier parts.

Some places in Africa are better than others for picking up spares. The high cost of imported parts means second-hand spares will almost always be the only viable option. Even official dealers for your vehicle are not guaranteed to have what you need, although they will generally direct you to the best second-hand source. The hammering a vehicle takes on African roads means most sizeable towns have a second-hand yard that can either come up with what you need or with a good alternative.

The best place we found for second-hand spares was Rufiki's in Nairobi. It is a massive yard absolutely stacked full of every part of every imaginable model — and at reasonable prices.

Tools

Working on your vehicle before you leave will give you some idea of what you are likely to need. Check through your workshop manual or talk to a friendly mechanic or off-road enthusiast to find out if you are missing something essential.

Heavy duty jacks and axle stands are a must. A high lift jack is a popular choice. As the name suggests it can lift to a greater height than standard jacks (they are one metre tall) and can also be used to get your vehicle out from deep ruts and can come in handy to take the strain out of breaking the bead when you are changing a tyre — but they can be difficult to use and are often unstable. It might be worth considering a bottle-jack as well for standard maintenance. An electric air pump is another sound investment.

Workshop manual

Do not leave home without one. A parts guide is also a useful but not essential companion.

Oils

You are likely to get through more than in normal conditions — so be prepared. Engine oil is generally available but gear oil and brake and clutch fluid are more difficult to find. You will find everything you need in a big city like Abidjan or Nairobi but don't count on it elsewhere.

Regular maintenance

Servicing should be carried out more frequently than at home. In particular, keep all oil levels topped up. You should also get into the habit of a regular mechanical check every day. This shouldn't take long — it is just a matter of keeping an eye on things and looking out for advance warnings of problems to come.

A typical daily check would include: engine oil level, radiator water level, clutch and brake fluid levels, battery level, corrosion of battery leads, fan belt tension, spark plug leads secure, shock absorbers, steering damper, brake cylinders and brake hoses, exhaust system, general leaks or damage under vehicle, tyre pressure, tightness of wheel nuts. It may seem like overkill to suggest checking something like the wheel nuts every day but the heavy vibrations of corrugated roads means that they can loosen themselves at a frightening rate. We speak from experience!

Common problems

The poor state of the roads means that suspension is public enemy number one — careful driving and constant vigilance are the only solutions. All of our springs broke in the course of a ten month journey. In order to reduce the chances of this happening we would strongly recommend fitting new springs on older vehicles before you set out. Newer vehicles with coil springs are probably less trouble than those with leaf springs.

We also had the misfortune to suffer a broken chassis towards the end of the trip. There is no way of being certain this will not happen to any vehicle, but older ones are obviously more prone to such a problem; make sure that the state of the chassis has been carefully checked before you buy a vehicle. If necessary you can get it strengthened.

The poor quality of some fuel means your fuel filter is likely to get blocked more often — carry a short length of hose to blow through and clear any blockages when things get bad. We had to use this method frequently in both Ghana and Chad because of poor fuel.

The climate means that rubber parts can be more prone to perishing — clutch cylinders commonly pack up. These are the kind of lightweight spares it makes sense to carry.

Inventive repairs

If you do not have the right spares and none are available, do not despair. African mechanics are among the most inventive in the world — they have to be. Likewise, you will need to become rather more inventive yourself. Make sure that you take along a good selection of basics like screws, nuts, wire, etc. One excellent material in an emergency is coat-hanger wire!

Planning a trip in six weeks

by Anthony Ream

I had always wanted to drive from London to Cape Town so when a friend also said he was interested, I told him to let me know when he was thinking of going. Julian next spoke to me from China, where he was working, saying he had resigned from his job and would be back and ready to leave in the New Year. I left my job at Christmas and six weeks later we left for Africa.

Neither of us had any mechanical knowledge so we needed a simple vehicle which was, if possible, already kitted out to do an overland trip — but at a reasonable price. That ruled out a customised overland vehicle. December was spent reading four-wheel drive magazines and newspapers and looking at Land Rovers that seemed to have potential.

Just before Christmas we found our Series III 2.4 litre petrol Land Rover in *Land Rover Owner* magazine. It had been built in Kenya where it had been used on safaris before being kitted out for an overland trip from Kenya to Cameroon. From there it had been shipped to England and left in a garage.

Apart from the fact that Boris, as it came to be known, had done at least part of the trip before, he had what appeared to be an extremely tough chassis with two hi-lift jacking points welded on the back. Other equipment included two additional 45 litre petrol tanks under the front seats and eight 20 litre jerricans — all of which proved essential — a roof rack which had to be assembled onto the chassis, a bull bar and back tailgate on which to put one of the two provided spare wheels, an extra fan to cool the engine, split charging and eight boxes containing an unbelievable assortment of mechanical and electrical parts, cooking accessories, spare tarpaulin and an awning.

We had Boris checked by a local Land Rover garage which gave his engine the all clear — do ensure that a compression test is done to check all four pistons are working evenly and the engine is not burning oil — and confirmed that his bodywork was awful, which did not matter. Boris was bought on 22 December.

Christmas was spent reading the first edition of this book, the *Sahara Handbook* by Simon and Jan Glen, and David Bryden's *Africa Overland*, studying Michelin maps 953 and 955, and planning a route to avoid the rainy seasons, at the same time compiling lists of what needed to be done.

A good part of January and February was spent trying to familiarise ourselves with the basics of the Land Rover engine and kitting it out. We tried to break the work into four areas.

The first was work recommended by the mechanics' report such as new points, plugs, leads and trying to fix an oil leak. Then there was the servicing work we would need to do on the move in Africa such as oil changes, lubricating gear/transmission boxes, differentials and greasing points, cleaning and checking the radiator, its hoses and the water pump bearing and bleeding the brakes. One point to note about lubrication is that in the older Land Rover models, the oil in the gear box tends to leak into the transmission box every now and then so the surplus has to be drained off.

Third was the work necessary for camping. Julian, an electrical engineer, rigged up the split charging and put in a second heavy duty battery to run all the fluorescent camping lights, stereo and a spotlight as well as the reverse lights and a clock. The wiring of the latter two were to cause some interesting smoke effects in the cabin while we were travelling through CAR and Kenya respectively.

We also put on the roof rack, the awning, the cooker, which was attached to the inside of the back door, and designed a tap and piping system for our water storage which consisted of four 20 litre plastic containers included in the equipment which came with the Land Rover.

Finally there was work on security. As Boris came with the back windows boarded up, window locks, anti-bandit film on the inside of the windows to hold them together in the event of their being broken and hasps on the doors, the only security measure we had to take was buying padlocks and curtains.

We also took Boris on several trial runs which revealed that if we thought his brakes were dodgy, his steering was unbelievably slack. Tightening the steering box and the wheel bearings (we bought a 52mm spanner for this) made a slight improvement. Do remember to take spare hub seals as they tend to leak. It was actually not until Togo that we solved our steering problem by stripping out a steering relay unit from an abandoned Land Rover and using it to replace ours.

A trip to Surrey to do some off-roading resulted in our deciding to go on David Bowyer's 4WD course in Devon. This time Boris made it there and back and survived the course! However, we were told he would not make it to Cape Town, being substantially underpowered (and that was unloaded) and that he needed new shock absorbers and springs which we replaced on our return, along with a new carburettor.

The most useful part of the course was on self-recovery. Personally, I thought the course was useful — Julian less so, except for the excellent pub nearby. Our differing opinions were probably due to the fact that he had driven a Land Rover before while I spent most of my time cycling.

One useful tip the course did not give was that when driving in the desert where the sand alternatives between hard and soft, drive with your front wheels locked so when you hit soft sand you can immediately engage high range 4WD without losing momentum, simply by slamming down the yellow knob.

Our final preparations centred on organising our camping and storage arrangements. It was far cheaper to build our own rooftop tent rather than buy one, which would not have left us much change out of £500. All it takes is a piece of marine plywood (this is less likely to warp) which is secured onto the front section of the roof rack. This folded out over the bonnet, its far end resting on the two sandladders that were simply placed on the front bumper against the bull bar. A further rectangular support folded out from the plywood to rest on the spare tyre on the bonnet.

We then put a free standing tent on top with the bedding — a mattress, sheet, duvet and pillows. The tent was stored in the back while the front section of the plywood folded backwards onto the roof rack and was then covered by tarpaulin so that the mattress and bedding could be stored underneath it. This meant that we had a free-standing tent when we went camping and when the weather was good we could sleep on top with just the bedding. We also had a spare tent pole which we wedged into the roof rack from which we hung a mosquito net — but it would have been simpler to drill a hole in the plywood.

It was when it came to storage that we were less well prepared. Other Land Rovers had built boxes screwed down onto their roof racks in which they secured bulky but light items such as chairs, table, sleeping bags and backpacks. Some had built cupboards to run along the sides and in one they had built a false platform in the back which provided an additional storage area underneath as well as a space on which one of them could sleep.

The only item we had well arranged courtesy of Boris' previous trip was the cooker attached to a small collapsible table on the inside back door. We were right to buy a large wok, firelighters and a good selection of tins and basics for food — although you could also buy the latter at a similar price in Gibraltar, there is precious little once you enter Mauritania and Mali and tins are far more expensive where they are available. But we probably should have waited until Morocco where it was cheaper to buy Camping Gaz cylinders for the cooker — these are the easiest cylinders to refill in Africa. It would also have been a good idea to have bought a decent sized grille for cooking on open fires. In fact we never used our cooker after Nairobi.

We ended up packing on the afternoon we were catching the ferry to Spain — not a good idea. We had only been going five minutes when we had to stop as the back end was swaying so much. A stop at an industrial estate revealed the sides of one tyre practically collapsing under the strain of the weight. That was not a good time to discover the hi-lift jack was totally inaccessible. We had to limp to Kwik-fit where they put on one of our spares and removed the offending tyre leaving us with the hub and its inner tube. Very kindly they did it free of charge, openly admitting they would be stunned if we made it to Portsmouth let alone Africa. We caught the ferry with 20 minutes to spare.

Planning in six weeks is a rush but it's certainly possible provided you do it full time. The main disadvantage is the lack of time in selecting a Land Rover. With the benefit of hindsight we would have taken a diesel engine. They are cheaper to run than petrol engines and diesel was as available as petrol on our route, if not more so in Zaïre (the only country where, in places, diesel was more expensive). They also appear to fetch a good price in Southern Africa and are extremely reliable, although if something does go it tends to be quite major.

Lack of time also meant we had very little time to familiarise ourselves with Boris' capabilities. For example, we did not know what his fuel consumption was when fully loaded — and very little idea whether he could even make it to Cape Town. But spending much longer preparing is no guarantee you will not have the odd problem. One group of overlanders we met spent months rebuilding their diesel engine only to blow a piston in Spain which meant spending £400 on a reconditioned diesel. Another group, whose Land Rover was kitted out by one of the specialist overlanding companies, was stranded in the desert for six weeks waiting for parts.

All this shows that, whatever your problem, there is always a way of carrying on. The only advice we would give is not to rush

Africa, and not to be put off by all the stories you may hear. It is the most spectacular continent with so much to see. We could do far worse than to learn from the hospitality you will constantly be shown on the road.

Motorbike selection and preparation
by Bernd Tesch

It is hard to cross parts of Africa by motorbike so you need to choose the right one. If you plan to stay mainly on tarmac you can take any kind of bike but if you want to go from the north to either West or East Africa then you will need an Enduro.

The Yamaha XT 500 was the first Enduro and is still a good choice. It is light, very handy, simply built and works well in hot weather. The 500cc gives enough power but the Yamaha XT 600 is better because of its greater power and less vibration. Take spare brake-brackets for the back because the sand and mud will soon destroy them — when I went from Dakar to Mombasa we had to drive 1,000km without a rear brake! The Yamaha XT 600 Ténéré has a larger fuel tank but relies too heavily on plastic.

The BMW R 80 G/S (which was built until 1987) and BMW R 80/100 GS (built from 1988-1995) are the most frequently used bikes for overland travelling. Their advantages are power and durability, they are easy to repair and very comfortable on tarred roads where you will cover your longest distances. Their disadvantages are high price, high weight, low distance from the ground (not high enough against rocks) and the high cost of preparing them for a trans-African trip (fitting a bigger fuel tank, stronger shock absorbers and so on).

The new BMW R 1000 GS is a wonderful motorbike in power and design. But for trans-African routes you don't need such power and the centre of gravity is too high. The design of the frame will not protect the bike when you fall — we built a strong baggage carrier to help. Other motorcycles such as Honda-Enduros and KTMs are not frequently used for trans-African routes.

The harder the route the lighter a motorbike should be. When I travelled from Egypt to Sudan and on to Saudi Arabia I had to conquer the difficult southern Nubian desert. I made it with an XT 500 but would not have made it through with a BMW-Enduro. Avoid a road machine if you have to cross long distances off-road.

The choice will always be an individual compromise. But be very careful with road machines if you travel in the hot season on tarred roads because the compression (8:1) is normally too high and the heat will easily destroy the engine.

Additional equipment

A large fuel tank: Crossing the Sahara you need fuel for at least 500km and crossing Zaïre you should have fuel for 600km. Because there are very few large fuel tanks for motorbikes I invented two solutions of my own. You can add a holder for an extra ten litre jerry can on each side of the bike in front of your aluminium luggage boxes. But the best solution is probably to have an extra ten litre light aluminium box inside the boxes for petrol and/or water.

A solid fuel tank of up to 45-50 litres made out of steel is OK — but these are only available for BMWs and are expensive. There are a lot of fuel tanks made from plastic (mostly Acerbis) of up to 30-35 litres at a reasonable price. But they are not well designed for tourers and it is hard to fix a tank-rucksack to them.

Kevlar-Tanks (from Moto-Forms in France) are very big and strong. They are used for the motorcycle *rallyes*. But they are extremely expensive and are not allowed in countries like Germany because they have not been tested by the German authorities. Aluminium fuel tanks are very light but expensive. I use aluminium tanks on all my trips because of their weight and have never had problems. To be strong enough they should be made out of at least 1.5mm metal and be well fixed to other surfaces with rubber.

In practice it is unlikely you will have to repair a fuel tank on the road. But if you should need to repair plastic and aluminium tanks after a fall this is easily done with plastic/aluminium patches stuck with petrol resistant glue. Every African garage will be able to weld a steel tank for you.

A strong baggage carrier and boxes: The most important thing on your trip is to reach your destination safely. You will certainly fall with the motorbike several times but if you use a strong baggage carrier made out of steel with strong 2mm aluminium boxes you will fall onto these first. Both will protect your legs, body, the fuel tank and the bike. Welded baggage carriers are stronger and lighter than screwed ones. If you use soft luggage carriers they will not protect you or the contents.

An oil thermometer and oil pressure gauge: Highly recommended, especially in hot weather. These mean you can control the engine all the time.

Spares

Exactly what you take will depend on the type of motorbike, your route and the climate in the area you are travelling. In general it's best to travel with two motorcycles of the same type. In most cases you will need just one set of spares, which saves on cost, space and weight.

It is very important to carry the original repair manual and the spares manual, especially if you don't know much about repairing motorbikes. Because you cannot carry every spare part, it's a good idea to arrange with your motorbike dealer for parts to be sent to Africa when you request them by phone or fax (you will need to sort out payment arrangements before you leave). The best address to use for this is an embassy. Normally you have to pay high customs fees in Africa but if you show a visa for the next country you are visiting and explain you are exporting the spares again then you shouldn't have to pay.

On the mechanical side you will need a spare fuel line for petrol, a petrol filter, an air filter, an oil filter, a clutch cable, a clutch, a brake cable, a cylinder head gasket, 10 spokes for the back wheel, three for the front, a spare chain (preferably a dust protected ring-chain), a clutch and brake holder (normally mounted at the steering).

On the electrical side you will need a circuit diagram for the motorbike, black box, spark plugs, spark cable, electrical cable, fuses, condenser, bulb for the headlamp.

Also very important are fluid loctide, instant gasket material, puncture repair kit, good quality tools, wire and a spare ignition key.

Tyres
You will be driving on tarred roads more than you think, so don't take only cross-tyres. A wonderful compromise are tyres with trail profile. These are good for stones and for sand. Reduce the pressure if you hit deep sand but drive slowly through it if you do not have tube-holders (a maximum speed of 60km per hour). Start with new tyres and take one spare for the back (a new front one will last for 15-25,000km). If you aim to do a lot of off-road driving then take a tyre with trail or cross profile (like Michelin Desert). Remember you will save both your tyres and your life if you drive slowly off road!

Shipping to Africa and back again
The cheapest way to get your bike to Africa is to ship it by sea. But remember to add up all the costs — getting the bike to the port, costs of harbour and crane, unloading and storing the bike until you collect it. Go to different agents and compare the prices. The agent will want to know the size and weight of the complete chest.

The main problem with shipping by sea is that it is difficult to know exactly when your bike will reach its destination. It is easier — though more expensive — if you send it by plane. You should take off the front wheel and steering to pack the bike in a small container. It is best if you can find a plane in which you can travel at the same time.

Bringing back your bike from Africa is normally cheaper. It is possible to arrange shipping yourself but unless you have a lot of time it is easier to use an agent. Always write down the name of the individual you are dealing with — it once took me seven months to get a bike back from Africa by ship!

The main problems

Dust and water. Take care of the bike and check it each day before starting. Check and change oil regularly. Fasten screws whenever you are riding off road. Clean the air filter often. Overheating the engine is the most common mistake in summer. Driving through water that is too deep and through mud are the main mistakes in the rainy season.

Other mistakes include thinking you know the desert after the first 200 miles and starting to drive too fast — your maximum should only be 50 miles per hour.

Too much weight loaded too high and towards the back is also a problem. Most of the weight must be between the axles and low down. Otherwise you will keep falling when you are off-road and the front steering will be too soft in sand and mud. When it comes to weight you should not carry too much petrol and water (though both are important) or too much food (you need food for three days at the most).

Make sure you have a comfortable ride (take a soft sack for your back with a sheepskin on it). Drive slowly because tarred African roads have potholes and are often crossed by animals. I have seen an accident between a buffalo and a vehicle and have driven over a dog, snake, pig and chicken — even though I ride defensively!

You will love travelling in Africa by motorcycle — *Tuku Tuku* in Lingala or *Piki Piki* in Kiswahili. The experience means you always remain close to nature, the sky and the earth.

Bernd Tesch runs the Globetrott Zentrale shop and mail order service for overland travellers (see Suppliers *section on page 60) and is the author of* Afrika Motorrad Reisen *(see* Further reading *on page 306).*

Motorbike selection and preparation (2)
by Jason Polley
My daydream was to reach Timbuktu. All I knew was that my

journey would take me across the Sahara, passing through Algeria and Mali, and that there would be no trains, no buses — no roads as such. It would simply be a matter of bouncing over the sand dunes, one eye on the compass and the other on the land.

I was sure that a well-prepared off-road motorcycle could do the job — the only problem was that I didn't know how to ride one. So I took a course, read Robert Persig's *Zen and the Art of Motorcycle Maintenance* and attended evening classes on motorcycle mechanics. I didn't know a La Verda from a Lambretta, so I sought advice for a suitable machine for such a trip. Finally giving in to patriotism, I decided on a 1976 Triumph 750 Tiger.

First I took the bike on a test run to Bohemia. It went like a dream and we became firm mates. On our return I set to work modifying the machine to suit the demands of the desert. I started by replacing the points with a Boyer Bransden electronic unit, which proved faultless. I fitted a Norman Hyde oil cooler, a Norton oil filter and a new carburettor; Koni Dial-A-Ride springs went on the back and the forks were filled with heavy grade oil.

The dual seat was replaced with an old single police seat and I had special racking made to carry my luggage and two 20 litre jerry cans — my fuel capacity provided a range of over 700 miles. A terrific Baglux magnetic tankbag, which never slid about, held essential items. I ran on Avon AM24 Gripster tyres with heavy duty Michelin inner tubes — and I never had a single puncture in my whole trip.

Oil filtration was improved by adding a Norton Commando unit and in-line fuel filters went between the single carburettor and tank. The compression ratio was lowered to around 7.5 to 1, so that the bike would be able to run on low grade African petrol. I also put Slick 50 in both engine and gear box. Spare clutch and throttle cables were taped in position and most nuts replaced with Nylocks or glued in place.

I rode up and down the country to make sure everything worked and went on a few hikes to properly test the stove, water purifiers and other bits of camping equipment. Then I drew breath...

This preparation guide first appeared in British Bike Magazine.

Motorcycling kit

Space is at an absolute premium if you plan to travel by motorbike or bicycle. A complete list of equipment carried by previous travellers can therefore come in helpful. This is Jason Polley's motorcycling kit.

Bike spares and tools

Front and rear Avon Gripster tyres
2 x Michelin Enduro/Motocross inner tubes
Puncture repair kit and extra valves
Mountain bicycle pump and spare connector
Spokes and spoke key
DID final drive chain
2 x air filters
2 x oil filters
2 x throttle and 2 x clutch cables (one set taped in position)

Spark plugs
Boyer Bransden 'black box'
Clutch lever
Bulbs and fuses
Roll of wire and assorted connectors
Two litres of oil
Tube of instant gasket
Set of ring spanners and adjustables
Standard tool kit (screwdrivers, pliers, feeler gauges, tyre pressure gauge, needle file, etc)
Assorted nuts, bolts and washers
Hide and copper hammer

Medical

2 courses of penicillin
Sterilised needles and thread
Syringes and intravenous connectors
Bandages and plasters
Medicines for eye, ear and throat infections
Antiseptic and antibiotic creams
Dental kit
Multi-vitamin tablets
Butterfly sutures
Sachets of antiseptic cleaner

Rehydration medicines
Salt and sugar
Surgical scissors and scalpel
Medicines for dysentery, nausea and pain
Anti-histamine creams and tablets
Insect repellent
Sterilised swabs
Surgical forceps and tweezers
Maximum factor suncream

Water

Portable water filter
Filter bags
Sterilising tablets
Tincture of iodine

4 x four-litre water containers
Two-pint canteen
Canvas bucket

Cooking

Small petrol stove
Firelighters
Zippo petrol lighter
'Magic' candles (relight when blown out)

Mess tins
Swiss army knife
Teaspoon

Camping

Lightweight tent
Sleeping bag
US army poncho

100 feet of parachute cord
Waterproof torch

Clothing

Leather jacket and trousers
Cotton shirt and trousers
Paraboots
String vest

Thermal underwear
Cotton scarf
Gauntlets

Miscellaneous

Sewing kit
Maps and guidebooks
Compass
Dried meat

Camera and film
Mason's dust mask
Small survival kit
List of important addresses

Bicycle selection and preparation

by Phil Nelson

No book on overland travel in Africa would be complete without some reference to cycling — a mode of transport that is more popular than you might imagine. But there are plenty of practical questions that need to be addressed by anyone who has plans for such a trip. I found the answers to many of these the hard way — in the course of a two year bike ride through North and West Africa and South America. Information on cycling through the desert and on food and water can be found in the section *Cycling the desert* in Chapter Five. But there are some other more general aspects that are worth considering.

Bike selection: Most people cycling across Africa use mountain bikes, although some do still prefer tourers. The width of mountain bike tyres and their handlebars give much better performance and stability on the pistes. There are a number of good mountain bikes on the market. The choice is a very personal one — but the best of them would include Marin, Specialised and Ridgeback.

Aluminium bikes are becoming popular but, as with the racks, I would not like to have one that became bent. The most important consideration is probably the choice of components.

The chainset is significant and Shimano Deore equipment has to be the best available — as its price would suggest. But whatever you use, if you go far enough on bad roads it will take a beating. Once you get into the desert you will have to run dry as any oil quickly attracts sand and this will destroy even the very best equipment.

Tyres make a big difference and price bears very little relation to suitability. Cheaper gum walled tyres can be better than skin walls at taking the weight on bad roads. On desert pistes we deflated our tyres so they bulged and the surface area in contact with the ground was increased. Skin walls invariably split under this kind of treatment. Tyres with little tread proved to be the best at sitting on top of the sand — Chan Sheng and Michelin road tyres in particular. Overall we were able to cycle along about 95% of the 600 kilometres of piste from Tamanrasset to Arlit.

Camera: We did allow ourselves the luxury of carrying a camera, which we kept in a Campro CSS bag. All the film that we needed had to be carried in our panniers — and did not suffer any damage from the heat as a result.

Clothing: All of our clothing — and our bodies — became absolutely filthy as there was rarely an opportunity to wash. Perhaps the hardest aspect of travelling by bike is going for two weeks at a time without a decent wash — sweating every day in the same smelly clothes. On the piste it is not really possible to use toe clips. As the trip progressed, I found that I became increasingly sloppy about such things — normally cycling in flip-flops after my shoes became too smelly and started falling apart. Leather gloves were soon thrown away as well for the same reasons.

Leather in cycling shorts also proved to be less durable than shorts with towelling or synthetic material. Any shirt would do — although baggy ones are more comfortable. Certainly you must wear something on top in order to avoid sunburn. A hat is also essential to protect your head and sunglasses are a good idea even if visibility is impaired when they get coated in salt from your sweat.

Containers: All equipment should be kept down to an absolute minimum, although our initial planning did underestimate the quantity of some of the things we would need. For example, we only had one half-litre petrol container to carry fuel for our cooker. In the end we were forced to use an empty banana syrup bottle as well. Its poorly fitting lid was dangerous and we lost some of our precious fuel through evaporation. You really need to take one or two one-litre Sigg bottles.

First aid kit: An item that you cannot do without. Make sure you keep it handy in case of falls from your bike.

Panniers: We used Karrimor panniers, which served us well for the two years. Of course, they did need some maintenance — sewing the canvas, replacing the plastic holding hooks and the elasticated securing hook. After about a year, the aluminium strips holding the top hooks broke and needed brazing. In fairness all of our bags were heavily overused — we had 45 litre Iberians that were always overloaded. Carradice bags seem to be made of the most durable material. Both our Karrimor and Carradice bags proved to be excellent, with Karrimor having the better pockets. All of my bags survived being dragged under a truck in an accident in Argentina!

Racks: We both used Blackburn aluminium racks — and they broke. If I could chose again now I would go for a steel rack — the main reason being that if they do break they are so much easier to get repaired. We did not use low riders and were certainly glad of the extra clearance of our conventional front racks. We carried little at the front. With hindsight this was a mistake in our loading but it did at least give us somewhere to put all our water. In general it is absolutely imperative to keep the weight as low as possible — but above the axles — and have everything firmly secured.

Tent: We had a small tent with us which we seldom used in Africa. It rained just twice during our two months in Algeria and never during four months in the Sahel. Good quality sleeping bags were essential — as was warm clothing for the nights and early mornings.

Bicycle kit
The following is a list of equipment taken by Christian and Gilly Lee on their cycling journey from Victoria Station in London to Victoria Falls in Zimbabwe. See page 143 for an account of their crossing of the Nubian Desert and page 236 for cycling around the Masai Mara.

Bike spares and tools
Panniers — Overlander by
   Carradice
2 x spare tyres
10 x inner tubes
Puncture repair kit
Cables
Brake pads
Grease and oil
Bearings

Wire and straps
Pliers
Set of Allen keys
Cable cutter
Spoke tensioner
Set of spanners
Screwdriver
Bottom bracket tensioner
Front bearing spanner

Spokes

Box of nuts, bolts, etc

Chain link extractor

Toothbrush

Medical

Rehydration mix and spoon

Gauzes, bandages and creams

Suture kit

Malaria tablets

Antibiotics

Eye ointment

Paracetamol

Tooth repair kit

Water

2 x Travelwell Military water purifiers

2 x 10-litre water bags

Cooking

Colman's multifuel cooker (replaced with a petrol stove)

2 x spoons

2 x plastic bowls

2 x plastic cups

Saucepan

Petrol canister

Penknife

Camping

Northface tent (Tadpole)

2 x sleeping mats

2 x sleeping bags

Nylon string

Towel

Miner's torch

Miscellaneous

2 x horsecrops (for warding off dogs)

2 x whistles (as warning and a signal)

Binoculars

Compass

Camera

Heliograph

SUPPLIERS

Information, planning and consultancy

Africa Travel Centre, 4 Medway Court, Leigh Street, London WC1H 9QX; Tel: 0171 387 1211.

Cyclists' Touring Club, Cotterell House, 69 Meadrow, Godalming, Surrey GU7 3HS; Tel: 01483 417217. The best starting point for all cycling travel tips. Information supplied to members only.

Globetrott Zentrale, Bernd Tesch, Karlsgraben 69, D-52064, Aachen-Centrum, Germany; Tel: 0049 241 33636, Fax. 0049 241 39494. A shop and mail order service for worldwide overland travel. Bernd Tesch has travelled 103,000km in Africa.

Expedition Advisory Centre (Royal Geographical Society), 1 Kensington Gore, London SW7 2AR; Tel: 0171 581 2057. Publishes a great deal of useful information and organises occasional seminars for independent travellers.

Overland Ltd, PO Box 4007, Pangbourne, Berkshire RG8 7YN; Tel/Fax: 01734 845990. Supplies customised new vehicles for overland travel and offers advice to prospective clients.

Ovex, 6 Pickets Close, Bushey Heath, Hertfordshire WD2 1NL; Tel: 0181 950 2977 or 0181 368 0919. Consultant on vehicle selection and equipment for overland travel.

Vehicle and equipment suppliers

Obviously it is possible to buy a vehicle from all kinds of sources — both privately and from established dealers. The following is simply a guide to suppliers who are particularly sensitive to the needs of overland travellers.

Bernd Woick, Gutenberg Strasse 14, 7302 Ostfilvern 4, Germany; Tel: 0049 711 455038; Fax: 0049 711 4560526.

Brownchurch Ltd, 308-310 Hare Row, Cambridge Heath Road, London E2 9BY; Tel: 0171 729 9437. Supplies new vehicles and is probably the most comprehensive supplier of Land Rover parts and accessories for overland travel; also the best source for sand planks, rooftop tents, etc.

Därr Expedition Service, Kirchheimer Strasse 2, D-8016 Heimstetten, Munich, Germany; Tel: 0049 89 903 8015; also at Theresian Strasse 66, D-8000 Munich 2. Comprehensive equipment supplier with mail order service.

David Bowyer's Off Road Centre, East Foldhay, Zeal Monochorum, Crediton, Devon EX17 6DH; Tel: 01363 82666. Specialises in winches, tools and jacks.

Dunsfold Land Rovers, Dunsfold, Surrey; Tel: 0148 649 567.

Second-hand Land Rovers and helpful advice.

Globetrott Zentrale, Bernd Tesch, Travel equipment, Karlsgraben 69, D-52064 Aachen-Centrum, Germany; Tel: 0049 241 33636; Fax: 0049 241 39494. Supplier of all you will need for an African trip, including baggage carriers, aluminium boxes and large fuel tanks for motorbikes.

Land Rover Centre, Lockwood, Huddersfield HD4 6EL; Tel: 01484 542092.

Nomad, 3-4 Turnpike Lane, London N8 0PX; Tel: 0181 889 7014, Fax. 0181 889 9529. General travel equipment and supplies — including specialist travel pharmacy and medical packs.

P A Blanchard, Clay Lane, Shipton Thorpe, Yorkshire YO4 3PU; Tel: 01430 872765. Specialist in all types of landrover, including ex-military and ambulance type.

Simmonites 4X4, 755 Thornton Road, Thornton, Bradford, West Yorkshire; Tel: 01274 833351/834306. Second-hand vehicles and conversions.

Survival Aids, Morland, Penrith, Cumbria CA10 3AZ; Tel: 019314 71444. Personal equipment and clothing.

Tarpaulin and Tent Manufacturing Co, 101-103 Brixton Hill, London SW2 1AA; Tel: 0181 674 0122. Large range of rugged tents and camping equipment.

Off-road driving courses

David Bowyer's Off Road Centre (see above). There are now many places where you can get practical training in off-road driving in your own vehicle, but this is the longest established and one of the best.

Chapter Three

Organised tours

Many of the advantages of travelling in your own vehicle can also be gained by joining an organised overland tour — and with a lot less trouble and expense. Of course, you will need to sacrifice a degree of independence and be prepared to live and travel together with a large group. But there are many compensations provided by this means of travel which should be considered before making a final decision on your trip.

One of the main advantages is that you can leave all of the preparation and planning to the tour company. Although planning can be a lot of fun in its own right, if you don't have the time this could be the answer to your prayers. The company should brief you in good time with specific information on anything you need to do before you leave — visas, vaccinations and insurance — and will advise on what you should pack for the trip. After that, all you have to do is turn up at the departure point and join in with the fun.

Overland tours are also worth considering for those with limited time available to travel and with limited finances. Because the same route has normally already been taken by your driver or by another driver with the same company, it is possible to travel much faster. Experience also means the driver tends to know the best places to visit or to stay in each area and the best ways around bureaucratic hurdles — all making the journey faster and more efficient than it would be for independent travellers in their own vehicle.

Those who do opt for an organised tour will probably never realise just how much they have been protected from African bureaucracy. While they sit in the truck at a border post they will probably have no idea of the amount of paperwork and hassles being dealt with by the driver or courier. The experience of expedition leaders in dealing with borders also means that trucks tend to have fewer problems with officials than independent travellers who are facing things for the first time.

Economies of scale mean that whatever trip you choose it will be possible to do it for less with an organised tour. Fuel is one of the biggest expenses of any trip. Even allowing for the higher fuel consumption of a large truck, it works out a lot less to spread this between 20 than it is share it between two (the most common number sharing a smaller vehicle) or even four (the maximum). Costs of all of the equipment and spares are similarly spread across a much larger group.

With all trucks operating some kind of rota system, travellers can even find themselves with more spare time to explore at the end of the day than their independent counterparts. If you travel independently you have to take personal responsibility for all the daily tasks — motor maintenance, shopping, pitching camp, making a fire, purifying water, cooking, cleaning and so on. But in a large group such tasks can be more efficiently divided and shared out — which means that some days you will be working and some days you won't.

Security is one of the most significant differences between the two options. The biggest headache for independent travellers is the need for constant vigilance over their vehicle and its contents. This makes it very difficult to get away from the vehicle, so reducing the possibilities for hiking and visiting more inaccessible spots. This is one time when the cramped conditions of travelling with four people in a vehicle pays off, as it is possible to split into pairs taking alternate responsibility for it.

But with a truck, there will always be enough people around to ensure a permanent security rota while allowing other members of the trip to leave their gear behind and take off by foot, canoe, train or bus. Individuals can generally leave the tour at any time and travel independently (at their own expense) to a pre-arranged rendezvous point.

So with all the above advantages for organised tours it would seem that independent travellers with their own vehicles must need their heads examined. Why travel any other way? But of course there's a big downside which may cause you to think again.

First and foremost comes the lack of independence — which is why most of us consider doing a trip to Africa in the first place. Most tour companies will do their utmost to accommodate individual preferences in the itinerary — and most journeys are pretty well planned. Once the journey gets underway, the driver will generally allow a measure of democracy to rule, allowing the trip to deviate a little from the published route. But that isn't the same thing as finding a particularly nice beach and deciding to hang around for a week or so, or deciding to miss out countries altogether and take a completely different route across the continent. Only independent travel gives you complete freedom to do what you want. If you are on an organised tour, your preferences will always be subject to the approval of all the other people on the trip — and people are the other potential problem.

However well you feel you can get along with other members of the human race, there will come a time during the course of a six month trip when you really don't want to spend every day with that group of 20 people. You will always have one thing in common with the other people on a trip — you all want to travel through Africa. But beyond that there are no guarantees you will get along with them.

The truth is, you are unlikely to be landed with an entire group that you can't stand — and if you do maybe they aren't the problem anyway! It's also well worth making sure that you treat yourself to time out from the group whenever you get the chance.

You should certainly make a point of getting away from the group if you want to spend time mixing with local people — and there can't be many people who don't want to get a taste of African culture while they are travelling. But the safety and protection offered by a large group can also do a great deal to distance you from that culture. People will approach a large group in a very different way than they would if you were on your own or in a group of two or three people — and you are far less likely to make genuine friendships if you don't break out of the group from time to time.

The routes

There is an incredible variety of trips to choose from — both shorter tours and the original trans-African expeditions. The longer trips are typically from London to Nairobi, Harare or Cape Town and can be combined with a number of optional extensions. The eastern route has also opened up for the first time in many years and companies are now setting up trips between southern Africa and Cairo, via Ethiopia. It will be possible to link these with extensions into the Middle East and Asia.

The principal trans-African route starts in Morocco. The preferred option at the moment is to stay close to the coast and travel through Mauritania into Mali and Burkina Faso. In Niger the two routes converge and continue through Nigeria, Cameroon, Central African Republic, Zaïre, Uganda and Kenya, with some continuing through Tanzania, Malawi, Zambia, Zimbabwe and South Africa.

The expense and bureaucratic difficulties of West Africa mean that few companies offer comprehensive tours of this most colourful and lively part of the continent. Some shorter tours are available but this is likely to remain an area that is best explored independently. Southern and eastern areas, however, now offer a huge choice of excellent shorter tours.

There has been a big growth in these shorter tours over recent years, allowing you to fly into a region for a few weeks and get a taste of it in a concentrated burst. These days such tours represent the biggest part of the overall market. The most popular starting points are Nairobi, Harare and — more recently — Cape Town.

Shorter expeditions also mean you can add them into your schedule once you arrive in a particular area — so giving you even greater freedom of movement. An organised tour could easily fit in with other parts of your journey by combining it with a hired car.

It is worth bearing in mind that a wide range of expeditions are available when you arrive in the main centres and so do not need to be booked in advance. Such local tours can respond to changing conditions much faster than the London-based operations and so can sometimes provide a more interesting trip. Smaller companies in South Africa and Zimbabwe were offering expeditions into Mozambique long before the big international operators started considering it for their itineraries.

Organisation

Of course, the precise details of organisation vary from company to company. They will generally organise briefing sessions to introduce themselves and explain how the trip will work — the everyday practicalities of the trip and precisely what you need to do in advance by way of documents, vaccinations and so on. They will generally also offer or suggest a comprehensive insurance policy.

Most tours aim to make the experience feel as close to independent travel as possible. There is, therefore, a fairly democratic approach to deciding on day-to-day details. Members of the group will normally set up a rota to cope with all the daily chores — especially cooking and security.

Two or three people each day will be responsible for cooking all meals — although there will often also be a rota for cooks' helpers. Even when a company provides a cook as part of its team, you will be expected to help out with much of the actual work, with the cook acting more as an adviser.

Everyone on the trip will also be expected to volunteer for an additional job. These vary from company to company and according to the number of people on the trip. But they would typically include responsibility for things such as stores, fire-lighting, water purification, security, first aid and rubbish collection. Many drivers will also suggest the option of setting up a bar, one responsibility which tends to be a popular job!

You will normally have to pay a deposit on booking. Some companies ask for a kitty at the beginning of the trip to cover food and other communal expenses but others include this within the overall cost of the trip. It is important to be clear what is and what is not included in the basic price — this varies from transport only through to all food, camping, game park fees and other admission charges. Also remember to add in the cost of any air fares when you are budgeting your trip.

The truck will stock up with staples before it sets off and wherever supplies are easy to get. But most food is bought locally and shopping will generally be the responsibility of those on cooking duty for the day.

You will have to supply your own bedding but tents are normally provided. Sleeping is generally in shared two-person tents. Check availability of camp beds and mosquito nets.

Most companies use Bedford, MAN or Mercedes trucks, customised with their own seating configuration. They have very different layouts but all of them can accommodate a maximum group of around 20 people.

Some trucks pack luggage and tents into a separate trailer, making for more space in the truck itself — as luggage is generally locked away by all the companies during the day anyway (with access only at the beginning and end of the day), this makes little difference to access but it does make things a bit more comfortable.

It is worth checking out the seating design of trucks you are thinking of travelling with. Has this been organised simply to fit in the greatest number of bodies or does it look relatively comfortable and possible to get a reasonable view of your surroundings? Try to get a sense of the relative merits of forward facing and inward facing seats — different companies offer different combinations of these. You will be spending a long time in the back of that truck so you ought to be quite sure you are happy with the layout.

More than anything else, the success or failure of your journey will largely be in the hands of your driver. This is an incredibly demanding job, with a requirement to be also a motor mechanic, a diplomat, an actor, a social worker, an expert on everything and a friend to everyone. The larger companies have extensive training programmes for their drivers — including both workshop experience and travelling with another driver. Other companies without the infrastructure to offer that kind of training are forced to rely more on luck.

Some companies also provide couriers or cooks — although it is not always clear just how useful these are. On a short journey a good all round driver should be enough but on a longer trip a second team member is invaluable in order to help with visas and bureaucracy — sometimes travelling ahead to deal with the paperwork — and helping out with some of the driving.

Choosing a tour

You can pay anything between £1,500 and £6,000 for a trans-African trip. But the variations between them are not just a matter of cost. The range of choices offered by the overland operators can be quite bewildering. Make sure that you find out exactly what is included in the price and how the trip is organised.

Cost is an important factor to bear in mind. As with most things, the general rule is that the more you pay the more you get. The cheaper end of the market can also tend to have less experienced drivers and use older and less dependable vehicles. It obviously costs a lot less to buy an old truck and advertise for a few passengers than it does to keep a regular business going with a full back-up service. Drivers with the larger operators keep in constant touch with full-time staff, who can help out in the event of problems or emergencies.

One-off expeditions are less secure when the going gets rough. But it may well be that you are not looking for the gold star treatment. If your idea is to set off on an adventurous expedition and to make the trip as independent as possible — to the extent of accepting the possibility that the truck may not even make it through — then the cheapest end of the trans-African market may well serve your purposes.

It is also worth noting that although operators generally claim precise departure dates, some smaller companies may sometimes change these in order to make sure they can fill the seats. So if time is a priority — in particular on shorter journeys — it is well worth going with one of the more established operators.

The overland companies

ABSOLUTE AFRICA 42 Bollo Lane, London W4 5LT; Tel: 0181 742 0226
Company with 16 years' experience. Average age is 18 to 35.

1994 prices
London to Nairobi — 22 weeks for £1,150 + £350 kitty
Mombasa to Harare — 12 weeks for £850 + £250 kitty
Arusha to Harare — 7 weeks for £480 + £110 kitty
Also offers gorillas and game park tours and Victoria Falls to Harare.

AFRICA EXPLORED Rose Cottage, Summerleaze, Magor, Newport NP6 3DE; Tel: 01633 880 224; Fax: 01633 882 128
Company with 22 years' experience using Bedford trucks, with a crew of two on longer trips. Average age is 18 to 35. Older passengers accepted if 'young at heart'.
1995 prices
Dover to Mombasa — 22 weeks for £1,250 + £240 kitty
Mombasa to Victoria Falls and back — 5 weeks for £390 + £50 kitty
Also offers a gorillas and game parks safari, a 5-week tour of southern Africa and a 3-week tour of Morocco.

AFRICAN TRAILS 126B Chiswick High Road, London W4 1PU; Tel: 0181 742 7724; Fax: 0181 742 8621
Has been running trips since 1980 using Leyland trucks with one driver and no courier. No age limit quoted — most passengers 18 to 35. Seats face inwards.
1994-95 prices
Nairobi to Harare — 5 weeks for £480 + £100 kitty; 9 weeks for £800 + £255 kitty
Cairo to Nairobi — 12 weeks for £950 + £260 kitty
Dover to Nairobi — 22 weeks for £1,300 + £350 kitty
Also offers a gorillas and game parks tour.

AFRICA TRAVEL SHOP 4 Medway Court, Leigh Street, London WC1H 9QX; Tel: 0171 387 1211; Fax: 0171 383 7512
Also has offices in Sydney (Tel: 02 267 3048), Melbourne (Tel: 03 670 9533), Auckland (Tel: 09 520 2000), New Jersey (Tel: 800 631 5650) and Nairobi (Tel: 2 214 099).
Offers a wide range of long and short overland options including truck tours, rail tours, self-drive in Southern Africa, camping and coach tours, motorbike safaris, balloon safaris and game lodge safaris. Because the Africa Travel Shop represents a range of companies it can be a good place to start when shopping around for the trip that suits you.

BUKIMA AFRICA 55 Huddlestone Road, Willesden Green, London NW2 5DL; Tel: and Fax: 0181 451 2446
Company using MAN trucks with a driver/leader and a co-driver/mechanic. Some seats face forward, some inwards. Video shows held every Sunday at 1.00pm or phone for an appointment.
1995 prices
London to Mombasa — 22 weeks for £1,350 + £350 kitty
Nairobi to Harare — 6 weeks for £580 + US$180 kitty; 10 weeks for £895 + US$400 kitty
Also offers Accra to Mombasa, Cairo to Nairobi, a gorillas and game parks tour out of Nairobi and Victoria Falls to Harare (25 days).

DRAGOMAN Camp Green Farm, Kenton Road, Debenham, Suffolk, IP14 6LA; Tel: 01728 861133; Fax: 01728 861127
Has been running trips for 11 years using 16-ton Mercedes trucks with a crew of two. Trips not generally recommended for travellers outside the 18-45 age group though some older passengers accepted. Seats face forward. Discounts sometimes available on full tour prices. Phone for details of fortnightly slide shows at the Hogarth Hotel in Earls Court. Talks also held around the UK.
1995 prices
Nairobi to Harare — 5 weeks for £1,065 + £155 kitty; 9½ weeks for £1,780 + £415 kitty
Cairo to Harare — 16 weeks for £2,535 + £520 kitty
London to Harare — 22 weeks for £2,950 + 635 kitty; 26 weeks for £3,375 + £760 kitty
Very wide range of shorter tours including the bushlands of the Kalahari and Namibia, and the Kenyan game parks. Also offers various combinations of individual tours and tours of Asia with Africa. Introduced trips to Mozambique in April 1995.

ECONOMIC EXPEDITIONS 29 Cunnington Street, London W4 5ER; Tel: 0181 995 7707; Fax: 0181 742 7707
Small company with 22 years' experience specialising in budget tours. Average age is 18 to mid-30s.
1995 prices
London to Nairobi — 22 weeks for £1,480
Mombasa to Johannesburg — 6 weeks for £480
Cairo to Nairobi — 12 weeks for £970

ENCOUNTER OVERLAND 267 Old Brompton Road, London SW5 9JA; Tel: 0171 370 6845; Fax: 0171 244 9737

Company with 25 years' experience running overland trips using trucks and trailers for luggage storage. Longer trips have a second driver. No age limits quoted. Most passengers in their 20s and 30s. Seats face inwards.

1995 prices
London to Cape Town — 26 weeks for £4,385
London to Nairobi — 16 weeks for £2,710
Cape Town to Harare — 35 days for £1,285
Cape Town to Nairobi — 9 weeks for £2,025
Harare to Nairobi — 28 days for £960
Also offers a very wide range of other trips including Dakar to Dar es Salaam, Nairobi to Kampala, and a range of tours of Asia with Africa.

EXODUS 9 Weir Road, London SW12 0LT; Tel: 0181 675 7996
Company with over 20 years' experience using mainly Mercedes trucks. One leader/driver on shorter trips, a crew of two on longer expeditions. Age limit of 17-45 on trips of 4 weeks or longer. Seats face inwards. Phone for dates of slide shows held once a fortnight in London at 6.30pm.

1995 prices
London to Harare — 23 weeks for £3,140 + food kitty
London to Nairobi — 17 weeks for £2,490 + food kitty
Nairobi to Harare — 5 weeks for £990 + food kitty; 9 weeks for £1,550 + food kitty
Also offers Nairobi to Addis Ababa, Nairobi to Victoria Falls, Victoria Falls to Windhoek, a 24-day Rift Valley trip out of Nairobi and shorter tours in north Africa.

EXPLORE WORLDWIDE 1 Frederick Street, Aldershot, Hampshire GU11 1LQ; Tel: 01252 319 448; Fax: 01252 343 170
Company offering up-market tours using a mix of hotels, lodges and camping in small groups in north Africa, Kenya, Tanzania, Uganda, Ethiopia, Malawi, Zimbabwe, Zambia, Botswana and Namibia. Phone for details of slide shows in London and around the UK.

GUERBA 101 Eden Vale Road, Westbury, Wiltshire BA13 3QX; Tel: 01373 826 611; Fax: 01373 858 351
Also has an office in Nairobi (Tel: 2 218 783). Represented in Australia by Peregrine Adventures (Tel: 03 663 8611). In the USA contact Adventure Centre (Tel: 510 654 1879).
Has been running overland expeditions and shorter safaris for 15 years using Mercedes, AWD and Bedford trucks. Expeditions have

a crew of three — two drivers and a cook. Average age is 20 to 50. Seats face inwards. Slide shows every month — phone for dates. Videos also available for hire.

1995 prices

London to Cape Town — 31 weeks for £4,860 + £900 kitty
Cairo to Nairobi — 23 days for £1,330 + £235 kitty
Nairobi to Cape Town — 11 weeks for £2,080 + £400 kitty
Harare to Cape Town — 22 days for £790 + £170 kitty; 29 days for £960 + £155 kitty
Also offers London to Harare, Dakar to Cape Town, Gibraltar to Dakar and a wide range of shorter trips.

HOBO TRANS AFRICA EXPEDITIONS Wisset Place, Halesworth, Suffolk IP19 8HY; Tel: 01986 873124; Fax: 01986 872224
Has been operating since the 1970s. Uses Leyland Clydesdale or Freighter or Mercedes 16/17 trucks with a group leader and co-driver/mechanic. Passengers over 45 should check before booking. Average age is mid-20s. Seats face inwards.

1995 prices

London to Nairobi — 20 weeks for £1,350 + £345 kitty
London to Harare — 25-26 weeks for £1,725 + £380 kitty (with optional 7 day extension to visit Arusha)

KUMUKA EXPEDITIONS 40 Earls Court Road, London W8 6EJ; Tel: 0171 937 8855, Fax: 0171 937 6664
Uses MAN trucks with a crew of two. Age limits on some tours. 12 seats face forward, 6 face inwards. Cook included on some tours. Discount for early booking sometimes available. Videos screened at 6.30pm on Wednesdays.

1995 prices

Johannesburg to Harare — 6 weeks for £1,175 + £290 kitty; 3 weeks for £680 + £125 kitty
Harare to Nairobi — 10 weeks for £1,445 + £260; 7 weeks for £995 + £210 kitty
Also offers a wide range of shorter tours in eastern and southern Africa.

PHOENIX OVERLAND College Farm, Far Street, Wymeswold, Leicestershire LE12 6TZ; Tel: 01509 881818; Fax: 01509 881822. Small company using Bedford four-wheel drive trucks with a driver/mechanic plus courier. No age limit on passengers. Photographs of trips can be viewed by appointment.

1995 prices
Istanbul to Harare — 19 weeks for £1,450 + £395 kitty
Nairobi to Harare — 5 weeks for £475 + £110 kitty; 10 weeks for
£815 + £255 kitty
Also offers a 4-week tour of gorillas and game parks running from
Nairobi.

TERANGA EXPEDITIONS The Stables, Lockeepers, Menmore Lane,
Grove, Leighton Buzzard, Buckinghamshire. Tel: 0121 447 8222.
Company specialising in flexible expeditions of two weeks to six
months in West Africa. Uses Bedford trucks with split level forward
and inward facing seats and a crew of two. Video available.
1995 prices
N'djamena to Bamako — 4 weeks for £670
London to Kampala (via Congo and São Tomé) — 7 months for £2,600

TRACKS 12 Abingdon Road, London W8 6AF; Tel: 0171 937
3028/9; Fax: 0171 937 3176
Also has an office in Nairobi (Tel: 2 00 24). In Australia is
represented by African Wildlife Safaris (Free call 008 333 022). In
New Zealand contact Adventure World (Tel: 9 524 5118, Toll Free
Fax: 0800 652 958). USA west coast contact Safari Centre (Tel: 310
546 441 Toll free: 800 223 6046) — east coast contact Himalayan
Travel (Tel: 203 359 3711).
Company with 22 years' experience of African tours using Bedford
or Mercedes trucks. Two leader/drivers on longer expeditions. Seats
face forward. Average age is 20 to 50.
1995 prices
London to Nairobi — 15 weeks for £1,890 + £300 kitty
Nairobi to Harare — 10 weeks for £1,450 + £275 kitty
Also offers a wide range of shorter tours in southern, east, west and
north Africa.

TRUCK AFRICA 37 Ranelagh Gardens Mansions, Fulham,
London SW6 3UQ; Tel: 0171 731 6142, Fax: 0171 371 7445
Small company offering tours only in Africa using Leyland
Freighters. Seats face inwards. Average age is 18-40. Videos
screened on Wednesdays or call for an appointment.
1995 prices
London to Harare — 7 months for £1,880 + £480 kitty
Nairobi to Harare — 6 weeks for £450 + £190 kitty
Group discounts available on some tours. Also offers shorter tours
starting and ending in both Nairobi and Harare.

Getting along on the road

No matter how well organised you are, no matter how much reading and research you've done in advance, you're never going to be able to answer the big question about a truck tour. 'What are the other people on the trip going to be like? And am I going to be able to get on with them for weeks on end?'

That's pretty well what was going through our minds just before Christmas when we stepped off the plane in Cape Town and found ourselves in the middle of a South African summer. As luck would have it, we bumped into one of our fellow travellers on the bus from the airport. Rachel couldn't understand how we knew who she was — until we pointed out the tour company luggage label on her rucksack.

Over the next few days, as we waited for our truck to arrive at the end of its southbound trip from Harare, we began to wonder if everyone in Cape Town was heading north on our truck. A quick tour of the Cape peninsula introduced us to two more people on the trip — Kevin from San Francisco and Anne from Germany. Back at our hotel Rachel introduced us to Duncan and Rudi who, although they'd never met before, had already slipped into the role of truck entertainers which was to keep us laughing all the way to Harare. So by the time we had our eve of trip meeting there were already a few familiar faces.

Even so, at the start it's perfectly normal to feel you'll never remember everyone's name, what truck job they've volunteered for and how many vegetarians there are for when you're on cooking duty. But it's amazing how quickly you get to know each other when you're all loaded into the back of a Bedford truck.

Perhaps it's this sense of being all in it together that makes everyone so supportive. If you have a problem you're likely to find a queue of people who want to help you sort it out. After all, it's their trip too, and they're just as determined as you are that they're going to enjoy it.

But it's only fair to say we both felt very lucky when it came to the group we were travelling with, who turned out to be as friendly and varied a bunch of overlanders as you could hope to meet. We had people who had flown in from New Zealand, Canada, the USA, Turkey, Germany, the Netherlands, Switzerland and the UK. The range of jobs — which included a barrister, an accountant, a few engineers, three nurses and a systems analyst — and the fact our ages spanned from 21 to 45, also helped. The people you travel with are a big element of a truck trip — and different outlooks are as important as shared interests and objectives.

We also struck lucky with our driver — the one person who probably makes the biggest impact on how your trip turns out. Ian Ransom, an ex-Australian army man, was a rock solid driver and mechanic who knew the trip backwards. But he also joined in everything we did with enthusiasm and shared our ups and downs along the way. Wherever possible we were given choices about what we wanted to do and where we wanted to go.

The decisions were easier than you might think, though the democratic process was hastened by Ian's masterful presentation of the options. Well, what would you say if someone asked you whether you wanted to spend all day travelling in the back of a truck or take a sunset cruise with free beer along the Zambezi river?

The trip itself was spectacular. From Cape Town we headed up to the Orange River and Namibia where we took in a day's canoeing, a trek down Fish River Canyon and generally marvelled at the splendid isolation of the Namibian desert. Dawn on Christmas Day saw us breakfasting on barbecued chicken and chilled champagne in the shadow of the largest sand dunes in the world at Sossusvlei. (We managed the climb up and back before Ian cracked open the bottles.)

Further north we spent three wonderful days in Etosha National Park at the end of the dry season. With water incredibly scarce throughout the rest of the park, all we had to do was sit by the waterhole at Okaukuejo camp and watch an incredible variety of game coming to drink throughout the day and night. Birgit, a German nurse used to working nights, sat up from dusk to dawn and saw two rhinos mating. When we asked her what it was like she shrugged. 'Noisy,' she said.

From Etosha we headed towards Botswana where we left the truck behind for a three day trip into the Okavango Delta where we were taken along the tiny tributaries in *mokoros* — dugout canoes poled along by local villagers. There can be no more peaceful way to experience the rich bird and game life in this astonishing inland delta, where the Cubango river simply flows out into the desert.

Our trip ended in Zimbabwe where we took in Victoria Falls, Bulawayo, the Great Zimbabwe Ruins and the beautiful eastern highlands before finally heading for Harare. This was the end of the five week trip for around half of us who were flying back home to jobs and other responsibilities. The rest were carrying on with the truck and some new passengers on the journey north to Nairobi.

Having previously done our own 23,000 mile African trip in a Land Rover, it's only fair to admit we had reservations about going on an organised tour. Used to taking our own decisions, planning our own route, stopping for a few days on a nice beach if we felt like it, how would we cope with the whole trip being basically organised from start to finish?

The answer is that we had a thoroughly good time. It's a different type of trip, of course. But if you have a limited timescale and budget you can see and do far more on a truck trip than you could ever organise on your own. We were covering large distances incredibly quickly without ending up physically exhausted by the process of driving our own vehicle all day. When we arrived somewhere we were fresh enough to take advantage of it — Ian was the one who needed to rest! As an independent traveller you have to build a lot more time into your schedule to take account of this.

And if you really want to, you will find there is plenty of opportunity on an organised trip to help with mechanical chores like truck maintenance — extra hands always come in useful when changing wheels, fixing flats and running general checks.

There are no golden rules for making your truck trip a success — so much will depend on who you end up travelling with, where you go and what you see. In the end a lot of it will come down to you and how determined you are to make the trip work for everyone. Still, there are one or two pointers it's worth bearing in mind:

If someone does something you find irritating, then tell them at the first opportunity in the nicest possible way. Don't wait until it's bugging you so much that you blow your top!

Never resent the fact you have a job to do every day — everyone else has got one, too.

Take time out if you need to — you can't walk around in a group of 20 all the time. You might just discover something worthwhile for the others to go off and see.

Don't panic about cooking duty — there will always be people to help and advise you, and you'll never be expected to cope on your own.

Leave your preconceptions at home.

And last but not least — relax and enjoy yourself.

Bob Swain and Paula Snyder travelled with Encounter Overland on their Southern Cross trip from Cape Town to Harare in December 1994-January 1995.

Chapter Four

On the road

The long-awaited day finally arrives (more than likely later than you had originally planned) and you hit the road. Setting off with sandplanks on your roof and heart in your mouth, you may well be wondering what on earth you have let yourself in for. There are some exciting times up ahead. This chapter provides a few tips which should help you to make the most of your trip.

DRIVING TECHNIQUES

Needless to say, the conditions you will face are going to be quite unlike anything you would usually come across on roads in developed countries. When it gets tough, driving can be very tiring, so try to keep shifts behind the wheel relatively short. It will help, of course, if there are at least two people who can share the driving.

If road conditions worry you, then careful route planning should help keep the bad parts down to a minimum. But there will always be long stretches of the three main perils — sand, mud and corrugations — that you will not be able to avoid.

Unless you go out of your way to explore desert regions, soft sand will only play a minor part in any desert crossing. But inevitably you will ultimately find yourself bogged down in the stuff. As long as you have four-wheel drive you should not have too many problems. But resist the temptation of trying to free yourself against the odds with engine power alone — if you are well and truly stuck the chances are you will just find yourself digging deeper and deeper into the sand. Instead, you should make full use of those two essential items of desert equipment — shovel and sandplanks. First dig away all sand from the wheels so they are completely exposed and enough sand is removed from in front of the wheels for the planks to lie flat. If the vehicle has dug so deeply into the sand that the chassis has grounded then you will not be going anywhere until you have cleared the sand from under it.

When you have finished digging, set the sandplanks in front of the wheels and drive onto them and (hopefully) out of trouble. In the hot sun, you will often be tempted to cut short the digging and head straight for the sand planks — but don't, as you will simply find the vehicle digging itself straight back into the sand, undoing all your hard work. Of course, the very best option in soft sand is not to get stuck in the first place. Unfortunately there really is no other way to learn how to cope with it than by experience. In the early stages you should simply take it easy and keep your eyes open. In desert driving it is always sudden changes in terrain that cause problems. In particular, pay close attention to signs of soft patches in the tracks of other vehicles.

Corrugations are probably the most irritating and most common driving obstacle in Africa. Constant ripples on dirt roads or other hard surfaces, they are caused by vehicles travelling at speed. Which means that once you get out of a soft section and onto what ought to be a reasonable stretch of road, the fact that previous vehicles have taken the opportunity to speed up means the surface will inevitably have become corrugated.

There are only two ways of coping with corrugations — very fast or very slow. Neither option is particularly pleasant. Driving fast, you can skip across the tops of the bumps. This is generally the favoured approach, although it does give your suspension a hard time and removes much of your steering and braking control. The slower option can be quite tortuous but is often the only way. You will sometimes notice tracks running parallel to badly corrugated roads which are an indication of the surface local traffic prefers — though often there is not a great deal in it.

Driving in muddy conditions requires a completely different set of skills — and is perhaps the only major aspect of driving it is possible to practise before setting off. The most important tip is to let the vehicle do as much of the work as possible. Those who are too heavy on the gas in slippery conditions are likely to find themselves in deep trouble.

If you do not have much off-road driving experience there are quite a number of practical courses available which could prove useful. They will not necessarily provide you with African conditions, but will help to teach you just what your vehicle is capable of. We went on a one and a half day course at David Bowyer's Off Road Centre (see *Suppliers* section, page 60). It provided an excellent introduction and encouraged an understanding of the capabilities of our Land Rover.

You will be required to perform some pretty careful manoeuvres once you are in Africa — such as getting on and off some of the smaller ferries you are sure to come across whatever route you take. The smallest will just provide a couple of planks to drive up and onto the deck — take care.

Don't panic too much about tales you may hear of the need to rebuild bridges along the way. Generally speaking this should not be necessary. However, in some areas you may need to rearrange things a little. It may also be necessary to consider fording some of the smaller streams rather than risking a dangerous bridge. Once again, learn to read the tracks to see which option local traffic prefers.

BORDERS, POLICE CHECKS AND BUREAUCRACY

Dealing with officialdom is an important aspect of any visit to Africa. If you are taking your own vehicle then you massively increase the extent to which you will need to sweet talk your way across the continent. Borders mean customs and immigration checks and sometimes police or military searches as well. Once inside a country police and military stops can be a regular occurrence. Different countries will require a whole host of registration formalities and paperwork. Keeping on top of all this can become a major preoccupation.

At the end of the day, there is just one golden rule — keep your cool and keep smiling. A friendly response to the ponderous pace of African bureaucracy will always pay dividends. It is true some delays can seem pointless and almost designed to make you frustrated, but a positive attitude will ultimately help smooth the way and an aggressive manner can slow a snail's pace down to a dead stop.

You will at some stage certainly be asked for money at a border or police check. Since receipted administration fees are almost as common as 'dash', the best advice on this score is to play it by ear. Normally, if you have to fill in a form and are given a receipt it is legitimate. Requests for 'some money' mean a bribe. It is up to you how to handle it.

We will not deny there are some individuals and border posts that seem dedicated to giving you a hard time — although most that have a reputation have gained this simply from bad experiences of a few people long ago. Try to check with travellers coming the other way how things are at the time.

PLACES TO STAY

There will be times when you can take advantage of the facilities of
a campsite or even a hotel — but usually it will simply be a matter
of picking out your spot and pulling up for the night. Your choice
of where to stop will largely be determined by the landscape. Desert
and *sahel* (semi-desert) areas present few problems other than lack
of cover but in areas of dense vegetation it can be a problem finding
a space big enough for your vehicle, let alone a tent.

Bush camping

Zaïre can be very difficult, with solid vegetation right up to the
sides of the road. The only two options are to find a village and ask
for permission to camp or to find one of the 'gravel pits' which have
been dug out for material to build the road. The pits are few and far
between and can often have large pools of water (making mosquito
nets absolutely essential). You are also almost guaranteed to have
visitors as gravel pits are frequently sited close to a village. It can
also be very hard to find a spot for bush camping in both Namibia
and Zimbabwe as almost all land is fenced off.

In the north you can generally camp in *palmiers* (palm groves) but
as these are privately owned you should ask permission if possible.

Wherever you decide to stay, it makes sense to be as discreet as
you can. The less visible you are from the road the better — and
wait until the road is free of traffic before turning off, unless you
want to advertise what you are doing. Make sure you leave yourself
plenty of time to select a camping spot, as problems tend to multiply
once it gets dark. Some travellers stop as early as three or four
o'clock to make sure they have enough time to cook, clean up and
get settled before the light starts to go (which is 6.00pm anywhere
near to the equator and earlier on either side in the winter).

Please do not be hostile to curious visitors when you are camping.
Unlike most other travellers, those who have their own vehicles can
become very insular and begin to forget they are guests in the
communities they are driving through. People in many parts of
Africa will not necessarily have seen anyone like you before and
will quite happily sit and watch you for hours. Try to remember that
you must seem rather weird. Just as you want to see new things
throughout your journey, you present something equally new to
everyone you meet along the way. Of course it can be extremely
unnerving to be the object of curiosity, especially when you are hot,
tired and hungry — but try to be rational and not take it out on
individuals.

If you do not have any experience of travel in less developed countries, all this will probably seem like an over the top warning. You will probably think Africa is such a huge continent that you will spend long periods of time well away from any human life. Nothing could be further from the truth. Apart from the most extreme desert regions you will find you are never far from other people. Villages will always develop alongside a country's communications network; where there are few roads and tracks, the population will be concentrated along them.

Missions

Throughout the continent missions, hospitals and aid organisations will often let you camp in their grounds. Some have had bad experiences with travellers and will turn you down; some will expect you to pay a small fee (even, on occasions, a fairly hefty fee). A small donation will always be appreciated.

The reception you receive at missions will vary enormously. This will largely depend on their previous experience of travellers — so remember your own behaviour will affect the reception for those that follow. Many missions make a point of welcoming travellers but others — particularly on the main routes — have had their fill of ungrateful freeloaders. But off the beaten track you will generally be welcome — we stayed at one mission hospital way off the main road where the Italian nuns said we were the first travellers who had asked to stay since they arrived in the 1950s!

Campsites

Along the main Africa overland route there are quite a few campsites. They are not at all common, however, if you choose to take a loop around West Africa.

Campsites should be used whenever possible because they are great places to rest, check up on the vehicle and meet other travellers. Along the main routes most travellers stop at the same sites; this means you will be able to get all of the latest information on roads, borders, currency, fuel and general news.

We have included information on some of the main campsites under the reference sections on individual countries. We have also given tips in these sections on other places to stay. While some of this information may change over time, it is good to have some idea of the possibilities up ahead. On the road you will discover your whole day can often revolve around making sure you end up with a good spot to stay in the evening.

Hotels

However tightly you intend to budget, you will inevitably seek the luxury of a bed for the night from time to time. The extent you use hotels will vary totally according to your own preferences and finances. It may well prove to be the only option in larger towns.

Unless you are travelling by motorbike or bicycle and can take your bike into your room, the golden rule is only to use hotels with secure parking (all of the hotels in our reference sections are in this category). This is no problem in the more expensive Western-style hotels, but if you look around it is also possible in cheaper African hotels, which are much more fun anyway. Bring your own mosquito net and be prepared for an interesting range of livestock in the bedroom — cockroaches, lizards and all kinds of crawling things are par for the course. We only had bats in our bedroom once, however — at the Foyer des Militants in Abomey, Benin. They lived in the roof and flew in and out through a hole in the ceiling all night. Clapping your hands loudly tends to shoo them away while you are awake.

At the top end of the scale it is possible to splash out for less than you might think (and it does you a lot of good to have a luxurious break). Prices vary considerably from country to country — with the CFA zones tending to be the most expensive for top class hotels. As ever, check with other travellers for the latest information.

FOOD AND DRINK

Unless you are travelling on an organised truck expedition, you will need to give some thought before you leave to how you are going to eat on the road. And even on the trucks you will have to take your turn at preparing meals. How much effort you put into cooking is largely up to you, but eating a sensible and varied diet can not only help lift a long day's hot and tiring driving or cycling, but help you to keep reasonably healthy and therefore better prepared to cope with doses of the African runs, and other infections.

Stoves, burners and fires

The wide variety of camping stoves available means you can exercise a fair degree of choice, though bikers and cyclists tend to opt for small, lightweight petrol stoves or burners. These can be fussy to light but are fairly reliable, depending on how much you are prepared to spend, though even expensive models can let you down. We invested in an expensive Swedish Optimus petrol burner which developed fuel jet problems on our way down through

Europe. Then when we finally replaced the jet, the seal on the priming pump went, making it completely unusable. But others we met with petrol stoves had no problems, so perhaps we were unlucky. Several people have particularly recommended Colman petrol stoves (one, two or three burners) as proving very reliable, though they are rather bulky and so not suitable for bikers or cyclists.

Disadvantages of petrol are blackening of pots (though it does rub off much more easily if you smear the outside of your pans liberally with washing up liquid before you cook) and smoking when you first light up. This also applies to the cheap Chinese-made kerosene wick stoves you can find almost everywhere in Africa — though we bought one of these in frustration at our petrol model and soon wished we had had one all along. There is virtually nothing that can go wrong with them, and the small amount of fuel they burn means you can easily carry enough to last until the next source of kerosene. They are probably too bulky to be of much use to bikers or cyclists.

Beware of taking a meths burner as meths is not widely available. We met some travellers in Zaïre who scoured Kisangani for meths with no luck.

Gas stoves are probably the easiest, cleanest and most reliable option. We had ruled them out, having heard it could be difficult to get hold of gas bottles. It is true that the small Camping Gaz cartridges — *cartouches*, in French — are almost impossible to find. But otherwise you will be able to get a bottle filled in most towns. Many local families cook with gas (particularly in the Sahara) and most gas stoves these days have a choice of regulators to cover a range of gas fuels.

If you are likely to be off the beaten track for long periods, it might be worth having large gas cylinders fitted in your vehicle. This is a customising service offered by the Overlanders Club.

Finally, although open fires are harder to control for cooking, they are an instant focus when camping, particularly when it gets cold at night. If you don't have a fire grille, a few strategically placed rocks can provide a pot stand just above the flames, and not just potatoes but other vegetables can be roasted in no time, wrapped in foil with a few herbs or spices for extra flavour.

If you do build a fire, be sensible in dry areas where sparks may set grass or scrub alight. And never cut green wood for a fire, particularly in the desert and *sahel* areas or game parks — Africa has enough deforestation problems of its own without adding to them. If your transport allows you to carry firewood as you go, you can dry it out by lashing it to the roof rack or the front of your vehicle.

Other cooking equipment

Like everything else it is best to keep this down to a minimum. You will quickly learn to adapt what you have for a whole range of purposes, and cooking on the road is all about using your imagination.

Cyclists and bikers can choose from a wide range of lightweight billycan sets, though anyone selecting collapsible pots and pans should pay particular attention to handles and how they clip or hook on. If some plastic slot-on handles chip you will never get them to stay put again.

Obviously you have more choice with a bigger vehicle. We brought a saucepan which doubled as a two-tier steamer, a deep straight-edged frying pan and bought a third aluminium saucepan after the first three months as we got more adventurous with food. We also wish we had brought a kettle. Other favourites with travellers are pressure cookers, woks and, particularly if you are in a reasonable sized group, big cast iron cooking pots that can be left sitting on an open fire to stew away for hours.

Basics you need to consider are a decent sharp knife, a wooden spoon, something to strain boiled pasta or vegetables, unless you have a saucepan and lid that are suitable, a tin opener, bottle opener, sardine key (no, they don't come with the tin!) and possibly a chopping board, though this is not essential as there is very little skill involved in chopping vegetables in the air straight into the pot. Our plates and mugs were enamel though we would recommend plastic mugs for tea and coffee as enamel gets frustratingly hot. We also chose deep dishes rather than flat plates; they are easier to eat off without a table and safer for runny dishes. Take spares of cutlery — teaspoons love inaccessible corners in Land Rovers or dropping out of kit bags.

Anything else you use at home you can probably adapt from what you have brought with you. Whole spices can be ground-up successfully with a clean beer bottle in a saucepan; you can brew up tea or coffee in anything that holds hot water (though we did meet one couple who had brought along their Espresso coffee maker!); garlic is just as good chopped as crushed; and a serrated knife will double as vegetable peeler and even as a grater.

Food to bring with you

Even if you are planning a shortish trip you will not be able to bring everything you are going to eat, but it is a good idea to assemble a store box of basics and emergency supplies before you go. It will not take long before you realise what you need to carry, and what can be picked up on the road.

Good basic supplies to carry include salt (extra loss means you will naturally salt your food more); some initial herbs and spices to liven up vegetables, though you will replace these every so often with wonderful fresh local alternatives; tea and coffee; sugar (even if you do not normally use it — it has a high barter value and sweet tea is great if you are ill and cannot face food); rice and pasta; tomato puree (go for tubes rather than tins which can be wasteful and have a tendency to splatter you in horror-film red if you open them in the heat); stock cubes; oil in plastic firm-screwtop bottles; and flour or cornflour for thickening. Dried beans are also good if your cooking equipment is up to the longer cooking times needed. Even if all you can buy locally is tomatoes and onions you will be able to cook up an acceptable meal with this lot. You will be able to replace most of these basics in larger villages and towns on the way.

Slightly more luxurious items to take could include mustard, for livening up salad dressings; dried mushrooms or other vegetables to make pasta or rice dishes a bit more special; lemon juice in plastic bottles; dried fruit to nibble; jam for a quick breakfast with local bread; biscuits or crackers; and boiled sweets for when you need a burst of energy, though better by far when you are flagging is Kendal mint cake (the high glucose bar that goes into the supplies for every major expedition). Next trip we are taking plenty.

You should also carry some more substantial stores to allow you to eat even when you cannot buy local produce. We almost always had enough for four or five meals, just in case. With a Land Rover you can afford to carry tins, but cyclists and bikers should carry emergency packets of dried food for times of need. The dehydrated meals available from camping and outdoor shops are expensive, none too generous in size and do not offer much in the way of choice. So unless you are rich with a small appetite and not particularly interested in food, you will have to look at alternatives. Good buys, particularly if weight is a problem, are packet soups, packets of instant Chinese noodles and other dried 'instant' food.

If you have the space a few well chosen tins can always be turned into a meal. Smaller tins of tuna or ham can be added to rice or locally bought vegetables, and instant mashed potato and dried milk is a useful filler with a vegetable stew. Small packets of parmesan cheese are a wonderful addition to basic pastas.

Unless you are extremely lucky there will be times when you will be unable to cook anything hot because the weather, circumstances or fate conspire against you. On these occasions you will feel a whole lot better for having some provisions that can be turned into a cold meal. One of our great standbys was a tin of beans (the flageolet beans available in French supermarkets in West and Central Africa are best though kidney or haricot beans are also good), mixed with a tin of tuna in oil, some lemon juice, some fresh chopped onion or tomato if you have it, mustard and herbs, for a tasty salad.

Local shopping

If you are setting off from the north and crossing the Sahara, do not count on much variety. In the desert towns fresh produce is virtually limited to tomatoes, onions, garlic, chillies, leeks — and oranges, if you can afford them. In terms of dried and tinned food you are limited to sardines, packets of bland biscuits and tomato puree, unless you are prepared to pay prohibitive prices for imports.

Further south you will start to see aubergines, pineapples, mangoes, limes, bananas and other forgotten luxuries, though all of these will get cheaper as you keep travelling south. Potatoes are curiously absent from West Africa, apart from expensive European imports, but reappear again in Central and East Africa. This happens with all sorts of vegetables — in some areas local markets may offer a choice of only two or three different things, but a few miles further on, they will disappear and something else will be available. You get very imaginative after a while.

One important thing to bear in mind when buying anything fresh is that it will not stay fresh for long being transported around in African temperatures. Avoid hoarding too much fresh produce just because you have the space to carry it. African market traders are well used to people buying only small quantities. Fruit and vegetables are sold in small heaps — you negotiate a price for the heap you want.

Bread is almost universally available, though it is always sweetened in Ghana, and in out of the way areas in East Africa only chapattis may be available.

We became virtual vegetarians during our first trip, partly from necessity and partly from choice. In bigger towns meat will be available but outside of supermarkets is often crawling with flies, so if you are a dedicated carnivore wash everything very thoroughly. Chickens are sold live, so you have to be prepared to do your own strangling. Near rivers and lakes you will also see local fish on sale — if it smells fresh and the flesh is firm it is safe enough if cooked thoroughly.

Supermarkets for stocking up on supplies are variable to say the least. In ex-French areas you can splash out in expensive SCORE supermarkets and get just about anything you need. You can even buy imported French cheese, though it is often past its best and not worth what they charge for it. Elsewhere availability of some things will be limited, though one item definitely worth mentioning is the peanut butter sold in large tins in West Africa, which is superb for cooking. It is much darker and runnier than you will be used to and makes a wonderfully rich sauce with vegetables like aubergines or the cooking bananas that are universally available in Zaïre.

In the bigger towns in southern Africa you will have absolutely no problems shopping for food, though expect only basic foods in Mozambique — maize, bread, chickens and seasonal fruit and vegetables.

Storage containers

Choose these with care. Corrugations and other rough driving conditions will shake things around so much that jars will literally unscrew themselves, plastic lids will pop off, and tubes of tomato puree will puncture. You can minimise this by packing loose spaces in a food box with towels so things do not jump around so much, but it is also worth thinking about having the right containers. Plastic jars and bottles with deep screw tops are best. Tupperware style boxes should have very tight seals. Do not buy oil in a flip top bottle — it can get very messy. If you cannot get oil with a screw top then transfer it to a safer jar. You are only likely to forget this once! Another good option is old tins which can be washed out and used for storing things like sugar, tea and coffee if you bring some plastic sealing lids (on sale in most supermarkets next to the tinned pet food).

Cooking with one burner

If your choice of stove means you have only one burner you need not feel restricted to one pot meals. Rice or pasta boiled for a few minutes will continue to cook sitting in the hot water while you make up a basic vegetable sauce. Or if you are cooking with meat or beans, start off your rice or pasta about half an hour before you plan to eat and set it aside while you finish off your other dish. Always bring rice or pasta back to the boil and check it is done before straining. If you are cooking two dishes you can always prepare them separately and heat things up before you eat. In time you will get more than skilled at juggling pots. If you find yourself travelling in convoy, or meet up with other travellers in campsites or free camping, you can pool resources and end up with some really adventurous meals. Four one burner stoves mean four hot dishes to share.

Food and hygiene

Your general standards of cleanliness will undoubtedly drop as you travel, but food is one area where it is only sensible to exercise a degree of care. Flies are a source of more exotic stomach bugs than you could imagine, and they are everywhere in Africa. If you are cooking meat or fish make sure it is thoroughly cooked and wash all vegetables carefully. If you are washing vegetables to eat raw then use purified water. Basically, if you would not want to drink the water, then don't pour it on what you are just about to eat — the effects are the same.

Food storage boxes need to be kept reasonably clean. Food is something you use all the time so you will know if it's time for a clean out. Fresh vegetables are best kept out of plastic bags, which make them sweat and start to rot. An open cardboard box is a good idea, or tie them up in a cloth local-style to keep them as dry as you can.

Eating out

Ordinary priced African restaurants do not really offer much choice, except in the more populated areas of Senegal which is justly famous for its food. If you eat at a lot of roadside stalls you will sooner, rather than later, get bored with the ubiquitous rice and sauce, which is mainly what you will be offered. There are, of course, some wonderful exceptions to the rule and we hope you find as many as we did. Exploring the local food is an essential element of enjoyable travel.

Needless to say, Western hotels and restaurants can give you pretty much what you would get at home — but expect to pay for it. It can be a nice treat once in a while — but somehow the atmosphere can feel a bit sterile when you are used to life on the road. Better for a special occasion if you are in a big capital city is to check out the more expensive African restaurants where you can sample new and delicious tastes that sadly most Africans will never be able to afford. East Africa is a real treat for Indian restaurants, particularly for vegetarian specials, and while some are positively up-market there are plenty of cheaper café-style Indian restaurants which serve delicious food at prices everyone can afford. Most towns in southern Africa offer plenty of choice when it comes to Western style restaurants though it can be harder to find African food.

Local specialities that are worth looking out for include: *capitaine* or Nile perch (a meaty firm-fleshed fish widely available in Central Africa and served in a variety of ways, including kebabs), *chambo* (from Malawi — delicious lake fish, very meaty with large bones), *moambe chicken* (from Zaïre — chicken cooked in palm oil and spinach), *groundnut stew* (mainly in West and Central Africa — meat cooked in a dark peanut sauce), *jollof rice* (Sierra Leone and other parts of West and Central Africa — rice cooked with tomatoes and spices and, if you are lucky, with pieces of chicken or meat) and a host of specialities from Senegal, including *yassa* (chicken cooked with lemon and onions), *poisson farci* (stuffed fish), *thiebou diène* (a delicious dish of precooked meats or fish and vegetables on a bed of spiced tomato rice) and its poorer cousin *riz gras* — literally 'fat rice'.

Finally, a word on a basic staple meal accompaniment you are unlikely to come across outside of an African restaurant. *Fufu* in West Africa and *ugali* in East is a stiff paste made from a ground starch (maize, yam, cassava and plantain are all common) and hot water. Travellers' reactions to it are either enthusiastic or less than politely disdainful. We represent one each from the two most extreme responses. One traveller we met described eating it as, 'like swallowing when you've got a heavy cold'.

The African good (and not so good) beer guide

African beers may not have quite the same reputation as German lager, British ale or Irish stout, but after a hard day's driving on difficult and dusty tracks, the thought that there may be a cool — or even warm — beer somewhere at the end of the road tends to take a strong grip on the imagination.

In the north, you are better off sticking with purified water — the rare supplies of beer are both extraordinarily expensive and very poor quality. But once you cross over the magical divide into black Africa, all that begins to change. The bar at the Assamakka (Niger) border post is one of the most popular in Africa for overlanders. Suddenly there are large bottles of cool beer available — and the long wait in the heat for border formalities does not seem so bad after all.

But unearthing supplies can sometimes stretch your ingenuity to extremes. Guinea was the one country where we failed to find any local supplies at all — the canned beers available ranged from Dutch to Cypriot to Lebanese. And finding that was a job and a half.

After a hard day on the road, we would pull up in a town and approach a likely looking bar. We would ask if it was open. 'Yes.'

'Can we have two beers please?' 'There isn't any.' But all was not lost. Having exhausted the supply of bars, a local would wander up to us to ask if he could help. The answer was simple — to be led through a maze of huts in the back streets to a small house where a number of locals would be gathered. Open the fridge and bingo — a stack of ice-cold Lebanese beer. These were some of the best and most entertaining 'bars' we found anywhere.

Generally speaking you will find standard bottled lager throughout Africa — the changing labels as you cross the borders often concealing some remarkably similar brews. It is important to remember that if you buy beer to take away, you will have to pay for the bottle as well — and this can be more than the beer itself. It is worth getting into a routine of returning bottles whenever you pick up fresh supplies. If you are in a truck or a large vehicle, a crate would not go amiss. Bottom of the pile in terms of quality was Cote d'Ivoire's *Bock* — although it can come in useful for those who left the laxative tablets out of their medical kits! At the other, more pleasurable, extreme, in Ghana, the friendly 'drinking bars' offer three excellent local beers — *Star, Club* and *ABC*.

Ghana also gives away its colonial heritage with pints of good draught lager served up in classic dimpled English beer mugs. In fact, draught beer is far from unknown in a number of countries. The Portuguese history of Guinea-Bissau shines through with its small glasses of extremely tasty draught beer, poured from large ornate taps. At a few pesos a time, they slipped down extremely well in Bissau's delightful run-down pavement cafés.

Namibia's German heritage means it offers some of the best beer anywhere in Africa — all complying with the German purity laws which allow nothing but water, barley and hops to be used in the brew. Both draft and bottled versions are available of the two leading brews — *Hansa* (made in Swakopmund and easily the best) and the capital's *Windhoek* brand.

Southern Africa is generally better than most areas for the quality of its beer. The world famous live music scene in Zimbabwe is based on the beer halls, where appreciative audiences spend the night dancing and downing the ubiquitous *Castle* or *Lion* or the premium brands *Zambezi* and *Bollinger*. In Bulawayo, a brewery has even been set up by a Czech ex-pat. The draft and bottled *Hunter's* that it produces are both excellent — although we only managed to track them down at the town's Exchange Bar (the oldest pub in Zimbabwe and well worth a visit).

Pub culture has recently become a popular new focus of South African social life. The range of beers available has been supplemented with the opening of a number of new 'brew pubs' which all make their own beer on the premises.

Probably the most enjoyable bars of all are in Zaïre — where the lively African spirit is at its strongest. The bars are full of travellers, breaking their difficult journeys with a *Primus* or two and swaying to the ever-present African beat of the juke box. The more sedate bars of Nairobi will serve you with the now well-known brands of *Tusker* and *White Cap*, as well as a large selection of imported beers.

Of course there are also other drinks that you can try along the way. Bottled beer is often the preserve of the relatively wealthy. The locally produced alternative can be far more interesting — if rather dubious. Local beers in East and Southern Africa look rather like buckets full of dilute porridge and require a fair degree of bravery to sample — not least because they are often drunk communally from what looks like a plastic bucket. Less difficult to try is palm wine — a knockout brew tapped direct from the tree and widely available in West Africa for just a few pence. In Ethiopia you can try *tetcha*, a honey beer which tastes great. Probably the worst drink that we actually sampled was the fermented rice water on sale in the streets of N'djamena in Chad.

Whatever your preference, your time in Africa does not have to be dry.

Beer prices in Africa
from Anthony Ream

Country	Price and beer (UK£ 1994)
Benin	£0.25 Large La Beninoise
Botswana	£0.66 Castle
Burkina Faso	£0.32 Large Castel
Cameroon	£0.40 Large '33'
CAR	£0.46 Large '33' or Castel
Ghana	£0.30 Star
Kenya	£0.40 Tusker
Malawi	£0.20 Carlsberg
Mali	£0.60 Large Castel
Mauritania	£4.00 Small Carlsberg
Morocco	£1.50 Can
Namibia	£0.25 Windhoek (bought by the case)
Nigeria	£0.18 Large Star
South Africa	£0.21 Castle (bought by the case)
Tanzania	£0.36 Amstel

Togo   £0.25 Large BB lager
Uganda   £0.80
Zaïre   £0.66 Primus
Zimbabwe   £0.25 Black Label

MEDICAL

This is one area where it can be difficult to strike the right balance between justified concern and outright paranoia. Some health guides for travellers visiting out of the way places will frighten you half to death. In the end you will find your own levels of hygiene and personal care — and even then your standards will vary according to the different conditions you find yourself in. Most of the time all you need is common sense.

Health insurance

Do not even think of leaving home without it. For details of what is available see Chapter One *Paperwork* section.

Vaccinations

The bottom line is the list of compulsory vaccinations to get into the countries you plan to visit. See page 21 for information on vaccination centres and sources of advice on health for overlanders. Yellow fever is the one absolute must. However, cholera poses something of a problem — if a country insists you have a valid certificate, that generally means you will not get in without one. But the jab only lasts for six months so, if you are on the road for longer than that, you may have to face the hassle of finding a safe way to get your certificate restamped. The vaccine itself is not even effective in protecting you against cholera, and some doctors fear it may be harmful. For these reasons you are best to check with Western aid organisations or embassies if you need to renew your cholera certificate while in Africa.

Even if you hate the thought of needles there are other jabs you should certainly consider before you leave home. You may need top-ups for tetanus, typhoid and polio, and rabies and meningitis are now also increasingly recommended.

For protection against hepatitis A you should ask for the new Havrix vaccine. Two injections a month apart give protection for a year and a booster 6-12 months later will increase immunity for 10 years. You can have a course of jabs to protect you against the much more serious hepatitis B, but this is much less infectious than A and the course is expensive. Standard anti-HIV infection precautions are effective protection against hepatitis B.

Check out vaccinations at least three months before your planned departure date as some jabs come in two parts at spaced intervals (though if you are planning your trip in a hurry you can get away with less time than this). Remember to leave the short-term-effective jabs until as late as you can before you leave.

Advance health checks

The only thing we bothered with, and something we would strongly advise, was a thorough dental check. We paid a quick visit to our doctor, who said there was no need for an all-in check for anyone who was reasonably fit and healthy.

Malaria

This is something on which you must get professional advice, as the development of drug resistant strains is changing all the time. Follow instructions to the letter. At best, malaria is extremely unpleasant and debilitating. It is also the world's number one killer. For current information in the UK phone the Malaria Reference Laboratory on 0891 600 350 (calls cost 38p a minute cheap rate, otherwise 49p a minute).

Mosquito nets are essential unless you are restricting yourself to the desert or sahel. You will definitely need one when camping out anywhere near water, and only the more expensive hotels provide them. The *anopheles* mosquito, which transmits malaria, feeds at dusk and at night.

When you do get bitten, and you will, do your best not to scratch. A simple mosquito bite can easily become infected and end up as a tropical ulcer that can take months to heal. We both have exotic scars to prove it.

Bilharzia

Bilharzia is an extremely debilitating and potentially serious disease, carried by a tiny parasite which infests freshwater snails. If you drink infected river or lake water, or swim or wash in it, the parasite will pass through your skin or the lining of your mouth. Symptoms vary but can include the presence of blood in urine or faeces, fever and flu-like aches, and the enlargement of the liver or spleen. If there is a chance you may have it, have a blood test done at the earliest opportunity. The disease is much harder to treat when advanced — although it may not cause much discomfort if caught early enough. As a general rule, fast-running water is safe — but if in doubt, stay dry. However, you should not become paranoid about the disease. You will probably start off being very cautious and adapt as you learn what water sources can be trusted.

Health and hygiene

A lot of common problems can be avoided by being sensible about hygiene. There will, of course, be times when you are more or less dependent on local standards of hygiene. We picked up tumbu fly, a nasty though not dangerous parasite, from sheets in a middle range hotel in Tanzania, and amoebic dysentery (which was pretty awful) from skewered meat from a roadside stall in Chad. You can, of course, cocoon yourself by never eating from local stalls or restaurants, refusing unpurified water and only ever staying in Western-style hotels — but if that is how you feel you should question why you are considering an overland trip in the first place.

Weight loss

Travelling independently, we both lost weight dramatically and most travellers we met said the same. Generally this is nothing to worry about, but women travellers should be warned that periods can stop altogether with a sudden loss of weight. You are much less likely to lose weight on an organised truck tour. In fact, the high quality of food and standard three square meals a day mean you are more likely to put on the pounds than lose them.

Diarrhoea and dysentery

You will be a rare traveller indeed if you do not suffer from at least one bout of what is described in Ghana as 'runny stomach'. If you are affected it is generally best to avoid solids and drink plenty of fluids until the symptoms pass. Salt and sugar solutions, like Rehidrat, are a wonderful boost if you are dehydrated. Coke is said to help; alcohol and spicy foods are likely to make things worse. If you take a diarrhoea treatment make sure you stop after four days as it may conceal the fact you are suffering from something more serious.

If you get dysentery as opposed to diarrhoea you will know. There are several different types which you can identify to a certain extent yourself, but the best advice is to get medical help, even if you cannot get to a doctor until the symptoms pass. Both amoebic and bacillary dysentery will recur with potentially serious consequences if they are not treated with the right drugs. Both are common in Africa so local doctors will be well used to treating them.

Bites and open sores

It pays to be careful. Hot damp conditions slow down healing and as long as anything is open to the air, it is also at risk of infection. Your feet and lower legs are particularly at risk, simply from walking around in the dust, dirt or mud. Out of wet areas it is easy just to live in flip-flops but it only takes one bad experience to make you more cautious about footwear. You need to watch your hands, too, if you break the skin when carrying out any vehicle maintenance. Try to keep any cuts or grazes clean and dressed.

Most of the time all you have to do is be sensible. Keep open sores dressed and change dressings daily, particularly when on the road. Hot salt baths are good for drawing out infections — all you need is a bucket, something to boil water on and some salt. Also try not to scratch bites and, given that it is almost impossible not to scratch in your sleep, wash your hands and nails thoroughly before you go to bed.

More serious problems

Do not hesitate to see a doctor or take advantage of medical insurance cover if you think there is something really wrong with you. Some countries have perfectly adequate hospitals and health clinics; some facilities are so basic they will make you cringe. Trust your judgment but do not assume that health care will be bad just because it is African — after all, the doctors there are far more accustomed to tropical diseases than those at home.

Medical kit

If you skimp on this you may well get away with it. Alternatively it could be one of the biggest regrets of your trip. You can buy ready assembled kits for overlanders (see section on *Suppliers* page 60) but it usually works out cheaper to do your own. Having said that, you should budget for £200-250 for two, including the cost of malaria pills, for a fully equipped kit. We packed ours into a plastic storage box, but whatever you use remember that glass bottles risk being broken if they are not sensibly packed. Bikers and cyclists are much more restricted in what they can carry and this is where personal requirements are the starting point. However you are travelling, you must take any special medical needs into account, bringing more supplies than you think you might get through in the course of your trip. If you are on a regular course of medicines or drugs remember to note down the pharmacological name, rather than brand, of anything you might ever need to buy.

One other absolute essential is a pack of sterile needles, syringes and sutures — you can get one by mail order from the London School of Hygiene and Tropical Medicine, Gower Street, London

WC1E 7HT; Tel: 0171 636 8636. The pack also contains a range of Melolin dressings which are far and away the best you can get, as they do not stick to wounds or burns.

Other priorities are elastoplast (band-aids), pain killers, antiseptic solution and cream, something for diarrhoea, and some sort of sugar and salt solution for dehydration — we used sachets of Rehidrat which were recommended by our doctor and are available from chemists. Malaria tablets are utterly essential — you would be crazy to leave home without the tablets recommended for the areas you will be travelling through. You can find recommended lists for the rest of your kit in books on the subject — everyone should include a first aid and tropical health book in their medical kit. The best and most comprehensive book we have used is *The Traveller's Health Guide* by Dr Anthony C Turner (Roger Lascelles).

Worth thinking about are a clinical thermometer, elastic support bandages for strains and sprains, something for indigestion, eye and nose drops, oil of cloves for toothache, insect repellent, something to treat stings and burns, salt tablets (you can, of course, use ordinary salt in solution, but these do not taste as strong so are good for when you are feeling a bit off), cream or gel to ease the pain of sprains and muscle cramps, anti-fungal powder, cotton wool and buds, and both sun-screen and sunburn creams.

Vitamin pills are a worthwhile addition, not necessarily for their limited medical use, but because they have almost wonder drug status in some parts of Africa, and therefore have a high gift or swap value. When we were in Mali the clinching factor in protracted negotiations over a superb carved figure of a drummer was nothing more or less than a small bottle of Sanatogen multi-vitamin tablets.

Some of our most used and useful items were also the most basic. Long periods of driving in hot dusty conditions really get to your eyes and once you discover the benefits of an Optrex eyebath you will wish you had brought more. We carried a lot more in the way of gauze, lint and bandages than we needed, but since we each developed a tropical ulcer we got through more of these than you might expect — festering sores that take a long time to heal are not that uncommon, and when you are on the road dressings need to be changed every day.

Things we did not take but wish we had included a cooling cream for burns (straightforward antiseptic cream does not take out the sting); treatment for colds and sore throats (more common in Africa than you might think), more Dettol or other antiseptic/disinfectant (we took two bottles for 10 months) — and definitely more Optrex!

Finally, a word on antibiotics. Some doctors will give you short courses to take away with you, but most will be reluctant because of the dangers of self-prescribing. Since you can buy antibiotics over the counter in most African countries it is worthwhile talking over with a doctor or pharmacist what the sensible doses are for things like an infected cut or a bout of dysentery. If you end up taking antibiotics (however you get your hands on them) while you are on the road, make sure you get medical help if the treatment does not work.

Dental care

Definitely have a dental check before you leave home. Toothpaste and toothbrushes are available in cities, but because one of us has a recurring gum problem we erred on the side of caution and brought everything we were likely to need. When we saw some of the African versions of the toothbrush we were glad that we had. Oil of cloves is good for numbing toothache, though of course it will not solve any real problems.

Contraceptives

If you have sex with anyone other than your regular partner you must use a condom because of the risk of infection with the HIV virus which can cause AIDS, or Hepatitis B. Condoms are usually extremely difficult to get hold of in Africa, though there is reputed to be a black market stall in Abidjan that sells nothing else. Generally you would be advised to bring what you are likely to need — and more. In the more remote areas thorough searches at border posts which concentrate on your washbags and medical box do so for a reason. Presumably the opportunity to relieve travellers of the odd three-pack of Durex is regarded as one of the perks of the job.

If you are only having sex with your regular partner condoms are not your only choice of contraception. The only problem the pill is likely to pose if you stick to your normal brand is its keeping quality. You should refer to the guidance set out on the packet (normally store in a cool, dry place) and follow it carefully. This may rule it out for some travellers.

A coil will get round this difficulty, but you must have it fitted at least six weeks before you leave to check you are not at risk from infection or expulsion. Some women experience heavy and painful periods with a coil.

You can also use a cap which can be sterilised easily in a mug with an ordinary water purifying tablet. But you should think about the number of times you will be using communal toilet facilities or washing in the open air before making a decision to rely only on your cap while you are away.

One other possibility is to have an injectable contraceptive (Depo-Provera) which will last for two or more months. Side-effects can include irregular periods, or no periods at all — not necessarily a disadvantage on the road. Fertility can also be delayed for a year after the last injection. Another disadvantage could be needing another injection when you are miles away from anywhere.

If you are thinking of changing your normal method of contraception talk this over in plenty of time with your doctor or FPA clinic who will be able to give you expert advice.

Tampons and sanitary towels

You will be able to buy tampons and sanitary towels in most big towns in West Africa and more easily in East and Southern Africa. Problem areas are North Africa, desert and other remote areas and Zaïre. Take enough supplies to get you through early problem areas and you will be able to stock up later on. If you have a definite brand preference and lots of spare space it's not a bad idea to bring extra supplies. It might be worth considering a reusable menstrual sponge, though if you have not used one before make sure you practise before you leave so you know exactly what is involved.

Treating local people

At some time you will be asked for medical help. Aspirin is particularly useful as it is unlikely to harm anyone and is often seen as a cure for everything. Vitamin pills also enjoy a legendary status. Don't ever hand out antibiotics as you risk making someone seriously ill if you give them an inadequate dose or they fail to complete a course. Take care, too, when administering eye drops or bandaging sores for people as infection is very easily passed on as a result of trying to be helpful. We felt most helpless in a completely remote village in Chad when everyone who was ill or sick — from old people with cataracts to malnourished babies — was brought out for us to 'cure'. What they needed was not aspirin or sugar and salt solution, but a balanced diet and clean water supply. We could not give them that but gladly offered anything we had that might ease their pain in any way, even psychologically.

Health checks on your return

We did not bother — feeling fine, though culture shocked. But if you suspect you may have caught bilharzia, for example, you should certainly see a doctor. This also applies if you got malaria on your trip, or if you fall ill after you have come home.

WATER

Water is one of the most precious commodities there is in Africa. Even in many sizeable towns it has to be fetched and carried. You will quickly recognise the gracefully slow walk of African women, and sometimes children, carrying enormous weights of water on their heads — often for great distances. Men generally seem to regard themselves as above this and other mundane tasks.

Because of its value you must be prepared to respect local sources. Never do anything to a well which might contaminate it like throwing anything in to it, or washing yourself or your clothes close by. And even if you have the capacity to carry enough water to wash down your vehicle, or throw it away because it tastes stale, you should not do so in front of local people who spend hours every day fetching and carrying.

How much to carry

This will obviously depend on what time of year you are travelling, where you are and how dedicated you are to washing — both yourself and your clothes. In the desert at the hottest time of year you should allow six to eight litres for one person's daily intake, and even in January or February you will easily get through two or three. It is absolutely vital to drink as much as you need as you could run into serious problems if you do not. It is a good idea to keep a tally of how much you are drinking in desert conditions to make sure you are drinking enough. If your urine becomes concentrated in colour you could be heading for trouble. A good guide is that you should aim to be peeing as often as you do back home.

Cyclists will face the greatest difficulties in terms of how much they can carry, and bikers will also be restricted by weight. For this reason they are best advised to stick to the more major desert routes where they are likely to be able to get water from other travellers. But even travellers in the newest four-wheel drive vehicles should not strain them by trying to carry too much — water is heavy.

If you are in a vehicle in drier areas you are also likely to be stopped by local people who know perfectly well that overlanders normally carry more than they need. Even if we were only able to offer a little, we never refused.

Containers

It is possible to carry 20-litre jerricans on the sides of a motorbike. Home-made frames are the best way of fixing them to the sides of the bike. You will probably want one for fuel so maximum carrying capacity will only be 20 litres of water — unless you can find more on the way, and that only gives three days in desert conditions.

A range of water containers are available for cyclists but you will be unlikely to carry much more than 10 litres at a time. Every extra litre you take means an extra kilogramme to carry — and that is an important consideration when you are cycling. This means that you really do need to plan your route so you can find a source of water each day (this may mean stopping other vehicles in the Sahara).

In our Land Rover we carried 25 litre plastic jerricans (*bidons* in French) and found it really useful to have a small one-gallon container to drink from direct. In hot dry conditions wrapping a damp towel round your drinking water will help keep it cool. Keep damping the towel so that there is constant evaporation. Locally sold goat skins, or *guerbas*, also keep water cool by evaporation, but we were not keen on the taste of rancid animal fat which never really disappears no matter how often they are used.

Sources
Basically you need to use you head and your nose. If water is in any way suspect then filter and/or purify it. And remember the golden rule — filtering always comes first. Alternatively, use doubtful water for washing and hang on to purer water for drinking and cooking. Don't be greedy at small wells that serve a large area. Some wells become contaminated so if no-one locally is making use of a well, there is probably a good reason. Sometimes rivers or lakes may be your only source — but they are also likely to be places where local people wash both themselves and their clothes. We used river water solely for washing. But if you need to use it, filtering and purifying will make it safe to drink.

Purification
If water is cloudy then filter before purifying. When necessary we used simple 'filter socks' which are quick, easy and extremely cheap compared with the more elaborate candle or silver filters available. You may, however, want to consider one of the more sophisticated filters if you are likely to spend long periods in very remote areas, relying on rivers and poor wells for all your water. Cyclists are certain to need a decent filter because they are less able to carry supplies of good water and will be more likely to rely on poorer sources. Travelwell Military water filters have been recommended for cyclists and bikers (they have a larger capacity than the standard model).

An investment we were glad we made was in Micropur purifying tablets which come in a range of strengths from one to 20 litres. They are silver based and leave no taste at all, unlike chlorine or iodine based tablets. They are more expensive than standard tablets but are really worth it, especially if you are on a long trip.

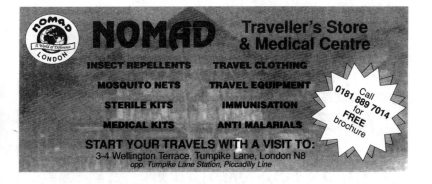

Part Two

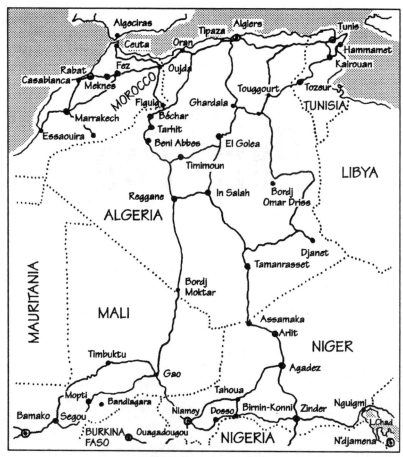

NORTH AFRICA

Chapter Five

North Africa and the Sahara

If your preconceptions of this area are of boring stretches of desert that are no more than an obstacle to the continent beyond, then think again. This is one of the most beautiful and awe-inspiring regions in the world. Crossing the Sahara overland is a truly wonderful experience — and an achievement you will never forget.

Before you reach the desert itself, the mountain ranges of North Africa provide a surprisingly lush green landscape. The ancient civilisations of the region make this a fascinating area historically and its vibrant culture means that towns and villages are full of life and colour.

Morocco has so much to offer it is easy to make this a trip of its own. Make sure you have enough time to spare to make the most of it before you move on. Excellent communications and a host of places to visit can mean an enjoyable holiday before the hard work begins. Tunisia can also offer pre-Saharan holiday facilities but without the same wealth of cultural diversity.

Once you move any deeper into the continent, you are in the largest desert in the world — the Sahara. Beyond and into the *sahel*, the scene changes to some of the saddest sights of Africa. The creeping desert means that crops fail year after year, leaving whole populations stranded and trying to scrape a living from the parched earth. Our most vivid experiences of the harshness of the *sahel* were in Chad but the story is much the same throughout this belt of land.

ROUTE GUIDE

The main starting points for a trans-African overland journey are South Africa (page 262), Egypt and Morocco.

At the time of writing in 1995, the Algerian routes across the Sahara had become impossible because of fundamentalist unrest in the north and Touareg separatism in the south. This situation looks as if it will remain difficult for some time to come. We provide information on travel through Algeria in case the situation improves, but right now the only western route is through Morocco, Western Sahara and Mauritania.

Before you can start on any trans-African journey you will, of course, have to get on to the continent of Africa. Unless you plan to take the overland route through the Middle East you will have to take one of the Mediterranean ferries.

By far the most popular crossing is from Algeciras in southern Spain to the Spanish enclave of Ceuta. This is a very short crossing. It does not require advance booking — although you may have to wait for several hours to get on. If you are travelling through Portugal, there is another short crossing from Faro to Tangier. If you want to sail directly from southern Spain to Algeria, there is a ferry operating from Alicante to Oran.

Some of the longer Mediterranean crossings can turn out to be excellent value for money. The savings on fuel used in driving the length of Spain or Italy make these crossings a lot cheaper than you might think. The two most popular long-distance ferries are from Marseille to Algiers and from Genoa to Tunis. There are also sailings from Marseille or Sète to Oran. If you prefer to take in Italy on your way, you can pick up ferries at either Naples or Palermo which go to Tunis. If you are aiming to start in Egypt, the best crossing is from Athens to Alexandria. Taking any of these crossings, apart from Algeciras-Ceuta, you ought to check out the sailings in advance with a travel agent (or check them for yourself in the *ABC Shipping Guide*). Many do not sail every day so it is well worth knowing the details before you set out.

An alternative to driving through Western Sahara and Mauritania is to ship your vehicle from Marseille or Casablanca to Nouakchott in Mauritania — although these boats do not take passengers. It is also possible to ship to other major ports in West Africa, such as Dakar, Abidjan, Accra and Lagos.

Allow plenty of time in Morocco before you make a start on the Mauritanian route across the Sahara. Although a final peace has yet to be agreed in Western Sahara, it is now firmly under Moroccan rule and is treated as an integral part of the country. There have been no reports of any problems from recent travellers, although convoys cross the most exposed section between Laayoun and Dakhla. These are organised from the police station in Laayoun. There are also three military convoys a week from Dakhla to Nouadhibou.

In 1995 Mauritania was not granting land entry visas but was allowing entry to overlanders turning up at the border with an air entry visa. It is generally possible to get one of these in Europe even though you should strictly speaking be in possession of a valid air ticket first. The border is currently closed to travellers wishing to head north from Mauritania to Morocco. Check the latest news on this with other overlanders.

The most difficult section of the route starts once you cross the border to Nouadhibou. It is strongly recommended you take a guide from here as it can be very difficult to follow the track around the salt pans. The soft sands here can be treacherous. The first 50km or so are the most difficult but you will probably need to keep the guide at least until you reach the sea at Nouamghar — although he may well want to continue the rest of the way to Nouakchott (150km along the beach and accessible at low tide only).

It is possible to head south from here and take a ferry from Rosso to Richard Toll in Senegal. But the faster and more popular route is to take the good tarmac road east to Néma. Ask at the police post for directions south from here as there is no clear road and various tracks to choose from. After a few kilometres the way becomes more defined. Driving conditions are very poor all the way down to Nara in Mali. Continue south on the dirt road to Bamako and your gateway to the rest of West Africa.

The eastern route into Africa starts from Alexandria, Port Said or Suez and then follows the main road along the banks of the Nile to Aswan. The only way to enter Sudan is on the Lake Nasser ferry to Wadi Halfa. There are two routes south to Khartoum — the easier one following the railway line and a more difficult one following the river. From here it is sometimes possible to head west to Nyala and CAR. But with the recent opening up of Ethiopia, the best route south is now via Kasala into Eritrea.

With some attacks on tourists in Egypt and extremely poor roads in Sudan, it is also worth considering the option of taking the three-day car ferry from Suez to Port Sudan. It is a relatively easy drive from here south to Kasala.

When the country is open, the two major desert crossings through Algeria are the Tanezrouft, leading down to Mali in the west, and the Hoggar, to Niger in the centre. The more difficult route to Djanet in the east makes for a breathtaking detour from the Hoggar route. If you intend to spend a lot of time in the desert and really want to explore, detailed routes are available in the classic *Sahara Handbook* by Simon and Jan Glen (see *Further reading*, page 306).

Previously the most popular route of all was to drive through Morocco, crossing into Algeria at Figuig. By taking the road around the western side of the Grand Erg Occidental (through Béchar, Taghit and Beni-Abbès), you will take in some of the most spectacular sand dunes in the entire desert. It is then possible to cross over to the main Hoggar route, either through Timimoun on the main road or from Reggane to Ain Salah on the piste further to the south.

The road south to Tamanrasset has a good tarmac surface running almost all the way. The section between Tamanrasset and Assamakka is likely to remain the most difficult part of the crossing for the foreseeable future. There is a lot of soft sand and the track constantly divides, making it difficult to follow. This is where two-wheel drive vehicles really start to get into trouble. Land Rovers and trucks have to tow Peugeots and the like out of trouble all along the route. The approach to the border post itself has the softest sand of all.

For those heading south, the bar at the border post in Assamakkais is legendary — offering the first taste of cold beer at a reasonable price. As soon as you enter Niger you know that you have crossed a divide that takes you from one culture to another. Suddenly you are in black Africa, where there is music in the air, laughter and beer in the bars, colourful clothes and exotic vegetables in the markets. The effect is one of the most striking switches of culture you will ever experience — most people want to stop and soak it up for a while. The best place to do this is Arlit, the mining town in the far north and the first place you reach after entering the country. It has the air of a wild frontier town with a party in every bar. Overland travellers are important to the local economy so there will be a lot of traders around you as soon as you hit town. Make the most of it; enjoy your arrival in Africa.

Once in Niger, life becomes a lot easier. After Arlit there are excellent surfaced roads linking all the main towns. The road to Niamey is another gateway to West Africa; the road down to Zinder takes you either down into Nigeria or out along the eastern road into Chad (permission to take this road needs to be obtained in writing from the Ministry of the Interior in Niamey).

The route around Lake Chad to N'djamena is an option that has been used in the past when there have been problems with access to Nigeria. It is also an extremely interesting area to visit, but it is very difficult. Current maps are impossible to obtain as the route changes constantly as the lake continues to shrink (and occasionally expand again). Try to update your information along the way — particularly before leaving Nguigmi and Bol (or N'djamena if travelling east to west).

MOROCCO

Area: 458,730km²

Population: 28.6 million

Capital: Rabat

Languages: Arabic and French are the official languages; some Berber also spoken.

Climate: Morocco has a complex variety of climates — Mediterranean in the north, Atlantic in the west, continental in the interior and desert in the south.

Visas: Not required by EU, Australasian, American or Japanese travellers.

Foreign embassies and consulates in Rabat: Algeria (Boulevard Front d'Oved; Tel: 765474); there is also an Algerian consulate in Oujda); **Australia** (13 bis Rue Jafaar As-Sadik; Tel: 71373); **Canada** (13 bis Rue Jaafar As-Saddik; Tel: 672880); **Cote d'Ivoire** (21 Rue de Teddens; Tel: 63151); **France** (Rue Sahnoun; Tel: 777822); **Mauritania** (2 Rue de Normandie; Tel: 770912); **Senegal** (Rue Cadi Ben Hammadi Senhadji; Tel: 754171); **Sudan** (9 Rue de Teddens; Tel: 761368); **Tunisia** (6 Avenue de Fez; Tel: 730576); UK (17 Boulevard de la Tour Hassan; Tel: 20905/6); **USA** (2 Avenue de Marrakech; Tel: 762265).

Other red tape: Green card cover on existing motor insurance is valid for Morocco. On arrival you must fill in a temporary vehicle importation declaration.

Banks and money: Unit of currency is the dirham, a relatively strong and stable currency by African standards. There are plenty of banks in the main centres of population. Do not fall for the tricksters in Algeciras (Spain) who will try to get you to change money with them, claiming that it is a public holiday in Morocco.

Public holidays: New Year's Day, Independence Day (March 3), Labour Day (May 1), Green March (November 6), Accession of King Mohammed V (November 18). The Islamic holidays of Aid el-Fitr, Aid el-Seghir and Mouloud are also observed, on dates varying from year to year.

Fuel: Readily available everywhere. Best to fill up in Ceuta where fuel is cheap — although prices in Morocco itself have also been falling.

Roads: Good; mostly surfaced apart from more remote desert tracks. Drive on the right.

Routes: Heading for Algeria most take the direct routes from Ceuta to Oujda or Figuig — but it is well worth exploring the High Atlas on the way. Fuigig offers a more convenient route into Algeria than Oujda, but the isolation of this border point does make it more prone to attempts at extracting a little extra cash from you. Stand your ground. Border disputes have closed both crossings in the past; check the situation before you set out. Heading for Mauritania, the only route is south from Agadir to Laayoun and the border at Nouadhibou.

Places to visit

The Atlas: The cool wooded slopes of the Mid Atlas and the arid and dramatic High Atlas are both essential elements in a trip through Morocco. The area around Azrou and Ifrane makes for a particularly pleasant base for a cool rest before heading south.

Erfoud/Rissani/Merzouga: A trip down into the far south of the country provides a view of remote Moroccan desert communities that few visitors ever take in — a beautiful and largely unspoiled Berber area.

Essaouira: An interesting old Portuguese town, which is now a sleepy fishing village. Good for water sports and fish restaurants (try Chez Sam).

Fez: The oldest and probably most interesting of Morocco's imperial cities, the old town of Fez is a maze of narrow winding streets. It has one of the biggest and best souks in Morocco. It is possible to see a wide range of craftworkers around every corner — and you should not miss a visit to the tanneries. There are magnificent panoramic views of the town if you drive up to the Merinde Tombs.

Marrakech: A fair bit off the main trans-African route but well worth a detour. Marrakech has a well-deserved reputation as one of the most fascinating cities in the world. The seething activity of the central square, Djmaa el Fna, at dusk is an unforgettable experience. Unfortunately, the city is also well-known for some of the worst tourist hassles in the world; fortunately the Moroccan authorities have recently been clamping down on the worst excesses of the traders and guides.

Moulay Idriss: Close to Meknès and named after the founder of Fez, this beautiful pair of villages on the side of a hillside are well worth a visit.

Volubilis: Situated to the north of Meknès, Volubilis offers some of the most extensive and best preserved Roman remains you are ever likely to see. An impressive sight, it was the second Roman city in Africa after Carthage.

Places to stay

Morocco is well served with good official campsites in all major cities and also has a good supply of reasonable small hotels. Camping outside official sites is allowed with the permission of the local authorities or the landowner.

Agadir: Has a luxury campsite at Boulevard Mohamed V. There is another campsite at Taghazouk, 12km on the Essaouira Road.

Casablanca: *The Oasis* campsite is at Beau Séjour. There are two campsites at Km 16 on the route d'Azemmour.

Ceuta: There is a number of good campsites at this classic starting point for trans-African journeys.

Erfoud: *Grand Hotel du Sud* — a magnificent but expensive old hotel; *Hotel Ziz* is a more modest option.

Essaouira: There is a campsite just outside of town by the sea.

Fez: There is a good campsite just outside the town at Ain Chket, which is very popular with overlanders. There are also campsites at Sefrou and Immouzzer to the south of Fez.

Marrakech: There is a campsite just off the Avenue de France, south of the railway station; Tel: 43 18 44.

Martil: Good campsite by the sea here, just south of Ceuta.

Meknès: There is a top-class international-style campsite just past the Royal Palace.

Oujda: It is possible to camp inside the central park, which is locked and guarded at night (you will need to give the guards a little money).

Rabat: There is a campsite by the beach at Sale, which is a big meeting point for overlanders.

Tangier: There are campsites at Tingis, Miramonte, L'Hélice Tripal, El Manar and on the Atlantic coast.

Sources of tourist information
Moroccan Tourist Office, 205 Regent Street, London W1R 6HB; Tel: 0171 437 0073.

Tourist offices in Morocco:
Agadir Place Prince Héritier Sidi Mohamed; Tel: 82 28 94.
Casablanca Rue Omar Slaoui; Tel: 27 11 77.
Fez Place de la Résistance; Tel: 62 34 60.
Laayoune Rue de l'Islam; Tel: 22 33 75.
Marrakech Place Abdelmoumen Ben Ali; Tel: 44 89 06.
Meknes Place Administrative; Tel: 52 44 26.
Mohammedia 14 Rue Al Jahid; Tel: 32 41 99.
Rabat 22 Avenue d'Alger; Tel: 73 05 62.
Tangier 29 Boulevard Pasteur; Tel: 93 82 39.
Tetouan Avenue Mohamed V; Tel: 96 41 12.

Guide books: *Blue Guide to Morocco*, Jane Holliday (A&C Black); *Fodor's Morocco*; *Independent Traveller's Guide to Morocco*, Christine Osborne (Collins); *Michelin Guide to Morocco*; *Rough Guide to Morocco*; *Insight Guide to Morocco*.

Journeys by boat on Lake Turkana and the Omo River
P.O. Box 39439 Nairobi, Kenya.
Tel. 254 2 218336/8 fax. 254 2 224212
Arrow House, Koinange Street, Nairobi

TUNISIA

Area: 164,150km²

Population: 8.7 million

Capital: Tunis

Languages: Arabic and French.

Climate: Mediterranean climate in the north; hot dry desert climate inland.

Visas: Not required by citizens of EU countries, Canada, Ireland, Japan, Switzerland and USA. One week visas for all others are available on arrival.

Foreign embassies and consulates in Tunis: Algeria (136 Avenue de la Liberté; Tel: 280082; there is also a consulate at Gafsa); **Canada** (3 Rue du Sénégal, Place d'Afrique; Tel: 796577); **France** (Place de l'Indépendence; Tel: 245700); **Morocco** (39 Rue du 1 Juin; Tel: 288063); **Senegal** (122 Avenue de la Liberté, Tel: 282393); **Togo** (23 Rue Lénine; Tel: 244511); **UK** (5 Place de la Victoire; Tel: 341444/341689/341962; also issues Nigerian visas); **USA** (144 Avenue de la Liberté; Tel: 782566).

Other red tape: International motoring documents required but no need for carnet. Green card cover on existing motor insurance is valid for Tunisia. Insurance is compulsory at the border for those who do not have any. Customs will issue a free circulation permit on entry. No compulsory vaccinations unless arriving from an infected area.

Banks and money: Unit of currency is the dinar, which is relatively strong; no problems with banks in main towns. You should declare foreign currency on entry in order to be able to export it legally — otherwise you need authorisation from the Central Bank of Tunisia. You cannot export dinar.

Public holidays: New Year's Day, Independence Day (March 20), Youth Day (March 21), Martyrs' Day (April 9), Labour Day (May 1), Anniversary of the Proclamation of the Republic (July 25), Women's Day (August 13), Political Change (November 7). The Islamic holidays of Aid el-Fitr, Aid el-Idha, Hejri and Mouled are also observed, on dates varying from year to year.

Fuel: Available in all main towns. Price is reasonable (but not as cheap as Algeria).

Roads: Mostly good surfaced roads. Drive on the right.

Routes: As long as the problems in Algeria continue it is unlikely you will want to enter through Tunisia. But once things settle down there you can take a ferry to Tunis and then either head straight across to Algeria along the north coast or head down through the interior to Tozeur and enter Algeria at Hazoua.

Places to visit

Boukornine: A forested National Park just 15km south of Tunis.

Ichkeul: National Park rich in bird life — particularly in winter. Situated 75km north of Tunis, it covers mountain, lake and swamp areas.

Kairouan: Most interesting town in Tunisia. Kairouan is an ancient walled city with excellent markets and one of the most important mosques in the world. This is also an important centre for carpet weaving, making it a good place to visit the looms and inspect the merchandise.

Tozeur: Delightful southern oasis town on the route to Algeria.

Tunis: The old walled town in the centre is well worth a wander, otherwise most of Tunis is modern. The main tourist attraction is the site of Carthage and its ancient ruins, just to the east of the city. Nearby is the beautiful old showpiece village of Sidi Bou Said — all white and blue buildings along tiny twisting roads, looking down on the sea below.

Zembra: Small mountainous island in the north, which acts as a stopping off point for millions of migratory birds.

Places to stay

There are plenty of opportunities for bush camping away from the main towns, and the palmeries in the south offer good camping spots. Since these are privately owned, you should ask permission to camp — if you can find someone. Otherwise there are few official campsites.

Hammamet: *Camping Simara* is a pleasant large campsite situated at the edge of town soon after you leave the motorway.

Tozeur: *Camping Belvedere* is a small site with few facilities; generally full of travellers.

Tunis: A large open area outside the ferry exit at La Goulette is used by most people arriving as an unofficial camping area.

Sources of tourist information
Tunisian National Tourist Office, 7a Stafford Street, London W1X 4EQ; Tel: 0171 499 2234.

Tourist offices in Tunisia:
Kairouan Ban ech Chouhada; Tel: 21797.
Nabeul Avenue Taieb Mehiri; Tel: 86737.
Sfax Place de l'Indépendence.
Sousse 1 Avenue Bourguiba; Tel: 25157.
Tozeur Avenue Abdul Kacem Chebbi; Tel: 50503.
Tunis 29 Rue Hatem Etlai; Tel: 289403.

Guide books: *Discover Tunisia*, Terry Palmer; *Rough Guide to Tunisia*; *Tunisia Today*, Jean Hurean (éditions j.a.).

ALGERIA

Area: 2,381,741km²

Population: 27.9 million

Capital: Algiers

Languages: Arabic, French, Berber, Tuareg. Most people speak some French in the north, less so in desert areas.

Climate: Desert temperatures are hottest in July and August when it can reach more than 50°C. In the winter months it is unlikely to go much above 30°C.

Visas: Required by all except citizens of Denmark, Finland, France, Iceland, Italy, Norway, Spain, Sweden, and Switzerland.

Foreign embassies and consulates in Algiers: Australia (60 Boulevard Colonel Bougara, El Biar; Tel: 60560); **Burkina Faso**, visas from the French Embassy; **Canada** (27 bis Rue Des Frères Benhafid, Hydra; Tel: 691611); **Cote d'Ivoire** (Immeuble le Bosquet, Hydra le Paradou; Tel: 602482); **France** (Rue Larbi Alik, Hydra; will also supply two-day CAR transit visas); **Ghana** (62 Rue Parmentier, Hydra); **Libya** (15 Chemin Cheikh Brahimi, El Biar); **Mali** (Villa No 14, Cite NNC/ANP, Chemin du Kaddous, Hydra; there is also a consulate in Tamanrasset); **Morocco** (Rue B Amani, Air de France, Route de Bouzareah); **Niger** (54 Rue Vercors, Air de France, Route de Bouzareah; there is also a consulate in Tamanrasset); **Nigeria** (27 Ali Boufelgued); **Tunisia** (11 Rue du Bois de Boulogne; Tel: 601388); **UK** (7 Chemin de Glycines; Tel: 605601); **USA** (4 Chemin Cheikh Bachir El-Ibrahimi; Tel: 691186).

Other red tape: Vehicle insurance is compulsory and must be bought at the border where available. Otherwise there are branches of the state insurance company SAA in all big towns. Carnet not accepted, *laissez passer* issued at border instead. You should check in with the police before attempting any particularly difficult desert pistes, this includes when you leave Tamanrasset to head south. There is no need to visit customs at Tamanrasset as all other formalities will be carried out at the border post, 15 kilometres beyond Ain Guezzam.

Banks and money: The Algerian dinar is not a strong currency, making this an expensive country at official exchange rates. There is a compulsory exchange of 1,000 dinars per person. The value of the dinar has fallen in recent years making the amount you need to change less than it was (about £80 in 1993). Both Oujda and Figuig have banks at the border where you will be required to change money.

Public holidays: New Year's Day, Labour Day (May 1), National Day (19 June), Independence Day (July 5), Revolution Day (November 1). The Islamic holidays of el-Ashura, Hejri, the Prophet's Birthday, Aid el-Fitr and Aid el-Adha are also observed on dates varying from year to year.

Fuel: Plentiful in the north; available in the main towns of the south. Stock up with more than you think you need before any long desert sections. Low cost and the need to burn up compulsory currency exchange make Algeria a good place to stock up on supplies before heading further south.

Roads: Good surfaced roads throughout the north and most of the way down the central route to Tamanrasset. Drive on the right. Desert pistes are of variable quality.

Routes: Although travel through Algeria has been regarded as unsafe for quite some time, trucks have started transiting the country once again — in convoy and as quickly as possible. Check on the latest situation before considering going through Algeria. Entering at Algiers, by the Oujda crossing from Morocco or one of the northern crossings from Tunisia, you will start out in the well developed Atlas region of the north. But the most popular overland routes into Algeria are at Figuig (from Morocco) or Hazoua (from Tunisia). These crossings mean you move straight into Algeria's arid interior. There are two main routes south — the Tanezrouft and the Hoggar. The main advantage of the Tanezrouft is that it is good firm going for most of the way, presenting few problems for any vehicle. But on the minus side it is more remote, has fewer settlements along the way, is used less frequently and includes what is generally reckoned to be one of the more difficult border crossings in Africa — at Bordj-Moktar, taking you through into Mali. The Hoggar route is by far the most popular. Although the road surface does come and go with alternate building work and flash floods, it is nowadays in better condition than it has been for many years — it should be possible to drive on surfaced roads most of the way to Tamanrasset. Between Tamanrasset and the border, however, you will face very difficult conditions — lots of soft sand and unmarked tracks. If you are going to run into trouble, this will be the place. Tracks often diverge over a very wide area as trucks search for firmer sand and as a result many people end up getting lost in this region. As long as you keep cool, keep a record of your movements and use your compass properly, you should not experience any real problems.

Places to visit

Ain Salah: Typical Saharan town with a small market. Make sure you head out on the good piste towards Reggane for about 50 kilometres to visit the petrified tree trunks — remnants of the times when the Sahara was a rain forest.

Beni-Abbès and Taghit: The most spectacular area you are likely to pass through for stunning dunes; this is the kind of scenery most people associate with the Sahara. An excellent introduction to the country for those entering at Figuig.

Djanet: This beautiful area is well worth the detour. The landscape is spectacular and local cave paintings are among the best in the Sahara. Only set out on this trip with at least two vehicles — this is not an easy route.

Ghardaia: Probably the most interesting town on the Sahara fringe, Ghardaia is made up of several separate settlements of the M'Zab. Founded by the strict Mozabite sect, this is an incredibly male dominated society. Many women are said never to have been allowed outside their homes. Despite this, Ghardaia is an interesting and bustling place. Its markets are probably the last place you will have a really good selection of things to buy in Algeria.

Hoggar Mountains: A remarkable range of volcanic mountains right in the centre of the Sahara. Hidden among them are green garden areas in small valleys, tended by the Touaregs. The area is also famous for its wealth of ancient rock paintings. Up in the heights is the Assekrem Monastery, the one place everyone wants to see — particularly at sunrise. The setting is quite unbelievable, with towering sheer-sided volcanic mountains all around.

Places to stay

It can be extremely difficult to find anywhere to camp along most of the northern strip of Algeria — and with fundamentalist attacks on foreigners it is extremely unlikely you will spend any time here, even if the Touareg situation further south improves enough to allow safe passage through the country.

THE ESSENCE OF AFRICA

1 E Paice	4 E Paice	7 H Bradt
2 N Cotton	5 P Cook	8 H Bradt
3 H Bradt	6 P Cook	9 N Dunnington-Jefferson

DRIVING THROUGH AFRICA

Above: In desert areas convoy driving is advisable (B Swain)

Below: A roof-top tent allows safe camping anywhere (B Swain)

ORGANISED AND INDEPENDENT TRAVEL

Above: People power in Namibia (B Swain)

Below: Knowing the location of wells is an essential part of desert cycling (N Cotton)

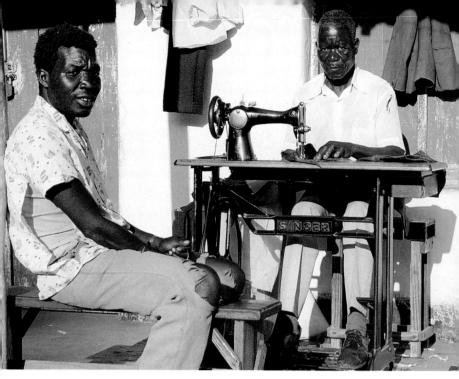

WORK AND REST
Above: Tailors, Malawi (P Cook)
Below: Vervet monkey (H Bradt)

Ain el-Hadjadj: A glorious spot to stop between El Golea and Ain Salah. The scenery is breathtaking here, as the road drops down from the Tademait Plateau. Come off the main piste just before it drops down and you will find some wonderful camping areas.

Ain Salah: *Zribat Camping* to the south of town is the best place to stay. But to be honest it is probably more pleasant to visit Ain Salah during the day and then head out into the desert for a peaceful night under the stars.

Algiers: It is very difficult to find anywhere to stay; sleep out of town if possible.

Assekrem: Camping in car park, no facilities. About 45 kilometres to the north, on the piste to Idilès, there is a series of beautiful sandy hollows just off to the side of the road. Inside them are pools and palm trees (only the tops of the trees are visible from the track). They are excellent places to camp.

Beni-Abbès: Campsite with beautiful views of the dunes.

El Golea: The private campsite on the main road as you enter to the north of town is fine but with fairly basic facilities; it is a friendly place. There is another official campsite on the way out of town to the south.

Gara Ecker: Unfortunately over-camped and strewn with litter. But this spectacular outcrop of rocks in the far south of Algeria does provide both an ideal windbreak and a majestic, if scruffy, setting to spend the night.

Ghardaia: There are several good campsites. The *Hotel Atlantide* has also been recommended.

Laghouat: There is a campsite and also a hotel with safe compound for parking.

Oran: The campsite here is reckoned to be a bit of a dump and rather expensive.

The Source: Camping about an hour out on the road to Assekrem from Tamanrasset; not highly recommended.

Taghit: Camp in palmerie; official site not recommended.

Tamanrasset: The old campsite on the edge of town on the road to Adriane has now been improved; it is large and a good place to meet other travellers. A second site has also been built recently and, for those on a bigger budget, the *Hotel Tahat* provides an expensive but luxurious option to break the journey.

Ténès: The wooded hillsides in this area to the west of Algiers provide some opportunities for camping.

Tipaza: There are a few campsites near here on the road to Algiers. There is a holiday village at Tipaza itself, which is a good place to stay outside of the main holiday season.

Sources of tourist information
Tourist offices in Algeria:
Algiers 5 Boulevard Ben Boulaïd; Tel: 641550.
Constantine 16 Rue Didouche Mourad; Tel: 941403.
Djanet Place du Marché; Tel: 735024.
Ghardaïa Rue Emir Abdelkader; Tel: 891757.
Oran 10 Boulevard Emir Abdelkader; Tel: 391611.
Ouargla Avenue Emir Abdelkader; Tel: 705183.
Sétif 13 Avenue du 8 Mai; Tel: 902502.

Cycling the desert
by Phil Nelson
Winter is the best, if not the only time to consider crossing the desert on any route — even so the temperatures can be murderous. We used to carry a couple of sheets and improvise some shade with them using signposts, piste beacons, burnt-out cars or our own bikes propped up against rocks. We would rest under this shade for about four hours in the middle of each day. By cycling four or five hours in the morning and another couple of hours in the afternoon, we covered about 120km a day on asphalt and about 50km on piste.

It is absolutely vital to keep to the main piste and to follow the markers whenever possible. Never cycle at night and always go back on your tracks as soon as you think you might be lost — no matter how strong the urge may be to go on. We made just such a mistake — and paid for it by having to survive on our meagre rations of water for five days when we lost the piste some 300km south of Tamanrasset.

The main problem we had to overcome was water — and being

able to carry enough of it in sections like that difficult one south of Tamanrasset. When we were planning our trip, we realised that at this stage we would need to have stocks to last 20 days at a stretch.

We increased our carrying capacity with a variety of plastic bottles held in panniers and in improvised wire cages. Our front racks and bike frames were given over entirely to carrying water. In this way we could each carry up to 15 litres — still not enough. Our supplies were soon exhausted and we were only able to survive by asking for water from passing vehicles.

Keeping to the centre of the piste we saw up to a dozen vehicles a day. We tried not to take too much water from anyone and never asked for it from motorcycles — but everyone was helpful. Algerian truck drivers were absolutely fantastic. They carried plenty of water and would sometimes stop to brew up tea for us. We saw some of them more than once and they occasionally shared their meals with us — which could be interesting. We were once fed gazelle and we met a French cyclist who said he had been served camel's testicles!

Europeans tended to have less water — but they could sometimes really make your day by giving you some fresh fruit. We felt like we had become celebrities, with people stopping to take our photos. We never felt we had been a burden on other travellers — although we could never have made it without their help.

Finding food that was easy to carry and that would also keep was often difficult. For the long ride down to the Niger border, we had to rely for our main meals on dehydrated food that we brought from home. We developed the practice of having a small breakfast and supper with a big dinner in the middle of the day. For breakfast we used to have sandwiches — bread was available in all the towns and stayed fresh for about three days if you kept it in plastic bags. Further away from towns, we used baby food in Algeria and managed to get porridge oats elsewhere.

We used to carry fresh vegetables for our main meals whenever possible and ate these with rice or pasta. Prior to Tamanrasset we also ate pulses — either lentils or beans that could be cooked up in bulk and then carried in screw-top plastic jars. They used to keep for three or four days — although they expanded in the jars with the heat and caused the jars to hiss as air was forced out. The first time this happened we thought there was a snake in the pannier bag and wasted several hours nervously prodding it with sticks!

The only tinned foods we could find in Algeria were peas and tomato paste. Meat was hard to come by — poor quality and pricey. Stocks were scarce everywhere, but in our experience El Golea was the worst — with trips to the so-called supermarket leaving you feeling like Old Mother Hubbard!

For supper we either had bread or biscuits together with some of the dates that we carried throughout North Africa for snacks. We could always get coffee, chocolate and milk powder to drink. But I have to admit that when we found that the only tea available in Algeria was green, we had supplies of British brands posted out to us!

NIGER

Area: 1,186,400km²

Population: 9.0 million

Capital: Niamey

Languages: French is the official language; main national languages are Hausa, Djerma and Tamacheq (Tuareg).

Climate: A two season climate, with the dry season from October to June and the wet season from June to September. It becomes very hot in April to June.

Visas: Not needed by citizens of EU countries and French-speaking Africa. All others can get visas from Paris, Algiers or the Niger consulate at Tamanrasset.

Foreign embassies and consulates in Niamey: Benin (Rue des Dallois); **French Consulate** (issues visas for Burkina Faso, CAR, Chad and Togo; Avenue François Mitterand); **Mali** (Boulevard de la Liberté); **Nigeria** (Rue du Président Luebke); **Tunisia** (Rue des Lacs, le Plateau; Tel: 722603); **USA** (Rue des Ambassades; Tel: 722661); the UK has closed its Niamey consulate — nearest representation is in Abidjan or Dakar.

Other red tape: At the Assamakka border from Algeria, officials may insist that you buy a *laissez passer*, even if you have a carnet (travellers coming from the south do not have the same problem). You will have to pay for this with either French francs or CFA, so make sure you are carrying some of these currencies (1990 cost was CFA10,000). More recent reports, however, suggest that the *laissez-passer* will only be issued to those without a carnet. You will also be required to buy vehicle insurance. A policy is available at the border that will cover you for all countries in West Africa. This represents a big saving over insurance bought country by country — and you will be asked to produce an insurance certificate everywhere in West Africa. A vaccination certificate for yellow fever is also compulsory. Checking in with the police is compulsory for every town where you stop overnight, and sometimes even for towns you just pass through. In Niamey you have to get stamped out by the police when you leave town, as well as registering when you arrive. Niger police checks will take up several pages in your passport. If you fail to get the right stamps you can be sent back for them.

Banks and money: Currency is the CFA (west). The CFA zone has no black market as this is a convertible currency. Banks in all major towns.

Public holidays: New Year's Day, Independence Day (August 3), Armed Forces Day (October 26), Proclamation of the Republic (December 18) and Christmas Day (December 25). The Islamic holidays of Aid el-Fitr, Aid el-Kabir and Mouloud are also observed, on dates varying from year to year.

Fuel: Available in main towns. Cheap black market supplies in Birnin-Konni.

Roads: Drive on the right. Mostly good surfaced roads after Arlit; some soft sand on route to Zinder. Desert tracks only in the northeast. Take care to find the good piste to Arlit at Assamakka or you may end up on the old piste to Agadez.

Routes: If coming from Algeria, the straightforward trans-African route simply crosses through Niger north to south — Arlit, Agadez, Zinder and through to Kano. The main alternative is heading southwest to Niamey and then north to Mali, south to Benin or west to Burkina Faso and all parts of West Africa. If coming from Mauritania, you will arrive in Niamey from Gao in Mali or Ouagadougou in Burkina Faso. The road from Niamey to Nguigmi, in the east, is surfaced all the way, taking you to the start of the difficult Lake Chad route (you need to get written authorisation from the Ministry of the Interior in Niamey to take this road).

Places to visit
Far too many travellers race through Niger. Take your time and enjoy this fascinating country.

Siesta time
In hot sahel countries, it makes sense to escape from the hottest part of the day. That is why in a town like Niamey everything closes down between 12.00 noon and 4.00pm. The only option you have is to do what everyone else does and find yourself a shady spot for a snooze. You are not even guaranteed being able to while away the time in a bar or restaurant. We tried this once and successfully managed to order a couple of Cokes. But having then brought us the menu, the woman serving us put her head down on the table and promptly fell asleep!

Agadez: One of the ancient crossroads of Africa, Agadez is the traditional starting point for caravans travelling north across the desert and is still the point of departure for camels driven across the Ténéré to Bilma. A bustling and colourful old town, it is however starting to attract some of the hassles associated with a booming tourist economy (particularly with traders and guides in the main square by the mosque).

Aïr Plateau: Just to the east of the new road from Arlit to Agadez lies this range of jagged peaks, which provide some of the most dramatic landscapes in Niger and some good opportunities to spot wildlife. There are gardens irrigated by springs in the valleys. This area has become dangerous recently with the Touareg separatist movement. Check on the latest situation before coming here.

Niamey: This bustling capital is worth a few days of anyone's time. Situated on the Niger River, it has many colourful markets and one of the best museums of national culture anywhere in Africa — admission is free. It is on a huge open-air site, taking in a large number of separate pavilions and exhibits — even complete re-creations of villages. The selection and prices of craft work for sale here are probably the best you will find in Niger.

The Ténéré: One of the most beautiful desert areas in the world, with rolling dunes over 650 feet high. The old salt road to Bilma and visits to the dead cities of Djado and Djaba provide a magnificent journey — but you must have at least two vehicles, a local guide and plenty of fuel and water. Once again, take advice on the current safety of this area before you go.

Places to stay
It is illegal to bush camp within 15 kilometres of a city area in Niger; you are likely to be moved on if you are seen doing so. Elsewhere there are plenty of opportunities for camping. Here are some of the best places to stay in towns.

Agadez: *Oasis Camping*, to the north of town on the old piste to Arlit, has gone downhill but there seem to be efforts to revive it. Check this site out first as it is very friendly and is in a more pleasant location. There is another site a few kilometres out of town on the main road to Arlit; this has less shade but may be the better bet now. The *Hotel Sahara* overlooks the old market and has safe parking.

NIGER POLICE CHECKS

Failure to check in with the police in Niger is unlikely to lead to you being arrested but it can certainly give rise to irritating delays. One set of travellers we met did not know this when they stopped at a hotel in Arlit. When they turned up the next morning and were asked why they had not checked in yet, it turned out the police knew their every movement! 'When we said we'd just arrived, they told us we'd stayed at such and such a hotel, and eaten twice in such and such a restaurant.

'They insisted on holding on to our passports until the end of the day which put us in one of those classic Catch 22 situations. We had to buy insurance to get our passports back, but we didn't have any CFA and needed our passports to change money. In the end we managed to talk them into giving us one of them back so we could get to a bank.'

Arlit: There is a good large campsite to the south of town on the main road to Agadez. The small campsite at the north end of town is described as 'horrendous' and just as expensive as an hotel. There is a good hotel with a locked compound for parking close to the police station.

Birnin-Konni: Campsite with bar and restaurant. Good place to arrange cheap fuel.

Dogondoutchi: You can camp at the *Auberge*.

Niamey: There are a number of good hotels to chose from with safe parking and swimming pools — expensive but worth it as a treat. On the road out to the west of town past the French Embassy is the *Hotel les Roniers*, which is highly recommended. In the centre is the *Hotel Terminus*. These are the two most reasonably priced of the good hotels. The *Grand Hotel* is more expensive but you can use the pool for a small fee. *Camping Touristique*, in the Yantala district on the road out to Gao, is the only campsite in Niamey. It is a large site but has very little shade (a big problem). Never wonderful, the facilities have gone downhill, and many overlanders have reported hassles with police here. *Camping Rio Bravo* is situated about 20km from Niamey out along the Gao road (just carry on past *Camping Touristique*). This site has been a little run down but it is in a much more pleasant setting and has plenty of shade.

Tahoua: You can camp at the *Campement*, behind secure fencing.

Zinder: There is no official campsite but there are some unofficial sites at private houses.

Sources of tourist information
Maison de l'Afrique: Rue de Viarmes 2, 75001 Paris, France.

Tourist office in Niger:
Niamey Avenue du Président Henrich Luebke, BP 612; Tel: 73 24 47.

MAURITANIA

Area: 1,030,700km²

Population: 2.2 million

Capital: Nouakchott

Languages: French and Arabic are the official languages; the main national languages are Hassaniya, Fula, Solinke and Wolof.

Climate: Mostly desert climate — very dry and extremely hot in the summer. Some rain along the coast in autumn.

Visas: Required by all except citizens of France and Italy.

Foreign embassies and consulates in Nouakchott: Egypt (32 Rue Oumar; Tel: 52192); **France** (Rue Ahmed Ould Mahmed; Tel: 251740; **Tunisia** (Tevragh Zeina, BP68; Tel: 52871); **USA** (BP 222; Tel: 52660).

Other red tape: Carnet required. On arrival you will be expected to fill out a currency and valuables declaration form and report to the police at the first sizeable town. There are a lot of checks travelling south from Nouadhibou. Travelling from Mali, this is Nema.

Banks and money: The unit of currency is the ougiya, which you are not allowed either to import or export.

Public holidays; New Year's Day, Labour Day (May 1), Africa Liberation Day (May 25), Mauritania National Day (November 11). Most Islamic festivals are also observed on dates varying from year to year.

Roads: Drive on the right. A few good surfaced roads; all others are desert tracks.

Routes: Mauritania now provides one of the main points of entry into Africa. See page 106 for details of the route. The only other time most overlanders will find themselves in Mauritania is if they are driving from Mali to Senegal in the rainy season (when the Kidira border is impassable). The only route (apart from taking the train) in such circumstances is to drive up to Néma in Mauritania and then along the main road to Nouakchott south to Rosso and across the River Senegal.

Places to stay

It's generally not a good idea to bush camp too close to Nouakchott.

Nouakchott: You can camp at *Tagit Vacances*, 10km north on the beach. Good fish meals at the fishing village on the way into town.

Sources of tourist information
Maison de l'Afrique Rue de Viarmes 2, 75001 Paris, France.

Tourist office in Mauritania
Nouakchott off Avenue General Nasser; Tel: 53337.

CHAD

Area: 1,284,000km²

Population: 5.5 million

Capital: N'djamena

Languages: French is the official language; the main national languages are Arabic in the north and Sara in the south.

Climate: The desert climate in the north is hot and dry all year round. Heavy rains come to the south in May or June to September, when many areas become completely cut off. Rains are not so heavy in the centre. Temperatures are extremely hot indeed at the end of May, just before the rains arrive.

Visas: Needed by everyone except citizens of Andorra, France, French-speaking countries in Africa, Germany and Zaïre. They are available from the French Embassy in London (the French Consulate is also the place to go in Niamey, Niger).

Foreign embassies and consulates in N'djamena: Cameroon; **CAR**; **Egypt** (Avenue Charles de Gaulle; Tel: 513660); **France** (Rue de Lieutenant Franjoux); **Germany** (Rue de Marseille); **Sudan** (Rue de Havre); **USA** (Avenue Felix Eboue; Tel: 516218).

Other red tape: Masses and masses of it. Fortunately Chad is a fascinating place with a lot of wonderful people — otherwise the level of officialdom would drive you round the bend. Be prepared for plenty of searches if you enter the country by the Lake Chad route — we were stopped and had every item removed from our Land Rover five times before we even got as far as the official entry point at Bol. When we did arrive it took another 21 hours to complete all the formalities. All of your documents will be meticulously inspected. You have to report to the *Sureté* when you arrive in N'djamena and go through two complete sets of registration procedures in two separate offices — once for immigration and once to register as a foreigner in the city. Having cleared that hurdle, you will also require written authorisation in order to travel any further in the country. You have to apply for this to the Ministry of Tourism, which then writes to the Ministry of the Interior which then issues the letter! All this can take a long time — but you will not get far without the right documents. If you want to speed things up you can try offering to deliver the messages personally from one ministry to the other. Take extreme care if you are using a camera as photography is strictly banned without a permit.

Banks and money: The unit of currency is the CFA (central). Don't count on being able to change money outside of N'djamena and Sarh.

Public holidays: New Year's Day, National Holiday (January 11), Easter Monday, Labour Day (May 1), Africa Liberation Day (May 25), Anniversary Republic (June 7), Independence Day (August 11), All Saints' Day (November 1), Day of the Proclamation of the Republic (November 20), Christmas Day (December 25). The Islamic holidays of Aid el-Fitr and Aid el-Adha are also observed, with dates varying from year to year.

Fuel: Seems to be available in main towns but it is expensive (although not quite as bad as the extremely expensive levels across the border in CAR).

Roads: Drive on the right. Only a few kilometres of potholed surfaced roads on either side of N'djamena. The rest are made up of sandy desert tracks in the north and very bad mud roads in the south.

Routes: If you are driving through Chad, the chances are you will either enter or leave on the difficult Lake Chad route, linking N'djamena with Nguigmi in Niger. From N'djamena you can cross straight into Cameroon. Otherwise, the main road south heads to Sarh and the border post at Maro; an alternative goes via Bongor and Doba. You will not be allowed to go to the north of the country but it may just be possible to take the long bad track across to Abéché and Sudan.

Places to visit

Bol: The main town on the north of Lake Chad has not changed for thousands of years. Catch it on market day (Wednesdays) and it feels as though you have wandered onto the set for a biblical epic.

Lake Chad: Hardly a lake at all these days, you will not see it from the soft desert tracks that criss-cross their way around it. But this really is a wonderful desert area and the survival of the people living here can make you feel very humble.

N'djamena: Dusty and desperately poor — with just a few expensive shops and restaurants for the ever-present aid workers and military advisors. There is an excellent museum close to the *Sureté* office.

Places to stay

No problems camping in the desert further north and there are plenty of bush camping opportunities further south. There are very few other options.

N'djamena: Apart from the hideously expensive *Novotel*, the only place you may be able to stay with safe parking in N'djamena is at the *Catholic Mission*, close to the main market. But they are loathe to let you stay for more than a night and it is expensive.

Sarh: The *Hotel de Chasse* is not cheap but it is an excellent place and has a first class restaurant.

Sources of tourist information

Maison de l'Afrique, Rue de Viarmes 2, 75001 Paris, France.

Tourist offices in Chad:

N'djamena Direction du Tourisme, BP 86; Tel: 28 17. Tchad Tourisme, BP 894; Tel: 34 10.

The Lake Chad route

Make sure you are well prepared if you plan to take the Lake Chad route; it is extremely difficult. Of course, the compensation is it is taken so infrequently that it does provide an insight into an ancient and more untouched world than you will encounter on the main Nigerian routes.

It is hard to give precise guidance on the route to take as this changes frequently depending on the size of the lake. As it contracts and (less frequently) expands, the routes change, keeping relatively close to the edge — although you are unlikely actually to see any water. The map provides two alternatives — the closest to the lake is the more recent.

The chances are there could well be another preferred route by the time you are in Chad. The best idea is to get a list of the villages you should pass through before leaving Nguigmi (or N'djamena). It is always possible to check your progress with locals, who can direct you by the names of places even if they speak no French.

Under 'control' in Chad

'Control!' There was that dreaded word again. By now we knew exactly what it meant — at least two hours spent in the sun removing every last item from the Land Rover, a search of the utmost detail by the military and then a futile attempt to fit

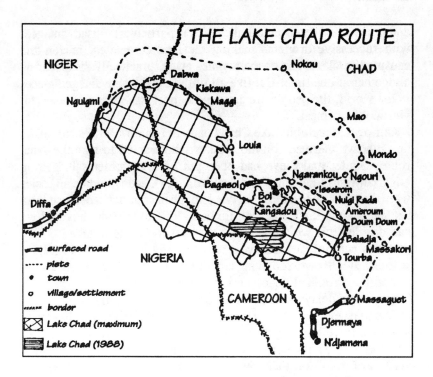

everything back inside again. And detailed really does mean just that; books would be leafed through page by page, individual packages opened, every last cranny peered into. Apart from the physical strain involved, a certain mental agility was also required to fend off the constant requests for *cadeaux* while all these riches were spread out on the ground. Try all that and keeping a smile on your face!

This was just one of the tiny villages along the Lake Chad route to N'djamena where we had to register with the *brigades* and undergo these minute searches. I suppose it wasn't surprising that this was the toughest place we passed through as far as military checks were concerned; it was only a month or so earlier a peace treaty had been signed with Libya after years of war over the northern territories.

Chad is such a sad country, born into conflict through its crazy colonial legacy. Like Sudan, its neighbour to the east, Chad is a huge country spanning two entirely different cultures. The Arab and Touareg north and the black African south have been pitted against one another under a variety of coalitions ever since independence. All this and years of drought have made Chad very down-trodden and poor. The area around Lake Chad is particularly disadvantaged, with successive droughts making the land completely barren and causing the lake to recede many miles away, practically disappearing altogether at one time. But like all of the most disadvantaged places in the world, the people are among the most generous and beautiful you will ever meet.

Our own assault on Lake Chad began in Niamey, where we linked up with two Germans on motorbikes who wanted to take the same route. Gűnter and Steve had been put off by problems in getting Nigerian visas in Niamey and decided Lake Chad would be an easier way through to Cameroon. We had also experienced some visa problems — at the Cameroon Embassy in Dakar. But above all we had decided this would be a more interesting route to take.

It was certainly a journey to remember. Apart from the military searches and the worst driving conditions we encountered anywhere, our time in Chad also introduced us to dysentery, rampant bureaucratic delays and the onset of the rainy season.

The journey really does require a four-wheel drive vehicle — two of them travelling together would be even better. The lack of supplies and water along the way means that bikes would find it very hard going on their own. It is doubtful whether Gűnter and Steve could have made it at all without us carrying some of their heavier loads through the soft sand.

We managed to get lost even before reaching the invisible border between Niger and Chad (it is many miles and two days further to the official entry point at Bol). Several times we tried the same stretch and each time the track seemed to disappear. Eventually we stumbled on the village of Bilabrim and got some helpful directions. But still we were not convinced we were on the right track.

That evening Paula ended up curled in agony with renal colic — the result of not forcing down enough water in these scorching conditions. Just as it seemed nothing could get worse, a gigantic black wall came racing across the desert towards us. We were engulfed in a fierce sandstorm which removed what few tracks there were to follow on this route.

But like all low points, the next day was bound to be a big improvement. Paula was feeling a little better and we chanced on a family of nomads. They were desperately poor and we dressed a horrifying open sore on one of the children. They told us (with no common language) that we were now in Chad and only a couple of kilometres away from the main piste. The head of the family immediately volunteered to come in the Land Rover to show us; once back on course, we managed to avoid getting lost again all the way to N'djamena.

Another village. Was it Maggi? We approached a group of villagers to find out. They greeted us with the enthusiasm and hospitality that is the hallmark of this area. But all too soon a soldier approached and barked *'Continuez! Continuez!'* The rifle grasped in his hands meant we were not likely to argue.

Racing off into the desert, we were remarking on the difference between civilian hospitality and military hostility when we realised the bikes were not following us. Soon Steve arrived. His passport had been confiscated while he was sent to fetch us. Apparently it was all he could do to stop the soldier firing at us as we drove off. The military idea of *'continuez'* in Chad takes you as far as the *brigades* post, not as far as the next village. Needless to say, that was one long hot *control*.

Bol had been described to us as the armpit of the universe. However, it seemed to us more like the town that time forgot — a remarkable desert trading post, practically unchanged for thousands of years. If you are ever likely to go this way, try to be here on a Wednesday. That is market day, when the place comes alive in its full medieval charm.

Walking through the market area at dusk, the air was thick with dust, filtering the golden rays of the setting sun. All around there were herds of long horned cattle and goats. The last few stalls that were open still had a small selection of vegetables. The rest of the traders were mounting their camels and starting the long haul back to their own villages. Several separate caravans were starting to form for the journey — some were setting up camp ready to make a start in the morning while others prepared to head home by moonlight.

Whatever time of day you arrive in Bol, you are unlikely to be able to get away again before the next day. This is where all the Chad entry formalities take place — immigration, police, customs, *brigades*. The opening hours are staggered as if they were deliberately designed to make it impossible to complete the process on the same day. It was 21 hours after arriving in town that we cleared the last hurdle.

When we finally got on our way, we found that we were invited to take a member of the *brigades* to the next village, Kandagan. It is not the sort of offer you can refuse. His route took us a much shorter but more difficult way than we had originally planned. Crossing what had once been the bed of the lake itself, we were constantly running through soft sandy stretches and up steep dunes (formerly islands). The routes around Lake Chad are constantly changing so you can only really rely on local knowledge for guidance.

N'djamena at last. At first it was a wonderful sanctuary but as the days went on, a kind of prison. Everywhere to stay in town is incredibly expensive and the bureaucracy means it can be very difficult to leave quickly.

Gűnter and Steve dodged straight across the bridge to Cameroon the next day. Being German, they did not need a visa. We did — and there is no Cameroon consulate in N'djamena and no way to get a visa at the border. We had no choice but to drive on south through Chad to CAR.

This is not as simple as it sounds. The catch is you need written permission to drive anywhere further than N'djamena. This permission must be requested from the Ministry of Tourism, which then asks the Ministry of the Interior, which then sends the letter to the Ministry of Tourism, which then hands over this precious document. At least that is the theory. Of course, in practice things are not nearly so simple. Weekends, a two-day bank holiday and a dose of dysentery for us both added to the chaos so that it ultimately took us 10 days to move on. With nobody allowed in or out of the town during the holiday, we began to feel trapped.

For all that though, N'djamena is a tremendous place — a dusty old town with none of the glitter of many capital cities. Apart from the outrageously ostentatious wealth of some traders, the military, the UN and some aid workers, it is very poor. It comes alive in the early evenings with small bars and stalls set up along the side streets and small fires crackling in the darkness.

By the time we left N'djamena the rains had broken. It was early June and the unbearable heat of the previous days had finally given way to sporadic downpours and a slightly cooler feel in the air. Overnight hundreds of frogs appeared, croaking noisily outside our room.

The condition of the mud roads deteriorated as we headed further south and the rains continued to get heavier. In Sarh we were told that a few days later we could have been stranded until the end of the rains. Spurred on by this we headed quickly for the border, taking the wrong turning along the way and leaving the country as we arrived — lost.

We were obviously the only vehicle that had attempted this route for a long time. The road got smaller and smaller until it was no more than a single file footpath across a field — with worryingly large patches of deep water to ford. We asked again and again and were assured that this was indeed the road to Maro. The novelty of seeing Westerners in their Land Rover out in the middle of nowhere could only have been enhanced when the fuel pump finally gave up at the quantity of water being forced through the engine — forcing a dive into the water below for some running repairs.

Chad was an eventful kind of a place.

EGYPT

Area: 997,739km²

Population: 60.8 million

Capital: Cairo

Languages: Arabic is the official language but English and French are widely spoken.

Climate: Mostly hot but cooler in the north from November to March. The little rain that falls is concentrated between December and March.

Visas: Required by all apart from citizens of most Arab countries and Malta.

Foreign embassies and consulates in Cairo: Australia (5th Floor, Cairo Plaza South, Corniche el Nil, Boulac; Tel: 777900); **Canada** (6 Mohamed Fahmi el Sayed Street, Garden City; Tel: 356 3548); **Cote d'Ivoire** (39 Rue El Kods El Cherif; Tel: 346 0109); **Eritrea** (87 Shahab Street, Al Muhandesein; Tel: 303 0516); **Tanzania** (9 Abdel Hamid Loutfy Street, Dokki; Tel: 704155/704286); **Tunisia** (26 Rue el Guezirah, Zamalek; Tel: 340 4940); **UK** (Ahmed Raghab Street, Garden City; Tel: 354 0850); **USA** (8 Kamal El-Din Salah Street, Garden City; Tel: 355 7371); **Zaïre** (5 Rue Mansour Mohamed, Zamalek; Tel: 340 3662); **Zambia** (22 El Nakhil Street, Dokki); **Zimbabwe** (36 Wadi El Nil Street, Mohandessin; Tel: 345 7221).

Other red tape: Standard international motoring documents are required. A carnet is absolutely essential — Egypt is one of the strictest countries in Africa for selling vehicles (if you have either Egypt or Kenya on your carnet you will automatically require a higher cover to meet the potentially astronomic duties if you do sell). You will need a permit if your vehicle is right-hand drive. Everyone has to register with the police at the Central Government Buildings in Cairo within a week of arriving.

Banks and money: The unit of currency is the Egyptian pound.

Public holidays; Unity Day (February 22), the Monday following Coptic Easter Sunday, Sinai Day (April 25), Labour Day (May 1), Evacuation Day (June 18), Anniversary of the Revolution (July 23), Suez Day (October 6), Victory Day (December 23). The Islamic holidays of Hejri, Aid el-Fitr, Aid el-Adha, the last day of Ramadan, Islamic New Year and the Prophet's Birthday are observed, on dates varying from year to year.

Fuel: Available along the Nile route and main centres of population.

Roads: All the main routes are good surfaced roads. Drive on the right. Outside of tourist areas road signs are in Arabic only. Travel permits are needed for some minor routes, available from the Travel Permits Department, corner of Sharia Sheikh Rihan and Sharia Nubar in Cairo.

Routes: Arriving either from Alexandria or Sinai (some overland truck operators offer expeditions to Africa via the Middle East), all roads in the north converge on Cairo. The most popular route south follows the Nile down to Aswan, where you put your vehicle on the boat to Wadi Halfa in Sudan. Overland crossing to Sudan is not allowed. But equally unmissable is the route following the Red Sea Coast, which is extremely beautiful. You can pick up the Nile route again at Qena. There have been a number of attacks on tourists in Egypt in recent years; although this has not been serious enough to close the country off to travellers, you should exercise caution. With safety in numbers, a convoy would be a good idea. Don't stray from the main routes.

Motoring organisations: Automobile Club Egypt, 10 Sharia Qasr el-Nil, Cairo; Tel: 74 33 55. Touring Club Egypt, 8 Sharia Qasr el-Nil, Cairo.

Places to visit
The Red Sea and the Nile are both beautiful. If you are in Egypt you should take in all of those famous places you always meant to visit — the pyramids, the Valley of the Kings, Luxor, Aswan. They are all breathtaking — but they also attract a lot of hassles. Enjoying yourself in Egypt can be hard work.

Places to stay
Finding a place to stay is very difficult. There are no campsites and the main road along the Nile is totally overcrowded. Not only are there people all the way but they also tend to be very persistent. The only real options are to drive into the desert well away from the road or to look out for hotels with secure parking. There are plenty of good, cheap hotels wherever you go along the main routes.

Sources of tourist information
Egyptian State Tourist Office, Egyptian House, 170 Piccadilly, London W1V; Tel: 0171 493 5282.

Tourist offices in Egypt:

Alexandria Saad Zaghlul Street; Tel: 807985.
Aswan Tourist Souk; Tel: 323297.
Cairo Adly Street; Tel: 3913454.
Luxor Nile Street; Tel: 382215.
Port Said Palestine Street; Tel: 223868.
Suez Canal Street; Tel: 221141.

Guide books: *Blue Guide to Egypt,* Veronica Seton-Williams and Peter Stocks (A&C Black); *Discovery Guide to Egypt,* Michael Haag; *Egypt Handbook*, Kathy Hansen (Moon Publications); *Fodor's Egypt*; *Self-guided Egypt* (Langenscheidt), *The Rough Guide to Egypt*.

SUDAN

Area: 2,503,890km²

Population: 29.4 million

Capital: Khartoum

Languages: Arabic is the official language; English is spoken by many officials.

Climate: Temperatures are very high, particularly in summer. Very little rainfall in the north from July to September; much heavier rainfall in the south from April to November.

Visas: Required by all and very difficult to get. Try to get your visa before leaving home as there can be a long wait at embassies in Africa — as much as two or three months.

Foreign embassies and consulates in Khartoum: France (Tel: 77619); **Germany** (Tel: 77990); **Uganda** (House 9, Block 9L, Street 35, New Extension; Tel: 43049); **UK** (off Sharia Al Baladiya; Tel: 70760); **USA** (Sharia Ali Abdul Latif; Tel: 74700); **Zaïre** (21 & 25 Airport Side-New Extension; Tel: 42424).

Other red tape: International motoring documents and vaccination certificate for yellow fever are required. Sudan is an extremely bureaucratic country; you will need to get permits for most stages of your journey. First of all you will need a permit to go from Wadi Halfa to Khartoum and then you must get one in Khartoum in order to travel anywhere to the south or west of the city. You must register at the Ministry of the Interior within three days of arriving in Khartoum.

Banks and money: The unit of currency is the Sudanese pound.

Public holidays: New Year/Independence Day (January 1), National Day (March 3), Easter, May Revolution Day (May 25), Christmas (24-26 December). All Islamic festivals are also observed on dates varying from year to year.

Fuel: Supplies are often very difficult to get. Stock up whenever you can. Queues for fuel in Khartoum can be two miles long!

Roads: Extremely bad — soft sand in the north and mud in the south. The only reasonable roads link Khartoum with Port Sudan and Khartoum with Shendi. Drive on the right.

Routes: Although the south has been impossible to go to since the early 1980s because of the civil war, overland entry to Ethiopia and Eritrea has now opened up. It is also sometimes possible to head west from Khartoum.

On the northern section you have two options — following the railway line across the Nubian desert and then continuing south to Atbara or taking the more interesting but more difficult Nile route. This presents a lot of awful driving conditions in soft sand with little more than the occasional track to follow; you will be away from the river for long stretches so you do need to be able to navigate — there are very few vehicles on this route. The compensation is that you will pass through some of the friendliest villages in Africa, meet and stay with many wonderful people and take in some beautiful desert scenery. Do not expect to be able to buy any food or fuel before Khartoum, but the locals will look after you — as everyone says, this is the friendliest place in the world.

If you are heading west, from Khartoum you will need to head to Nyala and on into CAR. It is then possible to head down to Bangassou and across to Zaïre to join the main overland route. This is an option taken by some of the overland truck operators. If you really do like it tough, it may be possible to head across from Nyala or El Fasher into Chad. All of these routes in western Sudan are totally dependent on the weather (they should certainly not be attempted between July and October; January until April would probably be the best months) and all require permits from Khartoum. If you wish to head south, you need to head east to Kasala in order to cross the border to Eritrea. An alternative way of reaching Kasala is to take the three-day car ferry from Suez to Port Sudan (via Jeddah, where you have to stay on the boat). From there you can head straight south to Kasala.

Places to stay
There are mostly only two choices — the wide open desert or asking permission to stay in a village. You are unlikely ever to be refused hospitality.

Sources of tourist information
Tourist offices in Sudan:
Khartoum corner of Sharia el-Baladaya and Sharia el-Huriyya.
Omdurman Tourism and Hotels Corporation, PO Box 7104; Tel: 74031.
Many large hotels can also supply tourist information.

Cycling the Nubian Desert: the Nile route

by Christian and Gilly Lee

We both felt pretty anxious about Sudan as we climbed onto what could hardly be called a boat, pulled on either side by two huge barges with roaring engines. This dragged us down Lake Nasser towards Wadi Halfa, a 24-hour journey, crushed from head to toe with bodies and piles and piles of merchandise, which was being taken back to the local markets of Sudan.

We could hardly find any space to sit, while we anxiously watched our bikes being slowly covered under a pile of pots, pans, carpets, skins, shoes, bodies and baggage. We retreated to an upper deck and found a small patch under a lifeboat where we could only lie flat and contemplate our new life.

When we arrived in Wadi Halfa we were faced with the task of trying to decipher where on earth all of those tracks led to in the sand. If you think of all the normal daily things in life — tarmac roads, electricity, running water, cutlery, loos, books, shops and most other 20th century things — and take them all away. Then you have Sudan.

So we pedalled off anxiously and after a few kilometres arrived in a shanty-like town which was confirmed as Wadi Halfa. We had been debating whether or not to ride across this 160km stretch of desert — all of the advice we had received was against. We got ourselves as well prepared as we ever could and decided to give it a go. We purified a massive amount of water (26 litres) and strapped our sloshing bags to our bikes. Another exhausting night was spent considering all the possibilities of what could go wrong.

We rose at 5.30am with butterflies in our stomachs and started to ride. Our first problem was choosing which track was the right one. We spent considerable time at this, asking people the way. We were busy taking compass bearings and eventually, after about five or six kilometres, the tracks seemed to converge and we had found our road to Dongola.

We were thrilled by our progress and began really to enjoy our biking. However, we soon became quite overawed by the desolation and the danger we had placed ourselves in. The desert is a powerful place emotionally — it leaves you feeling stripped naked and alone. Life felt very precious and family and friends filled our minds continuously. It was so barren but also so tantalisingly beautiful, with mountains of stark rock giving way to great plains of sand. The colours changed constantly during the path of the sun, from black charcoal greys to ochre yellows and, at times, almost white.

The riding was hard, the hardest yet. There was no road to speak

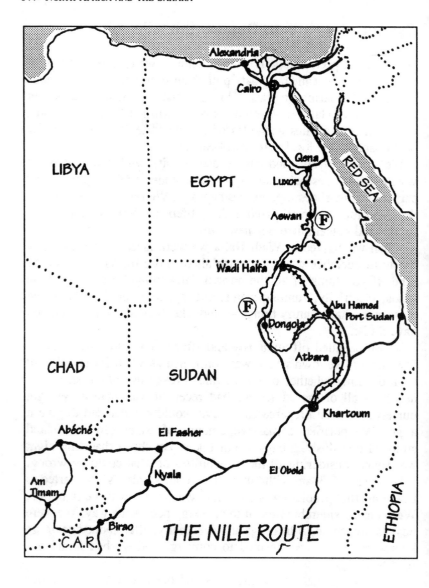

THE NILE ROUTE

of — just tracks frequented by Bedford trucks, the only form of transport here. They had churned and corrugated the track into a very bumpy boneshaking ride. Thank heavens we were fit — we needed to be. Surprisingly, in our first few kilometres we had a puncture. While we were repairing it, a large truck reassuringly stopped to check if we were all right. It was to be the only one we would see over the next two days.

We were lucky with the weather. The temperature range was from

30°-35°C in the shade (what a shame there wasn't any) with a cool wind blowing from the north (this wind blows until late March when it is replaced by a punishing hot wind from the south). We had completely covered ourselves with hats, scarves, cotton trousers, long-sleeved shirts, glasses, total sun block cream and a large piece of white cloth to cover our faces when sand storms blew up.

On our first day we managed to do 55km — but that had taken almost nine hours to complete and we were pretty exhausted and hungry by the end of it. Food is quite a problem in Sudan. There is nothing to buy — not even bread, our staple biking diet. We had brought some food with us from Egypt but were wondering if we were going to be perpetually hungry in this country.

We camped that night in the desert, ate our Egyptian lentils and vegetables and were stunned by the silence. When you stopped to listen to it, all you could hear were your own veins thumping.

The following day saw us up early and concentrating on the two yards in front of us that always demanded 100% of our concentration. By our reckoning it was another full day's ride across the desert before we would catch sight of the Nile again. When the time came when it ought to have appeared, it was impossible not to backtrack in our minds through all those turns and ask if we had really taken the right ones. After a long four miles, the Nile suddenly appeared and we were elated to see the thin green line of date palms and water; we both felt very proud of what we had achieved.

Without doubt our Fisher bikes had come into their own; this was the first time they had really shown us what they were capable of. Others would literally have rattled to pieces — but these battled through.

We were soon to discover the true hospitality of the Sudanese people. Now that the desert proper was over, mud villages appeared along the banks of the Nile, which we were to follow all the way to Dongola. Our appearance there must have been the equivalent of seeing a UFO go whizzing by. Once the villagers recovered their composure, we were inundated with hospitality and were offered overflowing proportions of tea and food and their own beds for the night. These people had nothing but were prepared to give us everything.

Although buying food was a problem, we soon learned that our bellies would be provided for. Simple meals were offered in abundance — their staple diet is *ful*, a broad bean that is mashed to a pulp and eaten by scooping up handfuls of the stuff with flat unleavened bread made from maize. It was impossible to return their hospitality. Money would have been a complete insult so we resorted to cigarettes and small bicycles we made out of wire. They seemed to go down well. We found it impossible to spend any money at all and had almost the same amount of money after eight days on the road.

We experienced the hardest day of our lives when we set out towards Delgo. After just two miles the track became soft sand. We had gone through this before but normally there was only a couple of metres of the stuff. We got off to push but this time it turned out to be altogether different. The metres turned into kilometres and the day became one long sweaty push as we dragged our heavily laden bikes through. By the end of the day we had travelled 27 kilometres — we had ridden eight and pushed the other 19. Had a truck come along we would have gladly hitched a ride. But none came and it tested our determination to the full. Magically, we were offered a meal and a bed for the night. Having been running on adrenaline, we collapsed in the sanctuary of this kind man's home.

We finally had to give up once we got close to Dongola. The sea of sand was now taking over and so we searched for a bus to take us the rest of the way to Khartoum. Well, you could hardly really call it a bus — more like a tank on wheels; 400km of riding felt like 4,000 — it was physically and mentally the most taxing section to date. We were pushed into the back and our bikes strapped to the top. Someone said 'Mind your heads', as we snuggled into our rather uncomfortable seats. We looked up at the roof, which was three or four feet above our heads, and thought that maybe he was getting a little confused with his English. About 30 seconds later we set off and very nearly hit the roof as we were catapulted around.

It was a terrible ride; 24-hours later we arrived in Khartoum, feeling like feeble wrecks, stiff as boards and aching all over. We thought the bikes would be handed over to us in small pieces but, except for a few large scratches, they miraculously seemed to be all right.

Christian and Gilly Lee cycled 14,415km from Victoria Station in London to Victoria Falls, Zimbabwe.

Chapter Six

West Africa

West Africa is often largely ignored by overland travellers — a shame as in many ways it offers the richest cultural mix of the whole continent. It is a lively and upbeat region of music, dance and good times — the kind of Africa many travellers hope to find.

What impressed us most was just how ready people were to stop and chat and make friends (a reasonable knowledge of French obviously helps, though it is surprising how little you can get away with). This makes it possible to learn so much more about the soul of the area — you are far more likely to have long meandering discussions here than anywhere else. The contrast is particularly marked with East Africa, where we always found it more difficult to break through.

Political debate seems to be more or less a way of life in West Africa — whereas it can be a difficult and dangerous subject in many other areas. On a beach in Ghana we were told of the limitations of local government policy. At the immigration post entering Senegal we were asked to explain the problems in Northern Ireland. In Togo, conversation turned to the importance of voodoo in the modern day and in Benin it was a lengthy debate on ancient philosophy.

What was important about such encounters was not that they took place but that they seemed as natural as breathing. Discussions about politics, art, culture and history were around every corner.

The biggest problem with West Africa is that it can be very expensive, particularly for fuel. Although prices are lower outside of the French speaking zones, a tour of West Africa can work out being more expensive than a complete trans-African trip. This is why most tour companies will not include a West African section on their trips. Though it has to be said that, in our opinion, the extra cost involved in taking in West Africa is well worth it.

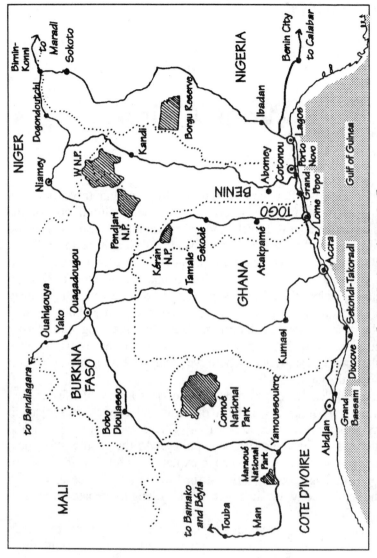

ROUTE GUIDE

The main route planning options are greatly influenced by budgetary considerations. They range from heading straight through Nigeria and on to Cameroon, to a complete loop out to Dakar and back. There are a series of shorter loops that can be taken as a compromise between these two extremes. Overlanders will have their own ideas on what they want to take in, but these are some of the most popular routes.

Nigeria

The quickest route of all is to head straight down from Zinder to Kano and then east to enter Cameroon at Mora. But it is well worth heading further south to take in some of the incredible variety of Nigeria. Make sure you visit Jos on the way down.

The Burkina Faso crossroads

Take the good surfaced road from Niamey or Bamako to Ouagadougou — which is a poor but bustling town. Burkina as a whole is well worth spending a little time in. You are now at the crossroads, with many options open. You can take the road northwest from Ouagadougou to Ouahigouya and cross into Mali to pick up the northern route there (see below). You can head on west to Bobo Dioulasso and across the border into Cote d'Ivoire — eventually heading back along the coast through Ghana, Togo, Benin and Nigeria. You can head straight down into Ghana on a shorter loop or you can cut back still further by simply driving down through Togo (so avoiding the high cost of visas and entry permits in Ghana — but also missing out on the cheaper fuel you are likely to find there). All of these routes are easy and on good roads.

Mali

If you take the Mauritanian route or the Tanezrouft route across Algeria this will be your starting point. Coming from Niger, the most straightforward way of coming into the country is to follow the river Niger up from Niamey to Gao (but check at the time as this road has been closed because of the Touareg uprising). and then take the main road to Mopti (or the detour via Timbuktu). Alternatively, you can enter from Ouahigouya in Burkina Faso and still take in the major sights of the Dogon Country, Mopti and Djenné, before heading on along the good surfaced road to Bamako. From Bamako you can quite easily head south into Cote d'Ivoire and then back east along the coast.

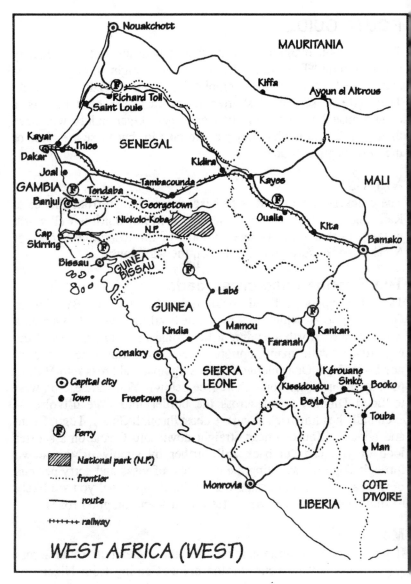

WEST AFRICA (WEST)

Further west

If you want to go beyond Bamako, the going gets a lot tougher. It is possible to head southwest from the city, crossing into Guinea on the road to Siguiri. Guinea is an absolutely beautiful country — but the roads are difficult and many bridges are in a bad state of repair. The other option is to head for Senegal. There are three ways of doing this — via Mauritania, loading your vehicle onto the train or taking the appalling track from Bamako to Kita, Bafoulabé, Kayes and Kidira.

Liberia and Sierra Leone

These countries have been closed to overland travel for many years because of bitter civil wars. They are unlikely to be open again for quite some time.

BURKINA FASO

Area: 274,200km²

Population: 10.1 million

Capital: Ouagadougou

Languages: French is the official language; most common national languages are Moré, Dioula and Peul.

Climate: A two season tropical climate, with a dry season from March to June and a rainy season from July to October. The transitional season between November and February is the ideal time to visit.

Visas: Required by all apart from citizens of Belgium, France, Germany, Italy, Luxembourg and the Netherlands.

Foreign embassies and consulates in Ouagadougou: Algeria (near Place des Nations Unies; Tel: 306401); **Canada** (Tel: 300030); **France** (Boulevard de la Révolution; Tel: 332270); **Germany** (Avenue Raoul Follereau; Tel: 306731); **Ghana** (west of Avenue Bassawarga; Tel: 307635); **Nigeria** (Avenue d'Oubritenga; Tel: 306667); **Senegal** (Avenue Yennenga; Tel: 333714); **UK** (Honorary Consulate; Tel: 306724); **USA** (01 BP 35; Tel: 306723).

Other red tape: Everyone must have a vaccination certificate for yellow fever. Motorists must have a *laissez passer* or carnet, driving licence, *carte gris* and motor insurance; there are regular police checks of these. A road tax will also be levied at the border. In theory everyone should also register with the police in Ouagadougou.

Banks and money: Currency is the CFA (west). Banking hours are 7.30am to 11.00am and 3.00pm to 4.30pm Monday to Friday.

Public holidays: New Year's Day, January 1966 Revolution (January 3), Easter Monday, May Day (May 1), Ascension Day, Whit Monday, The Assumption, All Saints' Day (November 1), Proclamation of the Republic (December 11), and Christmas Day (December 25). The Islamic holidays of Aid el-Fitr, Aid el-Adha and Mouloud are also observed, on dates varying from year to year.

Fuel: Available in most large towns; expensive.

Roads: Drive on the right. The main through route to Ouagadougou is a good surfaced road; most others are reasonable dirt roads.

Routes: Burkina Faso is at the crossroads of West Africa. The good main roads feed travellers through from Niger or Mali into Togo, Ghana or Cote d'Ivoire. But avoid the temptation to fly straight through this fascinating country — there is a lot more to explore. One highly recommended route is to take the road from Ouagadougou to Yako and Ouahigouya and then on to Mali.

Places to visit

Ouagadougou: A dusty low-rise town. Unlike most other African capitals, Ouagadougou feels as if it was an African village that just grew and grew. For film buffs, Burkina Faso is one of the centres of the African movie industry and Ouagadougou has an excellent air-conditioned film centre — home of the African Film Festival.

Places to stay

There is plenty of space for free camping in the bush away from the towns. So you only really need to find somewhere to stay if you are based in a major centre of population.

Ouagadougou: *Ouaga Camping* in the south of town is a pleasant enough site with good facilities but absolutely no shade.

Sources of tourist information

Maison de l'Afrique Rue de Viarmes 2, 75001 Paris, France.

Tourist offices in Burkina Faso:

Ouagadougou Hotel Independence, Avenue Quezzin Coulibaly; and Office Nationale du Tourisme Burkinabe; Tel: 31 19 59.

MALI

Area: 1,240,192km²

Population: 9.1 million

Capital: Bamako

Languages: French is the official language; main national languages are Mandingue, Berber, Tuareg, Peul, Bambara and Malinké.

Climate: Mali spans desert, sahel and tropical areas; this obviously creates big differences across the country. The three main seasons are: rainy season from June to September or October (average temperature in Bamako in August is 25°C); cool dry season from October or November to February (average temperature in Bamako in December is 25°C); hot dry season from March to June (average temperature in Bamako in April is 35°C).

Visas: Required by all except citizens of France and former French territories in Africa. Best places to get visas are the Mali embassies in Paris (89 Rue de Cherche Midi) and Algiers or at the consulates in Tamanrasset or Niamey.

Foreign embassies and consulates in Bamako: Algeria (on Ségou road, 4km after the bridge over the Niger; Tel: 225176); **Burkina Faso** (3 blocks north of Route de Koulikoro, just past the hippodrome; Tel: 223171); **France** (Square Patrice Lumumba; Tel: 226246); **Guinea** (Tel: 222975); **Mauritania** (Tel: 224815); **Morocco** (Tel: 222123); **Nigeria** (1km out the Ségou road after the bridge over the Niger; Tel: 224696); **Senegal** (Avenue Kasse Keita); **USA** (Rue Rochester NY and Rue Mohammed V; Tel: 22 54 70).

Other red tape: Mali has a bad reputation for bureaucracy — one that is not particularly deserved these days. The border crossing from Algeria at Bordj-Moktar can be difficult — but this is largely a result of its isolation. The road out of Gao towards Mopti is a classic checkpoint for everything possible — from insurance to fire extinguisher and warning triangle. You do have to register with local police when you stay in any town and get a tourist registration card from the immigration office in Bamako (CFA1000) but photography permits do not seem to be compulsory any longer. Standard motoring documents including insurance (carnet not essential if you buy a *laissez-passer* at the border) and vaccination certificate for yellow fever are also required.

Banks and money: Unit of currency is CFA (west). Banks in main towns; generally extremely slow.

Public holidays: New Year's Day, Fete de L'Armée (February 20), Democracy Day (March 26), Easter Monday, Labour Day (May 1), Africa Day (May 20), Independence Day (September 22), Christmas Day (December 25). The Islamic holidays of Ramadan, Tabaski and Mouloud are also observed, with dates varying from year to year.

Fuel: Available in the major towns only. It is relatively expensive — more than in all neighbouring countries except for Senegal and Cote d'Ivoire.

Roads: Drive on the right. Roads are mostly poor, apart from the main arterial route from Gao to Bamako. Desert pistes out to Timbuktu can be difficult and the road from Bamako to Senegal is awful.

Routes: The most common starting points are at Gao, having entered either from the Algerian border at Nara, from Mauritania, or along the Niger from Niamey. From Gao there is a choice between the desert piste to Timbuktu or the main road down to Dogon country and Mopti. An interesting alternative approach to Dogon country is to enter from Burkina Faso at Koro and then head towards the Bandiagara escarpment — climbing this sheer rocky face is one of those times when you realise just why four-wheel drive is so essential.

All travellers will converge on Bamako, where there is a choice of routes into Mauritania, Senegal, Guinea or Cote d'Ivoire. The road to Senegal (through Kita, Bafoulabé, Kayes and Kidira) is particularly difficult and has little traffic. It is, however, perfectly possible during the dry season and is a good way to pass through little-visited villages; four-wheel drive is necessary. An alternative but longer route goes up to Nioro and then west to Kayes. Both of these routes into Senegal can only be undertaken between February and June. This is when the river at the border is dry and vehicles can drive across; there is no ferry or bridge for the rest of the year. The only option outside these months is to drive north from Bamako to Néma in Mauritania and then along surfaced roads to Nouakchott and Dakar. You can also load your vehicle onto the train in Bamako and ride to Senegal. Cost of this in 1990 was 744 French francs per tonne from Bamako to Dakar (but FF919 from Dakar to Bamako) or FF497 from Bamako to Kidira. For passengers, the fares are FF246 for first class and FF164 for second class from Bamako to Dakar or FF118 for first class and FF79 for second class from Bamako to Kidira. The full rail journey takes about three days.

Places to visit
Bamako: Little to keep you beyond a day unless you want to take the time to explore thoroughly. It has a national museum (not as good as either Niamey or Dakar) and panoramic views from the 'piste touristique' to Koloumba. There are plans to rebuild the old market building which burned down in 1993.

Djenné: One of the best preserved and impressive of Mali's ancient trans-Saharan trading towns. It is mud-built in the classic Saharan style, including its wonderful mosque (actually a 20th century recreation of the original). There is an excellent market on Mondays. The nearby remains of Jenne-Jeno are said to be the oldest south of the Sahara. You can leave your vehicle with a guard on the eastern side of the river and cross to Djenné by *pirogue*.

Dogon country: Not to be missed — as long as you can avoid the more persistent attentions of the local guides. The ancient villages of the Bandiagara escarpment have changed little over the centuries and have to be seen to be believed. These villages can only be reached on foot, so it will be necessary to hire a guide in Bandiagara.

Gao: Largely a modern city these days, Gao was once the capital of the Songhai Empire and still has elements remaining from its glorious past.

Mopti: Formerly the most important commercial centre of the country, Mopti is a large town in the classic style of the region. It is built on three islands joined together by dykes and has an impressive mud-built mosque.

Ségou: A very pleasant town with an excellent market held by the banks of the Niger on Mondays.

Timbuktu: Not nearly as interesting as many travellers imagine it to be. The legend of this isolated trading spot is, however, enough to draw a steady stream of visitors across difficult pistes to reach it.

Places to stay
Can be a little difficult. There are few official campsites and many hotels that previously offered camping have been forced to stop — so the choice is generally either free camping or expensive hotels. Bush camping in most areas is good but it is not allowed close to towns.

Bamako: The safest place to stay is the former *Lebanese Mission* down from the central market. It has secure walled parking. Avoid the Youth Hostel which is a haven for con artists. If you are lucky you may be allowed to camp at the *Catholic Mission*.

Bandiagara: No official camping but you will soon be approached by guides who will take you to private camping at local houses (with generally poor facilities).

Bankas: Camping with bar, restaurant and warder at *Les Arbres* (Bar Ben) run by a Dutch guy called Hans. He can organise trips to the escarpment for you.

Gao: *Camping Dominique*, near the bus terminal.

Sources of tourist information
Maison de l'Afrique, Rue de Viarmes 2, 75001 Paris, France.

Tourist offices in Mali:
Bamako Boulevard du Peuple.
Gao Boulevard Askia.

Dogon country
The area around the Bandiagara escarpment is one of the most fascinating places in Africa, despite the ever increasing impact of tourism. The Dogon people and their traditional way of life have legal protection in Mali which has made them a favourite of anthropologists and archaeologists, as well as curious travellers.

In fact, Dogon country was our first real experience of Mali. After a remarkably laid back border crossing from Burkina Faso, we set off on a road to Bandiagara that wasn't even marked on the Michelin map. Coming from this direction your first sight of the escarpment, or *falaise*, is breathtaking. Even more so, when the road you are on seems to be heading straight for it, becoming increasingly rocky the closer you get. We joked about having to climb the sheer face of the escarpment — nervously.

By the time we had realised this was exactly what we were going to do, the surface of the track had deteriorated into an off-road enthusiast's dream — just a heap of rubble strewn with massive boulders. We slowed to walking pace as we climbed gradually upwards, negotiating hairpin bends and massive rocks at the same time. The views were spectacular.

When we finally drove into the town of Bandiagara we had our first taste of how tourism stamps its own particular mark on a traditional way of life. Heading for the police station to check in, we were besieged by locals chasing us on mopeds and bicycles, all offering to be our guide. In the end there was no problem — the police told us which one we were having!

You really do need a guide unless you are planning to spend more than a few days in Dogon country; even then you will probably be forced into it. The Dogon villages are of two sorts — those on the plateau at the top of the escarpment, and those at the foot of the cliff face. Many of the lower ones are completely inaccessible by road and you would be hard put to find them on your own. In any case, the whole tourist trade is so stitched up you would probably find it impossible to visit the more interesting villages without a guide.

The cliff-top villages are generally walled, with densely packed huts and smaller granaries with conical thatched roofs, but it is the villages at the base of the escarpment that are the most interesting. On the floor of the valley are the houses of the Christians and Muslims of the village, and actually clinging to the cliff face are the houses of the animists — those who follow the traditional religion. These are tall square mud-brick huts with flat roofs that you reach by a tortuous climb. You will easily recognise the local fetishist's house from its display of monkey skulls and bones, all neatly arranged according to size. Since by day the animists descend from their cliff-face homes to work in the fields of the valley floor, you can wander around quite happily without feeling you are intruding on anyone's way of life. You can also visit even older ruined villages and look up to see the remains of a chief's house, perched high above even the cliff-face village itself, and accessible only by rope.

You will certainly not be disappointed by a visit to Dogon country but you should expect to have to pay for every single extra, even after you have negotiated an 'all-in' price with your guide. You can even pay extra to share a meal with the *chef de village* — the local leader, not the cook. Although when we visited Teli, which is fairly typical of the lower villages, and were introduced to the *chef*, he was indeed preparing a dish of vegetables and chicken to share with a Dutch tourist who was paying for the privilege.

Bamako to Kidira

Anyone who has more than a passing interest in this area will find Sembene Ousmane's *God's Bits of Wood* compulsive reading. One of West Africa's most famous novels, it tells the story of the great railway strike on the Bamako to Dakar line, which was one of black

Africa's first real victories against colonial rule.

Our chosen route from Bamako out to Senegal was a little used track that hugged the railway almost all of the way. Most guide books and the Michelin map simply tell you to put your vehicle on the train between Kayes and Tambacounda, but you can get through with four-wheel drive, except between July and February — this is because to get into Senegal you have to drive across the Falémé River which is only possible in the dry months.

It is undoubtedly a difficult track. It took us five days to get from Bamako to Kidira and we felt pleased with ourselves whenever we got our average speed above 10 miles per hour. But the opportunity to travel through such a peaceful and remote area is not something you easily forget. The other thing about travelling slowly — and on this route you have no choice — is that you have the time to notice so much more. From Oualia, for example, we had moved into a Malinké area and were immediately struck by the brightly painted patterns on some of the village houses.

There was also a marked difference in how we were received, being seen more as a source of wonder than as *cadeaux*-bearing tourists. Waves of greeting were universal.

In terms of driving conditions this road offers everything — from crawling over enormous boulders and negotiating the sheer slopes of dried river beds to really soft sand. There is even a tiny ferry thrown in for good measure — across the River Bafing, which just a little further upstream joins with the Bakoyé to form the Senegal River.

Driving like this is so tiring we found it best to stick to really short shifts and take a decent break in the middle of the day. It was when we had stopped for a break one afternoon to brew up some tea that we saw the one and only vehicle we were to encounter on the whole route — a brand new Toyota driven by a European aid worker who stared at us in blank astonishment as he drove past.

Other than that single encounter we crawled on in solitude for five days to the Senegal border — even towns like Kayes didn't have much to offer in the way of supplies and we ended up drawing water from the river, with the inevitable insistent help from a young boy anxious to pick up his *cent francs*. Even if you never learn another word of French you will never forget how to say a hundred francs after you have been in West Africa.

In the end, the actual border escaped us completely. We suddenly realised we were already in Senegal when we reached the dried up bed of the Falémé and saw the beginnings of the border town of Kidira on the other side.

The customs officials apologised profusely after they got over their initial astonishment at seeing us drive up to their little shed. They only had one customs stamp, they explained, and that was down at the train station. We would have to wait until the train was checked through before we could get our carnet stamped. They were more than happy to chat to pass the time, and ended up insisting we explain the political situation in Northern Ireland in our high school French. Amazingly enough they seemed convinced they understood it all by the time the stamp finally arrived.

As we bade them farewell we asked if there was anywhere we could eat in town — after five days on the road without a chance to buy food we were utterly ravenous. They obliged by telling us how to get to their favourite restaurant, where a group of men were sitting outside on a trestle bench, eating from a huge communal bowl of rice and sauce. That simple meal has to be one of the best we have ever eaten, washed down with our first beer since Bamako, and accompanied by friendly questions about where we had come from and who we were.

Those memories of Kidira were reinforced more than two weeks later when, having travelled through Gambia and back into Senegal, we finally left the country to cross into Guinea-Bissau. The Senegalese customs official smiled in recognition at our initial entry stamp on the carnet. 'I worked at the post in Kidira for two years before I came to work here,' he explained. 'There's a wonderful restaurant on the road that leads to the station. I wonder if you know it...'

SENEGAL

Area: 196,722km²

Population: 8.7 million

Capital: Dakar

Languages: French is the official language; the main national language is Wolof.

Climate: Dry from December to May; hot, humid and wet from May to June. The dry season is shorter in the south and east of the country.

Visas: Visas are required by all apart from citizens of France and French-speaking African countries. You can get visas from a French embassy when there is no Senegalese representation. Make sure you get a multiple entry visa if you aim to go across Gambia and back into Senegal in the south.

Foreign embassies and consulates in Dakar: Algeria (5 Rue Mermoz; Tel: 224527); **Cameroon** (157 Rue Joseph Gomis; Tel: 213396); **Canada** (45 Boulevard de la République; Tel: 239290); **Cote d'Ivoire** (2 Avenue Albert Sarraut; Tel: 210163); **Ethiopia** (24 Boulevard Pinet Laprade; Tel: 212763); **France** (1 Rue Assane Ndoye); **Gabon** (36 Rue Assane Ndoye; Tel: 211529); **Gambia** (11 Rue de Thiong; Tel: 214476); **Guinea** (Rue 7, point E; Tel: 218606); **Guinea-Bissau** (Rue 6, point E; Tel: 245922); **Liberia** (20 Boulevard de la République; Tel: 225372); **Mali** (46 Boulevard de la République; Tel: 210473); **Morocco** (43 Boulevard de la République; Tel: 216927); **Niger** (km 5, route de Ouakam, point E; Tel: 240089); **Nigeria** (Rue 1, point E; Tel: 216922); **Sierra Leone** (13 Rue Castor, Clinique Bleu); **Tunisia** (Rue Seydon Nourou Tall); **UK** (20 Rue du Docteur Guillet; Tel: 237392); **USA** (Avenue Jean XXIII; Tel: 234296); **Zaïre** (16 Rue Leofro Benuis Fannce; Tel: 251979); **Zimbabwe** (Avenue KM 6 Cheik Anta Diop, Fann Mermos; Tel: 230325/222135).

Other red tape: Standard motoring documents and vaccination certificates for yellow fever are required. There are spot checks on roadworthiness of vehicles.

Banks and money: The unit of currency is the CFA (west).

Public holidays: New Year's Day, Easter Monday, Senegalese National Day (April 4); Labour Day (May 1), Ascension Day, Whit Monday, The Assumption, All Saints' Day (November 1),

Christmas Day (December 25). The Islamic holidays of Korité, Tabaski and the Prophet's Birthday are also observed, on dates varying from year to year.

Fuel: Availability is not really a problem but prices are exorbitant — stands alongside CAR as our highest prices ever.

Roads: Variable — from excellent to bad. Drive on the right.

Routes: Entering from Mali at Kidira, you can take the poor track to Tambacounda and then continue on the main road to Dakar; alternatively there is a reasonable surfaced road up to Richard Toll where you can join the main road from Mauritania. The easiest way down to the beaches of Casamance is to cut across Gambia to Ziguinchor; from here it is just a short hop either to the coast or into Guinea-Bissau. It is also possible to begin or end your journey at Dakar, as this is a good port to ship your vehicle from.

Places to visit

Cap Skirring: Excellent beaches down in the southern Casamance region. Parts are now getting a little too developed with tourism but you can still find some pleasant spots.

Casamance: Beautiful forested swamplands rich in wildlife, based on the Casamance River. Either Cap Skirring or Ziguinchor make good bases to explore from.

Dakar: A modern African city with a strong line in street hustlers. Despite that, it makes a welcome break to enjoy the comforts of city life. In particular, you should remember that Senegal has the best reputation in Africa for its food. If you splash out on a meal anywhere, you should make it here. Soumbedioune is one of the most colourful areas of town with its fishing *pirogues* and craft workshops. The national museum is well worth a visit, with an ethnographic collection covering the whole of West Africa.

Isle De Gorée: This famous old centre of the slave trade is just off the coast at Dakar. Regular trips are available to visit the island, with its fort, 18th century buildings and three museums.

Kayar: Extremely picturesque fishing village just to the northwest of Dakar. In the early evening the beach is full of colourful fishing *pirogues*.

Niokolo-Koba National Park: Good game reserve with elephant, leopard and other game.

Saint Louis: The 19th century capital of both Senegal and Mauritania — and it does not seem to have changed one bit since then. Saint Louis is a gorgeous sleepy old colonial-style town with none of the hustle and bustle of Dakar.

Places to stay
There are good opportunities for free camping in most parts of the country, but avoid anywhere close to a town.

Cap Skirring: You can camp on the beach below the various hotels and campements for free. The people at the *Campement Paradise* are particularly helpful so you can park in front of their patch and use their facilities (bar and restaurant included).

Dakar: Plenty of hotels but the only ones with safe parking anywhere near the centre are expensive. If you feel like a treat, the most central one with good parking is the *Novotel* on Avenue du Barachois. One cheaper option is *Chez Charlie* — although this is several kilometres out of town on the Route de Rufisque. It does have safe parking behind locked gates — it also features its own small private zoo!

Joal: Just after passing Mboudiènne, between Nianing and Joal, there is a small track leading across to the beach. There are a few holiday homes here and it is an excellent spot for camping. Local fishermen will sell you fresh fish for your supper.

Rufisque: *Auberge Quatre Vents* is on the main road out of Rufisque towards Dakar. A very strange place run by long term Spanish and French colonials, but it does have car parking and excellent food. It is fairly cheap and they have even been known to allow camping.

Sources of tourist information
Délégation générale au tourisme du Senegal, Avenue Georges V 30, 75008 Paris, France.

Tourist office in Senegal:
Dakar Place de l'Indépendence.

Guide books: *The Gambia and Senegal* (Insight Guides); *Senegal Africa Handbook*, Christa Mang (Bradt).

Easter Sunday at Mboudiènne

One of the problems that faces every long term traveller now and again is the need to apply for another batch of visas. This can mean spending longer than you want to in a large expensive city, when you would much rather be on the road or in some small village out in the countryside.

Dakar is just such a large city — it has more than its fair share of hustlers and is particularly expensive, with few opportunities for cheaper accommodation. We knew that the visa trail meant we would be stranded here across the Easter weekend, with every embassy shut down for the next four days, so we decided to head out of town to find a quiet beach to camp for the weekend. That may sound easy enough, but Senegal's coastal strip is so well developed that we were nearly as far south as Joal before we found the clue we had eagerly been looking for — a small, little-used track winding across the 400 metres between the main road and the sea. It turned out to be a great find.

With the beach to ourselves, apart from flocks of egrets and armies of sand crabs, we were able to forget the hurly-burly of Dakar and just listen to the waves as they lapped the shore. A group of boys soon passed by to sell us fresh red mullet and our little paradise was complete. We got to know one of them — Philippe — particularly well over the next few days and on Sunday he invited us to his village Easter dance. First of all we went to visit his mother and then moved on into the centre of the village, where it was apparent we were the only outsiders who would be privileged enough to be there.

The six drummers were warming up, weaving a wonderful and complex pattern of sound with their wide range of instruments. The tones stretched from the large drums spread out on the ground to the small talking drum of the leading entertainer of the troupe.

The early stages of the dance were aimed at the children. They loved every moment as the lead drummer encouraged them with one game after another. Gradually the women started to join in and the steps became more sophisticated. One by one they would leap into the ring and take centre stage for a while. The men were nowhere to be seen — the drums of this region are traditionally an accompaniment for women's dancing.

For several hours they whirled around the patch of ground, colourful dresses flying and feet rhythmically pounding the earth as their arms shot into the air. Every now and again they would try to encourage a man to dance but after a few reluctant steps he would quietly sneak off to the sidelines again. But then came one of the key dances of the day, which had the assembled villagers hooting with laughter. A male had finally joined in — dancing with a woman's traditional steps. At the same time one of the women started imitating the man. Then the men marched in with a very different and more restrained dance. It was the signal for all to relax and enjoy themselves.

As dusk came, a natural break gave the mothers time to put the smaller children to bed before the real business of the evening festivities could begin. The fiery sounds of drumming filled the air around the shoreline all through the night.

GAMBIA

Area: 10,689km²

Population: 959,300

Capital: Banjul

Languages: English is the official language but some French is also spoken; the national languages are Wolof, Mandinka and Fula.

Climate: Cool dry season from December to April (24°C in Banjul), followed by a warmer dry season and then the rains between June and October. Temperatures are higher inland; rainfall is higher on the coast.

Visas: Required by all apart from citizens of the UK, the Commonwealth, Belgium, Denmark, Germany, Finland, Greece, Iceland, Ireland, Italy, Liechtenstein, Luxembourg, Netherlands, Norway, Spain, Sweden, Switzerland, Tunisia, Turkey and Uruguay.

Foreign embassies and consulates in Banjul: Guinea-Bissau: (Wellington Street; Tel: 28134); **Liberia** (Cameron Street); **Mauritania** (12 Clarkson Street; Tel: 27690); **Senegal** (corner of Cameron and Buckle Street; Tel: 28469); **Sierra Leone** (Hagan Street); **UK** (48 Atlantic Road, Fajara; Tel: 95133/4); **USA** (Kairaba Avenue, Fajara; Tel: 392856).

Other red tape: Standard motoring documents and vaccination certificates for yellow fever are required. The officious nature of policing in Gambia comes as a particular shock because it is surrounded by the smiling and helpful ways of Senegal. There seems to be a sour taste in everyone's mouth here when dealing with Westerners — which in part must come down to different colonial experiences.

Banks and money: The unit of currency is the dalasi. Not particularly strong; successive devaluations have made it the sort of currency you need to carry in a suitcase.

Public holidays: New Year's Day, Independence Day (February 18), Good Friday, Easter Monday, Labour Day (May 1), Christmas Day (December 25). The Islamic holidays of Ramadan, Aid el-Fitr, Aid el-Kabir and the Birthday of the Holy Prophet Maulaud Nab are also observed, on dates varying from year to year.

Fuel: Available at prices way below the exorbitant levels in Senegal.

Roads: Drive on the right. The only top-class surfaced stretch links the airport with the tourist hotels. The southern route along the river is also good; otherwise the roads are poor.

Routes: In such a tiny country the options are simple — you either cut across while heading along one of the main two routes linking Senegal or you head up river (and then on to Tambacounda or Guinea). Car ferries cross the river at Banjul, Farafenni, Georgetown and Basse.

Places to visit

Steer clear of the tourist beaches and head up river. It is amazing just how untouched most of the country is by the package holiday boom — most people really do seem to find it impossible to prise themselves off the beach. It is when you start to explore the delightful interior of the country that you will discover its heart. Make a point of checking out some of the glorious music of the Gambia — it is home to some of the very best *kora* playing and *griot* singing in Africa.

Places to stay

The tourist economy is totally geared towards package holidays so it can be difficult to find a good place to stay near to the coast. There are one or two quiet spots along the beach where you can camp — but they are few and far between.

Tendaba: Pleasant campsite on the north bank of the river.

Sources of tourist information
Tourist office in Gambia:
Banjul Government Tourist Board, Bedford Place; Tel: 8321.

Guide books: *Discover The Gambia*, Terry Palmer (Heritage House); *The Gambia and Senegal* (Insight Guides).

I'm sorry, madam...

After Dakar, Banjul comes as something of a shock. Instead of tarmac roads you have badly potholed and cracked surfaces to drive on and the whole feel of the place is scruffy and downbeat. Just one little incident sums up Banjul for us.

We had picked up a wonderfully uplifting pile of mail in Dakar and had already written some letters back to family and friends. Finding the post office was the easy part. Buying the stamps was where we failed. The women behind the counter shook her head as we held out our letters and asked for stamps for England. 'I'm sorry, madam,' she said with absolute sincerity. 'I'm afraid we don't have any stamps...'

GUINEA-BISSAU

Area: 36,125km²

Population: 1.1 million

Capital: Bissau

Languages: Portuguese is the official language although Creole is widely spoken; the main national languages are Balante and Fulani.

Climate: Heavy rainfall with an average temperature of 20°C. The hottest months are April and May.

Visas: Required by all; they are easy to get in Dakar.

Foreign embassies and consulates in Bissau: Algeria (Rua 12 de Setembro; Tel: 211533); **Belgium** (Avenida Amilcar Cabral); **France** (Rua Eduardo Mondlane; Tel: 21 2633); **Guinea** (Rue 12 at Rua Osvaldo Vieira; Tel: 212681); **Nigeria** (Avenida 14 Novembro; Tel: 212782); **Senegal** (Praça dos Herois Nacionais; Tel: 212636); **UK** (Avenida Pansau Na Isna); **USA** (Bairro de Penha; Tel: 2273).

Other red tape: Standard motoring documents and vaccination certificate for yellow fever are required.

Banks and money: Unit of currency is the Guinea peso — weak and prone to high inflation.

Public holidays: New Year's Day, January 20, March 8, Labour Day (May 1), August 3, September 12, National Day (September 24), Republic Day (November 14), Christmas Day (December 25).

Fuel: Available in Bissau but do not count on it elsewhere. This is one of the cheapest places in the region to stock up on supplies.

Roads: Not too good. Surfaced roads are mostly potholed. Drive on the right.

Routes: There are several road links with Senegal in the north — the main one leads down from Ziguinchor — although you can avoid the two ferries on this route by entering further up country. The ferries only take one vehicle at a time and only operate at high tide — and foreigners tend to be hit for excessive charges. The only access to Guinea (Conakry) is to take the main road east to Koundara.

Places to visit
Bissau: Bissau is a wonderful small old Portuguese town. Faded and

dusty now, it is still full of charm. It is a good place to wander around and stop to sit on the veranda of one of the many local bars, sipping a draught beer and soaking it all in.

Places to stay
It can be difficult to find good accommodation. There are plenty of opportunities for bush camping in the countryside (and on the edges of Bissau).

Sources of tourist information
Tourist office in Guinea-Bissau:
Bissau Centro de Informacao e Turismo, CP294, Avenida Domingos Ramos; Tel: 213282

Travels in Guinea-Bissau
True to form, the road running south to the Guinea-Bissau border was deteriorating badly. Practically the only thing you can count on when it comes to African roads is that, however bad they may be in the interior of a country, they get even worse when you try to leave. With no signs to show the way, as the red dirt track split into two yet again, the badly potholed road was the only indication we had that we were on our way out of Senegal.

The status of our first check in Guinea-Bissau was never quite clear, although our passports and driving licences were carefully scrutinised. We also picked up a hitch-hiker here who spoke a little English — which was to prove useful. Our French had kept us going so far but we didn't have a word of Portuguese between us.

At that border post we suddenly felt as if we had been transported to some obscure little Latin American state. It wasn't just a matter of hearing Portuguese spoken for the first time. Unusually for West Africa, all of the soldiers were bearded; with rifles casually slung over their shoulders, they lounged around on benches or leaned against walls, eyeing us with a complete lack of interest. The pace of officialdom was barely discernible.

Our hitch-hiker explained we would have to wait. The customs office was closed and the police chief was having his lunch. We settled down on a bench and made a few attempts at conversation but everyone was happy to sit silently in the shade. It was an hour before anyone moved.

But it was all we could do to keep a straight face when the time finally came to have our passports stamped. The police officer facing us sported two badges of office on his khaki shirt, a Boy Scouts of America badge was neatly stitched to his top pocket and his right sleeve bore a German Red Cross emblem. If it looks official, then wear it!

Bissau itself is a lovely town. Wide tree-lined avenues give a wonderful impression of space; street cafés sell cheap glasses of draught beer. After passing through tourist-conscious Senegal, it is so relaxing just to sit out on the main street and only generate the mildest of passing interest.

A trip to the bank revealed that the recent massive devaluations in the peso had at least made a positive impact on local employment prospects. There were two women at the cashier's window — one paying out money and the other painstakingly making up large bundles of notes by tying them with string!

After the expensive fuel prices in Mali and Senegal, it was a relief to discover we could fill up for as little as 90p a gallon. And although most guide books claim food and other goods are in short supply, the bustling central market proved a good place to pick up everything we needed — and even the government shops were full of goods. But they were nothing compared with the Aladdin's cave of Western goods filling the plush supermarket run by the British Honorary Consul (who happened to be Dutch!). The shop is important to UK and Commonwealth travellers as you need to get a letter of introduction from the supermarket boss in order to get a visa from the Guinea embassy. Unfortunately for us, he was away on business when we were in Bissau, but his helpful wife took us down to the embassy to find out what we should do.

'They will need a letter signed by the British Honorary Consul?' she asked tentatively.

The Guinean first secretary waved her hand dismissively. 'Or the Consul's wife,' she said. 'It is the same thing.'

Back at the supermarket, the Honorary Consul's wife managed to find a copy of the last letter of introduction that had been written — for a Canadian some months earlier. Offering us the letter together with a bottle of Tippex, she suggested we might just like to add in our own names. We suggested in turn that it might make a better impression if it were retyped.

So that was how we found ourselves sitting in the office of a Dutch supermarket, typing our own letters of introduction. They were duly stamped and taken round to the embassy and the visas were produced first thing the next morning.

In the meantime, we had to find a place to spend the night. We drove out of town and eventually found a cleared area with piles of gravel for road construction. We had learned by now that gravel pits are often the best camping spots to be found.

We had just stopped to check it out when two young men approached us, introducing themselves as Francisco and Lopeste. They were positively delighted by our attempts to mime a conversation and eventually joined in with the game when they realised that we really were too stupid to understand Portuguese. Eventually they mimed for us to follow them down a little track to the side of the pit which led to a grassy shaded clearing, surrounded by trees and well out of sight of the road. It was the perfect place to camp.

The following hour was one of the most enjoyable of our whole trip, with endless stories being played out for our benefit. At least half of them were lost on us but that didn't seem to matter. Francisco's boundless energy and enthusiasm explored every possibility of communication — exaggerated theatrical mimes, drawing in the dust, comic whistles and other amazing sound effects, all accompanied by his rapid Portuguese commentary. If you want to meet the African Harpo Marx, Francisco is your man.

One story we did manage to follow was about the cashew trees surrounding us. We had already noticed an unfamiliar fruit being carried by the local women, which looked like a cross between a plum and a capsicum pepper. They were cashew fruits. Francisco insisted on fetching one for us to taste. It was deliciously sweet — not unlike a plum but with a mustier taste. He then mimed the stirring of a large pot and what can only have been a fermenting brew to judge from the drinking motions and comic staggering walk that followed.

'*Muito saporito,*' he said and burst into peals of laughter; Lopeste smiled and nodded his head sagely. Francisco and Lopeste are the kind of people we will never forget, and Guinea-Bissau the sort of country that, in all its eccentricity and warm-heartedness, will stay with us forever.

GUINEA

Area: 245,857km²

Population: 6.4 million

Capital: Conakry

Languages: French is the official language; the main national languages are Susu, Malinké, Fulani and Peul.

Climate: A tropical climate with length of rainy season determined by altitude and location. Rains occur mainly between May and October. The highest rainfall is on the coast.

Visas: Required by all — available in Dakar, Bissau, Bamako and Abidjan.

Foreign embassies and consulates in Conakry: Algeria (5th Avenue and 1st Boulevard; Tel: 441505); **Congo** (Route Donka; Tel: 46 2451); **France** (8th Avenue and 2nd Boulevard; Tel: 44 1655); **Ghana** (Corniche Sud; Tel: 44 1509); **Guinea Bissau** (Route Donka; Tel: 46 2136); **Liberia** (Cité Camayenne, Route Donka; Tel: 46 2332); **Mali** (Corniche Sud; Tel: 46 1418); **Morocco** (Southern end of Corniche Nord; Tel: 44 3710); **Nigeria** (Corniche Sud; Tel: 46 1343); **Senegal** (Corniche Sud; Tel: 46 2834); **Sierra Leone** (Route Donka; Tel: 44 3738); **Tanzania** (Cité des Ministres at Donka; Tel: 46 1332); **USA** (Second Boulevard/Ninth Avenue; Tel: 41 1520).

Other red tape: Standard motoring documents (carnet not essential — but a *laissez-passer* must be obtained when you get your visa if you do not have one; price £15 in 1990) and vaccination certificates for yellow fever are required. Photography permits are supposed to be compulsory and you may well be challenged in towns if you do not have one. Trying actually to get one from the *Sureté* is, however, likely to prove more trouble than it is worth. Personally we found travelling in Guinea to be an utter joy, with nothing but help, co-operation and friendship from officials. More recent reports do, however, speak of hefty demands for money from some officials.

Banks and money: Unit of currency is the Guinea franc — it has gone through many reincarnations over the years as its value continues to fall. This version was introduced at parity with the CFA franc as a first step to entering the system — but its value quickly slipped and was worth less than half the value of the CFA franc by late 1989. The only banks are in Conakry, Labé and Kankan.

Public holidays: New Year's Day, Labour Day (May 1), May 14, Assumption Day, Independence Day (October 2), Army Day (November 1), November 22. The Islamic holidays of Lailat el-Miraj, First day of Ramadan, Aid el-Adha, Hejri, el-Ashura and the Prophet's Birthday are also observed, on dates varying from year to year.

Fuel: Not available at filling stations. All supplies are through the black market. Prices are at a European level — lower than in Cote d'Ivoire, Mali or Senegal but higher than in Guinea-Bissau.

Roads: Drive on the right. Mostly very poor. Surfaced roads are generally badly potholed. Bridges are often in a very bad state of repair, causing you either to deviate through streams or rearrange the surface of the bridge.

Routes: The main entry points are at Koundara (from Guinea-Bissau and Senegal; the first section of this road is very badly corrugated), Siguiri (from Mali) and Beyla (from Cote d'Ivoire). If you are entering from or leaving to Cote d'Ivoire, be warned that the road south of Beyla is extraordinarily bad (and by Guinea standards that really is saying something). The best route is to head east from Beyla to Sinko. From here there is an excellent dirt road leading across to the Guinea customs at Tienkoro and then on to the Ivoirian customs post at Booko (the road and these posts are not marked on most maps — but they are there).

Places to visit

Guinea is one of the most beautiful countries in Africa — it is also one of the most friendly. The combination makes a visit a real highlight of any African trip. Having been pretty well isolated from the outside world until the mid-1980s, people are even keener than elsewhere to make friends and help Western visitors.

Conakry: A lively and very African capital city. Check out the Guinean music, which is particularly good.

Kankan: The second town of Guinea; has a large market.

Kérouané to Beyla: Utterly beautiful mountain area. Unfortunately the road is extremely bad.

Kindia: The beautiful mountains in this area have many streams and waterfalls. Of particular note are the Santa Falls, about 20 kilometres to the east.

Labé to Mamou: Two of the largest provincial towns — but would be small by most standards. Everywhere you go you will find small dusty trading centres like these. This entire Fouta Djalon mountain region is stunning. It is the surrounding countryside rather than the towns that are most worthy of exploration.

Places to stay
There are few places to stay apart from taking advantage of free camping opportunities. Luckily there is no shortage of such places, mostly in wonderful settings.

Sources of tourist information
Tourist offices in Guinea:
Conakry Secrétariat d'Etat de l'Information et du Tourisme, BP617; and Office du Tourisme, Square des Martyrs.

Travels in Guinea
It is hard to summarise our feelings as we drove the last stretch towards the Guinea border. When you are travelling fairly quickly through the smaller countries of West Africa, the sadness at leaving a country you have grown used to — where you have finally learned how to handle the currency and got to know something of local life and customs — is heightened by the sense of heading into the unknown.

The unusual history of Guinea had already given us a healthy respect for its people. Unique among the former French African colonies, it rejected de Gaulle's offer of joining a French Commonwealth, declaring that it preferred 'poverty in liberty to riches in slavery'. Poverty was certainly what it ended up getting when the French reacted by pulling out completely, cutting all investment and destroying all existing records. For most of its independent life, Guinea has existed in almost total isolation.

But since the mid-1980s it has increasingly opened up to the outside world — although when we visited early in 1988 it had lost none of its special and independent charm. Everywhere we went felt both easy-going and free. Isolation was still such that in the seven days allowed us by our visas, we didn't come across a single European.

It was only when were given our visas in Bissau that we knew for sure that we would be able to enter by the land border. Early in 1988, information on what to expect was sketchy to say the least. In the end, that border was probably one of the most laid back we encountered. We chatted happily about our trip for quite a while before finally setting off. It was only then that we realised they had not even bothered to stamp our passports — the first time this had happened in Africa.

It was midday by the time we reached the official border town of Koundara and checked in with the local *gendarme*. We asked him where we could change some money and get something to eat. He shook his head and smiled.

'We don't have a bank,' he said. 'But if you go into the shop just there, you can change some money. Don't accept less than 800 Guinea francs for 500 CFA. And if you want to eat you must go to my friend Monsieur Gou. His restaurant is around the corner on the other side of the street.'

Guinea francs in pocket, we set off to find Monsieur Gou. Thrilled to be addressed by name, he pulled out all the stops to please us. Or was it just that we were his first customers of the week? The fact that he set off for the market after we had ordered seemed to answer the question!

Setting off through Guinea, the roads proved to be pretty dire — with atrocious corrugations finally giving way to badly potholed tarmac. A rapid succession of bridges in an appalling state of repair made things just that bit more hazardous. Fortunately, tracks leading off to the side would generally show where the locals preferred to ford small rivers rather than take any chances on the bridge.

At the police check in Seriba, we were asked to wait a moment so that we could take one of the policemen into Labé, where his child was ill. He soon arrived — carrying a ghetto blaster, an orange carrier bag and a live chicken. The chicken was unceremoniously dumped in the back of the Land Rover where it squawked loudly every time we went over a bump — and there were plenty of those.

Before long we came across a truck that had broken down in the road. The passengers were sitting and glumly waiting while the driver dismantled the entire transmission. Our policeman spotted a friend among the crowd who begged for a lift. He was not to be put off when we pointed out that we only had three seats and the back was fully loaded. '*Pas de problème*,' he said. 'I'll get on the roof.'

We had hardly gone any distance at all when another police check turned up yet another deserving case for a lift — a *brigade mobile* who was no longer so mobile since his transport had broken down. He scrambled up on the roof beside policeman number two, taking with him a bottle of cloudy liquid.

Our first passenger sniffed disdainfully. 'It's bad to drink alcohol,' he said. 'What is it?' we asked. 'TTM,' he explained, though we were none the wiser. 'You make it from sugar, yeast and water. It's very strong.' His teetotal credentials were soon underlined when he asked us to stop in a village and he hopped out to treat the three of us inside to cans of Vimto and a bag of cough sweets.

Whatever TTM may be, it certainly made the two policemen on the roof rack forget their worries. All the way to Labé we could hear them screeching with laughter and bursting into song. Stuck inside with a squawking chicken, a disapproving official and a can of Vimto, we couldn't help but silently wish them the best of luck. When they finally bade us farewell, they first rushed off to find four cans of ice cold beer to present as a parting gift. It was a welcome antidote.

In the days that followed, we became increasingly worried about making it to the border before our visas ran out. The roads were awful and the bridges were even worse. We lost count of the number of times that we rearranged those loose planks of wood before inching slowly across.

On one occasion we stopped to consider a particularly dodgy bridge over a particularly deep-looking river. We were still standing there, trying to weigh up the options, when a local man on a bicycle approached from the opposite direction. He stopped and came over to us. '*Pas de problème,*' he said, pointing at the river. 'You can get through it with a Land Rover.'

When he saw we were still not convinced, he laid down his bicycle, rolled his trousers up to his knees and waded into the river to show us exactly how deep it was. He smiled, remounted his bicycle and rode off into the distance.

Several people passed us that evening as we set up camp, many simply greeting us and continuing on their way. But one man stopped and came across, a rifle and a rough canvas bag slung over one shoulder. He had a few words of French so we were able to chat for a while. Then he fished around in his bag and hauled out a huge hunk of wild honeycomb which he held out for us to eat.

'Is it sweet?' he asked as we tasted it. We nodded enthusiastically. It tasted like the best honey in the world — almost painfully sweet but with a smoky undertone. He was delighted by our response to his gift and wished us all the best before continuing on his way home.

In the space of just a few days we had come across a side of

Africa that we had not previously been lucky enough to experience. We met with warmth and a willingness to share from ordinary people in most parts of Africa, but in Guinea it was special. Maybe it was because we were such a novelty or maybe it was just that Guinea is like that anyway, with its extra special dimension to every meeting and to every conversation.

SIERRA LEONE

Area: 71,740km²

Population: 4.6 million

Capital: Freetown

Languages: English is the official language but Krio (Creole) is the most widely spoken; the main national languages are Mende and Temne.

Climate: Very wet in the rainy season from May to October. Temperatures on the coast in the dry months are often cooled by sea breezes.

Visas: All travellers require either a visa or an entry permit. There is little difference between the two — it just depends on your nationality which one you will have to get. You will probably need to get an extension at the immigration office in Freetown.

Foreign embassies and consulates in Freetown: Cote d'Ivoire (1 Wesley Street; Tel: 23983); **France** (13 Sankoh Street; Tel: 22477); **Gambia** (Wilberforce Street); **Ghana** (16 Percival Street; Tel: 23461); **Germany** (Santanno House, Howe Street; Tel: 22511); **Guinea** (4 Liverpool Street; Tel: 22331); **Italy** (Wilkinson Road; Tel: 30995); **Liberia** (30 Brookfield Road; Tel: 40322); **Mali** (15 Lightfoot Boston Street; Tel: 41994); **Nigeria** (Siaka Stevens Street; Tel: 24202); **Senegal** (9 Upper East Street); **UK** (Standard Chartered Bank Building, Lightfoot Boston Street; Tel: 223961-5); **USA** (corner of Walpole and Siaka Stevens Streets; Tel: 226481).

Banks and money: The unit of currency is the Leone.

Public holidays: New Year's Day, Good Friday, Easter Monday, Republic Day (April 19), Whit Monday, Christmas Day (December 25), Boxing Day (December 26). The Islamic holidays of Aid el-Fitr and Aid el-Adha are also observed, on dates varying from year to year.

Roads: Poor. Drive on the right.

Sources of tourist information
Tourist office in Sierra Leone:
Freetown Lightfoot Boston Street.

LIBERIA

Area: 99,067km²

Population: 3.0 million

Capital: Monrovia

Languages: English is the official language.

Climate: Tropical with temperatures averaging 25°C. Rainy season from May to October and dry season from November to April.

Visas: Required by all.

Foreign embassies and consulates in Monrovia: Cameroon (Congotown; Tel: 261516); **Cote d'Ivoire** (Congotown; Tel: 261284); **France** (UN Drive; Tel: 221122); **Ghana** (11th Street; Tel: 261477); **Guinea** (19th Street; Tel: 261711); **Nigeria** (Tubman Boulevard; Tel: 261093); **Sierra Leone** (Congotown; Tel: 261301); **UK** (UN Drive; Tel: 221055); **USA** (111 UN Drive; Tel: 222991).

Other red tape: Vaccination certificate required for yellow fever.

Banks and money: The unit of currency is the Liberian dollar, which is fixed at a rate of one to one with the US dollar (which is also legal tender in Liberia). There are few banks outside Monrovia.

Public holidays: After years of civil war an interim government was announced at the end of August 1995. Fixing public holidays is unlikely to be an early priority in a country which has been devastated by conflict, but if you are planning to travel in Liberia you may be able to get some information from the Liberian Embassy in London (see section *Embassies for African countries* in the UK page 27). Before the recent conflict Liberia celebrated eight national public holidays as well as the main Christian holidays.

Fuel: Supplies are poor.

Roads: Poor. Drive on the right.

Routes: Liberia has been out of bounds for a while, as a result of civil war. Once the country reopens you will be able to enter from Sierra Leone and go on to Guinea or Cote d'Ivoire via Monrovia. To be honest, however, Guinea is such a beautiful country that it would be hard to justify making the detour unless you have a pressing reason.

Sources of tourist information
Tourist office in Liberia:
Monrovia Broad Street.

COTE D'IVOIRE

Area: 320,763km²

Population: 13 million

Capital: Abidjan

Languages: French is the official language; the main national languages are Dioula and Baoulé.

Climate: There are two climatic regions. In the south the temperature remains at a constant of about 30°C all year round and has heavy rainfall; there are four seasons — a long dry season from December to April, a long rainy season from May to July, a short dry season from August to September and a short rainy season from October to November. The north has a broader temperature range; it has a rainy season from June to October and is dry from November to May.

Visas: Required by all except EU nationals and citizens of Norway and French speaking Africa. In 1994, three month single entry tourist visas cost £15.

Foreign embassies and consulates in Abidjan: A wealth of embassies makes this one of the key cities for collecting visas. **Algeria** (Boulevard Clozel; Tel: 322340); **Belgium** (Rue Lecoeur, Immeuble Alliance, 4th Floor; Tel: 322088); **Benin** (Rue des Jardins; Tel: 414484); **Burkina Faso** (2 Avenue Terrasson de Fougères; Tel: 321313); **Cameroon** (Boulevard Botreau Roussel, Immeuble Général, 3rd Floor; Tel: 322087); **Canada** (Immeuble Trade-Center, 23 Avenue Nogues; Tel: 212009); **CAR** (Avenues des Combattants, Immeuble Atta 1, 4th Floor; Tel: 323646); **Denmark** (Boulevard Botreau Roussel, Immeuble le Mans, 5th Floor; Tel: 331765); **France** (Rue Lecoeur; Tel: 212566); **Gabon** (Boulevard Carde, Immeuble Hévéas, 6th Floor; Tel: 322312); **Germany** (Boulevard Botreau Roussel, Immeuble le Mans; Tel: 324727); **Ghana** (Avenue Général de Gaulle, Immeuble Corniche, 5th Floor; Tel: 331124); **Guinea** (Avenue Crosson Duplessis, Immeuble Crosson Duplessis; Tel: 324600); **Guinea-Bissau** (Cocody; Tel: 415436); **Japan** (Rue Gourgas, Immeuble Alpha 2000, 12th Floor; Tel: 212863); **Liberia** (Avenue Général de Gaulle, Immeuble CNA, 8th Floor; Tel: 324636); **Mali** (Rue du Commerce; Tel: 323147); **Netherlands** (Boulevard Carde, Immeuble Harmonies, 2nd Floor; Tel: 227712); **Niger** (Avenue Achalme, Marcory); **Nigeria** (Boulevard de la République and Avenue Janot; Tel: 223082);

Norway (Boulevard Général de Gaulle, Coté Hilton; Tel: 222534); **Senegal** (Rue du Commerce; Tel: 322876 — also issues visas for **Gambia**); **Switzerland** (Rue Gourgas, Immeuble Alpha 2000, 12th Floor; Tel: 321721); **UK** (3rd Floor, Immeduble Les Harmonies, Angle Boulevard Carde et Avenue Dr Jamot; Tel: 226850-2; also issues visas for **Sierra Leone**); **USA** (5 Rue Jesse Owens; Tel: 210979); **Zaïre** (23 Boulevarde Clozel, Immeuble 29, 3rd Floor; Tel: 222080).

Other red tape: Standard motoring documents and vaccination certificate for yellow fever are required.

Banks and money: Unit of currency is the CFA (west). On arrival you should declare currency other than CFA and French francs. Banks in main towns but can be difficult to change anything other than French francs in some areas outside of Abidjan. Banking hours are 8.00-11.30 and 14.30-16.30 Mondays to Fridays.

Public holidays: New Year's Day, Easter Monday, Labour Day (May 1), Ascension Day, Whit Monday, The Assumption, All Saints' Day (November 1), Peace Day (November 15), National Day (December 7), Christmas Day (December 25). The Islamic holidays of the end of Ramadan and the Prophet's Birthday are also observed, on dates varying from year to year.

Fuel: Available in all large towns. It is very expensive — prices are lower in all neighbouring countries.

Roads: Drive on the right. Good surfaced roads on main routes with mainly good dirt roads elsewhere.

Routes: The main routes all converge on Abidjan, coming from Accra and Kumasi in Ghana and Bobo-Dioulasso in Burkina Faso. The best road to Guinea is not even marked on the Michelin 953. You should take the main road from Abidjan to Yamoussoukro, Daloa, Man and Touba. About 85 kilometres further north take the minor road to Booko; an excellent dirt road in fact continues from here across the border to Sinko. This route means you can avoid the utterly atrocious roads in Guinea south of Béyla.

Places to visit

Abidjan: A huge modern city — one of the most important in West Africa. The chances are you will stop here for a few days as this is a great place to get all the visas you need for the next section of your journey. The most interesting area to investigate while you are here is the African heart of the town in Treichville. Otherwise, it is a very Westernised place indeed, with all modern facilities. The ethnographic museum at Adjamé has a rich collection of exhibits.

The coast: There are many excellent beaches all along the coastline — take your pick. Major places like Grand Lahou and Sassandra are dominated by holiday villages.

Comoé National Park: Situated in the northeast, the most common game to be seen are buffalo, antelope and wild pigs.

Man: One of the most attractive towns in the country and a good centre for exploring the surrounding area — famous for its rich cultural traditions of masks, carvings and dances.

Yamoussoukro: Has to be seen to be believed. The birthplace of President Houphouet-Boigny, Yamoussoukro has been built up from a small village to a major modern town with huge buildings on extraordinarily wide boulevards lined with street lamps and dotted with artificial lakes. The plan was to make it the new capital, but it has proved more difficult to attract the diplomats and business interests to move here than it was to build this white elephant of a town. Pride of place goes to the outrageous Basilica of Our Lady of Peace, one of the largest domed cathedrals in the world, looking so out of place with its classic and opulent European styling in this jungle setting.

Places to stay

Abidjan: *Camping Coppa Cabana* is a friendly place along the coast road leading out of Abidjan to the east. Run by two Breton brothers who came travelling but never got away again, it offers good food and a bar as well as a place to camp. There are plenty of international-style hotels with safe parking if you feel ready to splash out.

Bingerville: There is just one hotel with safe parking — but it is comfortable and very reasonable.

Grand Bassam: The beach here has been recommended for camping in the past. These days it is a dangerous spot and should be avoided.

Menolé: One of several small villages along the western coast that have been recommended for a lengthy stay.

Orès-Krobou: There is a small African hotel with safe parking here, on the road from Agboville down to the Abidjan-Yamasoukrou highway.

Touba: Drive up the *route touristique* to Mount Zaala. From the top there is a magnificent view of the surrounding area and a couple of tourist bungalows. It's a good place to camp.

Sources of tourist information
Cote d'Ivoire Tourist Board, 21 Saxe Avenue, 75 007 Paris, France; Tel: +33 45 67 3538.

Tourist offices in Cote d'Ivoire:
Abidjan Boulevard Générale de Gaulle; also try Office Nationale de Tourisme, Cité Administrative Tour E, BP V 184; Tel: 32 00 88.

Guide books: *Ivory Coast Handbook*, Regina Fuchs (Bradt).

GHANA

Area: 238,533km²

Population: 17.2 million

Capital: Accra

Languages: English is the official language; main national languages are Twi, Fante, Ga, Ewe, Dagbeni, Hausa and Nzima.

Climate: Hot and dry in the north, humid in coastal and forest regions. The rains arrive in late April or early May and last through until September.

Visas: Citizens of non-Commonwealth countries require visas; citizens of the UK and other Commonwealth countries require an entry permit. There is no difference between the two — both require the same amount of form filling and photographs and both are expensive.

Foreign embassies and consulates in Accra: Australia (2 Milne Close, off Dr Amilcar Cabral Road, Airport Residential Area); **Burkina Faso** (772/3 Asylum Down, off Farrer Avenue; Tel: 221988); **Canada** (46 Independence Avenue; Tel: 228555/566); **Cote d'Ivoire** (9 Eighteenth Lane; Tel: 774611); **France** (12th Road, off Liberation Avenue); **Germany** (Valldemosa Lodge, Plot 18, 7th Avenue Extension, North Ridge Residential Area); **Guinea** (11 Osu Badu Street; Tel: 777921); **Liberia** (Switchback Close off Neru Road; Tel: 775641); **Mali** (Crescent Road, Block 1; Tel: 775160); **Netherlands** (89 Liberation Road, Independence Circle); **Niger** (E 104/3, Independence Avenue); **Nigeria** (Tito Avenue; Tel: 776158); **Senegal** (Rangoon Avenue); **Sierra Leone** (C 135/3, Asylum Down); **Switzerland** (9 Water Road, North Ridge Area); **Togo** (Cantonments Circle; Tel: 777950); **Uganda** (174, 7th Ringway Estate); **UK** (Osu Link, off Gamel Abdul Nasser Avenue; Tel: 221665); **USA** (Ring Road East; Tel: 775348/9); **Zaïre** (Third Rangoon Close).

Other red tape: Standard motoring documents and vaccination certificate for yellow fever are required. It is also necessary to register with the immigration authorities at the first opportunity (Sekondi coming from the west and Accra from the east); the stamp you get in your passport will be required at subsequent police checks.

Banks and money: The unit of currency is the cedi; despite many hefty devaluations, it is still not a particularly strong currency.

Public holidays: New Year's Day, Independence Day (March 6), Good Friday, Easter Saturday, Easter Monday, Republic Day (July 1), Christmas Day (December 25), Boxing Day (December 26), Revolution Day (December 31).

Fuel: No problems if you search around; much cheaper than neighbouring countries.

Roads: Drive on the right. The coastal highway is a very good surfaced road; elsewhere it is pretty patchy.

Routes: The most-used route is along the coastal highway, linking Lagos and Abidjan. The other main route that is used is to head northwest from Accra to Kumasi. From here it is possible to head back down to Abidjan or continue north to Ouagadougou.

Places to visit

Accra: A bustling low-rise, old-style African town — so different from a modern city like Abidjan. Accra has a real lived-in feel — the way you would like all African capitals to be. The way to enjoy it is just to wander around. The central market typifies the feeling of the town.

Axim: Site of a 17th century Portuguese fort.

Busua Beach and Dixcove: Beautiful beach at Busua, with the delightful Dixcove just a few hundred yards away by foot (quite a bit further by road). Dixcove has an old English fort and is one of the most pleasant places along the whole coastline.

Kakum: 20km north of Elmina which is on the Sekondi to Accra road, this rainforest reserve has platforms to view salt licks and walking safaris to see forest elephant.

Kumasi: Former centre of the Ashanti kingdom and now a centre for business and education in Ghana. Visit the National Cultural Centre, which combines a museum, theatre, art gallery, craft workshops, farm and zoo.

Sekondi-Takoradi: A lively port, this is a very pleasant town with a busy central market area.

Places to stay

Can be difficult to find anywhere to camp, although plantation areas

DIXCOVE AND BUSUA BEACH

Relaxing on a beautiful sandy beach in Ghana with an ice cold beer, it feels like some deserted Caribbean island — not at all the same as the fast-moving French lifestyle of the surrounding countries. The lazy sound of the reggae beat gently thumping out of the local 'drinking bars' only serves to emphasise the illusion.

If it's a beautiful beach that you want and crowds that you don't want, then Busua Beach in the west of the country is the place to head for. Busua does have a small holiday complex of bungalows but they are mostly empty. They are cheap to rent if you like the idea of relative comfort for a while — otherwise just camp by the beach. This is the kind of restful place you will want to take full advantage of and just hang around for a while. A short walk over the headland is Dixcove — an idyllic fishing village with an old Portuguese fort.

Shortly after arriving we decided to take a quiet stroll around Busua. This was the cue for Francis Boston to step in and take charge. Francis was a young boy with very firm ideas about the tourist delights of the village — and an equally firm conviction that nobody's backyard or kitchen should be protected from the tour. He did indeed provide an interesting guide to the preparation of manioc, fish-smoking, extracting coconut oil and the village's own coconut processing machine.

Finally, his elder brother James appeared on the scene and offered to sell us some lobsters from the next day's catch — three for a pound. When we told him we didn't have a large enough pot he agreed to cook them for us at no extra charge.

Sure enough, the next day he dropped by with the most delicious lobsters ever — and even threw in a couple of lemons for garnish. Just one more plus for such a perfect place. The only sadness of the day was when we met James later in the bar and he told us how he saved all his money when he was younger to start a new life abroad. He got as far as Heathrow airport where the immigration authorities put him straight onto the next plane back to Accra.

can come in useful. When staying in hotels, it is important to note that Ghanaians eat incredibly early in the evening — by 7.00pm the restaurant is likely to be closing down!

Accra: Various hotels available with safe parking at reasonable rates. The *Zeus Hotel* is a good one on the main road into the centre of town; it has a very pleasant rooftop bar.

Busua Beach: Paradise. Busua has a quiet holiday camp right on the beach with bungalows to let. It is also possible to camp there and use the facilities. Take a break and stretch out on this beautiful beach and before long you will be offered fresh lobsters and fish for next to nothing by the local fishermen.

Sources of tourist information
Tourist office in Ghana:
Accra Kojo Thomson Road; Tel: 65461.

TOGO

Area: 56,785km²

Population: 4.3 million

Capital: Lomé

Languages: French is the official language; main national languages are Ewe and Kabre.

Climate: The main rainy season is from April to July, with short rains coming in October to November.

Visas: Not needed by citizens of EU and West African countries, USA or Canada. All others can get visas from French embassies if there is no Togolese representation.

Foreign embassies and consulates in Lomé: The most important office in Lomé is the **French** Consulate (not the Embassy, which is in a different building), in Rue du Colonel le Roux (Tel: 212571). This office issues visas for Burkina Faso, CAR, Chad, Cote d'Ivoire, Djibouti, Mauritania and Senegal. Also represented in Lomé are: **Belgium** (294 Boulevard Circulaire; Tel: 210323); **Gabon** (Tel: 214776); **Ghana** (Route de Palimé; Tel: 213494); **Nigeria** (311 Boulevard du 13 Janvier; Tel: 213925); **Tunisia** (Rue de Méinas; Tel: 212637); **USA** (corner of Rue Pelletier Caventou and Rue Vauban; Tel: 217717); **Zaïre** (325 Boulevard Circulaire; Tel: 215155).

Other red tape: Vaccination certificate for yellow fever, driving licence, motor insurance, carnet or temporary importation certificate (available at border) are all required. Be prepared for a lot of police road checks.

Banks and money: Currency is CFA (west). Banks in main towns.

Public holidays: New Year's Day, Liberation Day (January 13), Economic Liberation Day (January 24), Triumphant Return (February 2), Easter Monday, Victory Day (April 24), Independence Day (April 27), Labour Day (May 1), Ascension Day, Whit Monday, Martyrs of Pya (June 21), The Assumption, All Saints' Day (November 1), Christmas Day (December 25). The Islamic holidays of the start of Ramadan and Tabaski are also observed, on dates varying from year to year.

Fuel: No problem with availability; mid-range price — higher than both Ghana and Benin but slightly lower than Niger.

Roads: Drive on the right. Coastal highway is first class; north south road is good; others are fair.

Routes: Togo is such a small country that you are not presented with a great choice of routes. Some will enter from the north and drive the length of the country — otherwise it will just be a matter of a short hop along the coastal highway and those beautiful beaches.

Places to visit

Kéran National Park: Togo's only wildlife reserve.

Lomé: As a free port, Lomé is a bustling centre of trade. In many ways, it is the most typical of West African cities. The heart of town is the huge *Grand Marché* — a colourful sea of traders selling vegetables, fruit, fish, clothing, material, music cassettes, fetishes, etc. The beaches along this stretch of coast are also excellent.

Places to stay

Atakpamé: *Hotel du Roc* has safe parking but is expensive.

Lomé: All of the best places to stay are outside the town. *Chez Alice* is a classic and pleasant travellers' campsite, about 10 kilometres east along the coast road. It also has good communal meals and cheap rooms. Along the same stretch of beach are two other sites — *Robinson Plage* and *Campement Ramatou*. A few kilometres further down the road at Baguida is *Petit Alexandre*, which has also been recommended. *Foyer des Marines* is a hotel with parking in Lomé itself — but the only report we have is from travellers who left as soon as they booked in because the rooms were so awful.

Sekodé: Has a good cheap hotel with safe parking near the airfield.

Sources of tourist information

Haut Commissariat au tourisme du Togo, Rue François 1er 23, 75008 Paris, France.

Tourist office in Togo:
Lomé Office Nationale du Tourisme Togolaise, BP 1289; Tel: 21 43 13.

BENIN

Area: 112,600km²

Population: 5.3 million

Capital: Porto Novo is the official capital but Cotonou is home to the machinery of state and is the effective capital.

Languages: French is the official language; the main national languages are Fon, Yoruba and Bariba.

Climate: Humid with a steady temperature of around 27°C in the south; drier with greater extremes of temperature in the north. There are four seasons in the south — dry from January to April, a rainy season from May to July, a short dry season in August and another rainy season from September to December. In the north it is dry from November to June and rainy from July to October.

Visas: Required by all apart from citizens of France and French-speaking African countries.

Foreign embassies and consulates in Cotonou: Algeria (route de l'Aéroport; Tel: 312991); **Chad** (Akpakpa district); **France** (route de l'Aéroport; Tel: 312638); **Ghana** (route de l'Aéroport; Tel: 300746); **Niger** (behind the post office; Tel: 314030); **Nigeria** (Boulevard de la Marina; Tel: 301142); **UK** (Honorary Consul; Tel: 301601); **USA** (Rue Caporal Bernard Anani; Tel: 300650).

Other red tape: Standard motoring documents are required. Crossing on the coastal road, travellers have reported problems at both borders, with demands for bribes. We have experienced no particular problems ourselves — apart from having to wake up a customs officer who was stretched out asleep on the counter!

Banks and money: Unit of currency is the CFA (west). Banks in major towns.

Public holidays: New Year's Day, Good Friday, Labour Day (May 1), Independence Day (August 1), Armed Forces Day (October 26), Benin Day (November 30), Christmas Day (December 25), Harvest Day (December 31). The Islamic holidays of Aid el-Fitr and Tabaski are also observed, on dates varying from year to year.

Fuel: Reasonable supplies; cheaper than Togo or Niger but much more than the incredibly cheap fuel in Nigeria.

Roads: Drive on the right. The coastal highway and the main north to south road are good.

Routes: The coastal road to Togo and Nigeria and the north to south road to Niger are the only through routes.

Places to visit

Abomey: Previously the centre of the Kingdom of Abomey, this is the most interesting historical site in Benin. A separate palace was built here by each of the 12 kings in the line; three of these have now been restored and can be visited. An excellent museum has been set up in the grounds and a range of craft workshops provides a good opportunity to buy local bronzes, textiles and so on, at good prices.

Cotonou: A busy town with lively markets; colourful scenes of fishermen with their *pirogues* along the beach.

Ganvie: Remarkable village built on stilts in the lagoon north of Cotonou. In theory you should hire an official *pirogue* for your visit at Abomey-Calavi, but if you go a little further up the lagoon you can get a much better deal with private individuals.

Grand Popo: Glorious beaches here along the main road close to the Togo border.

Ouidah: Old fortified town with narrow streets and former Portuguese fort.

Pendjari National Park: Situated in the north of Benin, this is one of the best places in West Africa for game.

Places to stay

There are plenty of good places for free camping in the north of Benin but it can be a little more difficult in the more heavily populated south.

Abomey: *The Foyer Des Militants* (straight out on the road north of the market) has been recommended; but we found the parking not to be as secure as we would like and there were bats flapping about our room!

Azohoue Aliho: Extremely wacky small hotel here on the dirt road from Ouidah to Alladah.

Cotonou: There is a simple campsite on the north side of the coast road about a mile west of the junction with the main road up to Abomey.

Grand Popo: It is possible to find some excellent camping spots on these beautiful beaches.

Sources of tourist information
Maison de l'Afrique, Rue de Viarmes 2, 75001 Paris, France.

Tourist office in Benin:
Cotonou Onatha (official tourist office), BP 89; Tel: 31 26 87/31 32 17.

THE KINGDOM OF ABOMEY
Many travellers manage to skip Benin — or just whizz through along the coast road from Lomé to Lagos. That's a sad loss as it is a fascinating country. Among the many places to go, perhaps the most unmissable is Abomey and a visit to the palaces of the ancient Fon kingdom.

Each of the 12 kings of Abomey built a new palace. Several of these have been restored so far. The grounds include a museum and some of the best craft workshops in West Africa (good prices and quality for bronzes and weaving in particular).

A guided tour takes in such gory delights as a throne made from human skulls and a wall made from a mix of mud and the blood of vanquished warriors. Animist traditions and a powerful kingdom came forcefully together in this region which also gave birth to voodoo.

An Egyptian philosopher and Monsieur Cosmos
We were finally on our way into Benin, driving beneath the banners proclaiming the eternal truth of Marxist-Leninism in the glorious People's Republic. Of course, everything has changed since then. The collapse of the political order of Eastern Europe created a string of consequent changes around the world — including Benin.

Our delay at the border had been a purely local matter however. The customs officer had decided it would be pleasant to take a quick nap and when we arrived he was stretched out on the counter fast asleep. No amount of polite attempts to rouse him were of any use. It was only when a colleague stormed in and hauled him to the floor that we had any hope of getting our carnet stamped.

The political banners continued to flash by as we passed the glorious Grand Popo beach and all along the coastal highway. As we were planning to head north to Niamey, we then turned off along the unsurfaced shortcut from Ouidah to Allada. It was along this stretch that we came across the zanier side of life in Benin.

We hadn't gone far when we heard the all too familiar sound of a police whistle from the side of the road. You are frequently brought to a halt by a whistle throughout West Africa — although this was to prove to be our only police check in Benin. On such a minor road, we were an unusual enough sight to warrant a complete sift through our documents.

The young officer led us across to the police hut and presented us to his chief. During our travels we have come across a vast range of intellectual attainment among the police and military — everything from complete illiteracy to well-educated and inquiring minds. But nothing had prepared us for the police chief in this backwater of the People's Republic — he had a post graduate degree in Egyptian philosophy!

As it happens Paula is also a philosophy graduate (medieval logic a speciality) so the conversation in the roadside hut moved away from carnets and passports and onto Aristotle, Plato and Thomas Aquinas. The conversation was so enjoyable that time flew by and before we knew it dusk was approaching. Our philosopher encouraged us not to camp tonight but to stop instead at a hotel he could recommend just along the road. With Benin looking like such an interesting place, we decided to give it a try. We drove on to the village of Azohoue Aliho and found the hotel — with safe parking for the Land Rover. It turned out to be an unmissable stop when Rose and Virginie, the two young women running it, introduced us to the wicked and fast-moving delights of African ludo. 'Normal ludo is only for *les petits*,' added Rose.

Before long we were introduced to the man supposedly responsible for the hotel while the owner was away. Monsieur Cosmos was totally out of his skull as he worked on his latest creation — he claimed to be an artist and was indeed surrounded by canvases of mediocre quality. Like many people around the world, Monsieur Cosmos had his own tale to tell of his travels in Europe. 'I went to London once,' he said, eyes spinning and unable to focus on anything before him. 'I spent 10 days there training to be a croupier.'

With Egyptian philosophy, African ludo and an alcoholic croupier painter called Cosmos, all within hours of each other, the People's Republic already looked like being one of the strangest and most individual places we would visit. We weren't disappointed.

NIGERIA

Area: 923,768km²

Population: 98.1 million

Capital: Abuja — but many government offices still remain in the former capital, Lagos

Languages: English is the official language; the main national languages are Yoruba, Hausa and Ibo.

Climate: The south is hot and humid with a long rainy season lasting from March until November. The north has far greater extremes of temperature, with its Saharan influences; the rains last from April until September.

Visas: Everyone needs a Nigerian visa. The Nigerian Embassy in Algiers is reputedly one of the best places to try; there are also embassies in both Lomé and Cotonou.

Foreign embassies and consulates in Lagos: Algeria (26 Maitama Sule Street, SW Ikoyi); **Australia** (2 Ozumba Mbadiwe Avenue, Victoria Island; Tel: 618703); **Cameroon** (Elsie Permi Pearse Street, Victoria Island; you will need a letter of introduction from your own embassy — be prepared for delays; there is also a consulate in Calabar at 6 Ezuk Nkapa Street); **Canada** (4 Idowu Taylor Street, Victoria Island; Tel: 262 2513-6); **Cote d'Ivoire** (08-5 Abudusmisth Street, PO Box 7786, Victoria Island; Tel: 161 09 36); **Egypt** (182 B Kofo Abayomi Street, Victoria Island; Tel: 618029); **France** (Queen's Drive, Ikoyi; Tel: 603300); **Gabon** (Tel: 684566); **Gambia** (162 Awolowo Road; Tel: 682192); **Germany** (15 Eleke Crescent, Victoria Island; Tel: 611011); **Ghana** (21-23 King George V Road); **Guinea** (8 Abudu Smith Street; Tel: 612206); **Kenya** (52 Queens Drive; Tel: 682768); **Mauritania** (41 Moshalashi Drive; Tel: 684439); **Namibia** (PO Box 8000, Victoria Island; Tel: 619323); **Niger** (15 Adeola Odeku Street; Tel: 612300); **Senegal** (14 Kofo Abayomi Road; Tel: 614226); **Sierra Leone** (31 Wazin Ibrahim Street; Tel: 614666); **Tanzania** (8 Agoro Odiyan Street, Victoria Island; Tel: 613594/613604); **Togo** (Plot 976, Oju Olobun Close; Tel: 617449); **UK** (11 Eleke Crescent, Victoria Island; Tel: 619531/7); **USA** (2 Eleke Crescent, Victoria Island; Tel: 2610097); **Zaïre** (23A Kofo Abayomi Road, Victoria Island; Tel: 614834); **Zambia** (11 Keffi Street, South West Ikoyi); **Zimbabwe** (Plot 1189, 6 Kasumu Ekemonde, Ikoyi; Tel: 619328).

Other red tape: In the past there have been a lot of police checks, with the road from Lagos to the Benin border made up of one long search. However, the news is that these have largely disappeared. Carnets are generally stamped without problems despite the fact the Nigerian Automobile Association is not recognised by the AA in the UK and so Nigeria is not entered on carnets (the RAC enter Nigeria on carnets, however, and the AA seems now to be following). Some problems with this on leaving Nigeria have been reported, all solved with a spot of 'dash'. Nigeria is the last country where you will be able to use the West African insurance policy available when you enter Niger or Mali. One recommendation for the rest of your trip is to get a policy from the Manilla Insurance Company (head office in Calabar but with a branch office at the Cameroon border at Mfum-Ekok). They will issue a three month policy valid everywhere in Africa. Standard motoring documents and vaccination certificates for yellow fever are required. Take care to remember that the last Saturday of the month is litter day — everyone is expected to lend a hand clearing the streets; anyone attempting to drive between 8.00am and 10.00am will be pulled over and sternly dealt with.

Banks and money: The value of the naira has plummeted over the years, making Nigeria an extremely cheap place to visit.

Public holidays: New Year's Day, Good Friday, Easter Monday, National Day (October 1), Christmas Day (December 25), Boxing Day (December 26). The Islamic holidays of Aid el-Fitr, Aid el-Kabir and Mouloud are also observed, on dates varying from year to year.

Fuel: Easily available and incredibly cheap.

Roads: Generally good. Drive on the right.

Routes: The fast through-route for trans-African trucks generally cuts down from Zinder in Niger to Kano, then west to Maiduguri and through into Cameroon at Mora. This is an extremely easy and quick route. More interesting is to continue south to Jos and then on down to Calabar. The minor road from Calabar to the border at Ikang is very good, making this a popular point to enter Cameroon. The formalities at Mfum-Ekok can be very difficult, making Ikang an even more attractive alternative. Many travellers also enter Nigeria along the coastal highway from Benin. The whole southern route from Lagos to Cameroon (via either Enugu or Owerri) is extremely fast.

Places to visit

Jos: A very pleasant town at high altitude, making this a good place to cool down after the heat of the north.

Kano: One of the most interesting places in Nigeria, Kano was founded over 1,000 years ago and was a major objective of the trans-Saharan trading routes. The old Kurmi Market is wonderful and still acts as the focus for traders arriving from afar with their laden camels. If you are in Kano at the end of Ramadan, the display of traditional horse riding is not to be missed.

Yankari: Game reserve with a smattering of elephants and baboons but the big attraction is the warm springs which make this a good place to wash the dust off. Camping charges are less than US$1 a head.

Places to stay

You should be cautious of bush camping near cities in Nigeria — particularly in the west. In rural areas it should be all right to camp — but the best option is to talk to the local head man and ask if you can stop in his village. In towns, hotels are the best bet. You will easily find a reasonable hotel in every town — and they are incredibly cheap. Immediately after devaluation in 1988 good hotels were charging about £8-9 a night for a double. More recent reports suggest prices have not increased much.

Banchi: The tourist camp just down from the Central Hotel has camping and rooms.

Calabar: The *Metropolitan Hotel* offers complete luxury at around £15 for a double room. This could be your most comfortable night for a long time to come.

Jos: No official campsite; hotels are the best bet here. The *Hill Station Hotel* (Tudun Wada Road) is a beautiful old colonial-style place.

Kano: *Tourist Camping* is the only place to stay; it can be difficult to find. A private company at the site changes money at the tourist rate (with official blessing) — making this a good place to change.

Lagos: Victoria Island is a good area for hotels.

Sources of tourist information

Tourist Department, Nigeria High Commission, 56-57 Fleet Street, London EC4Y 1JU; Tel: 0171 353 3776.

Tourist offices in Nigeria:

Kano Ministry of Home Affairs and Information, Zaria Road; Tel: 2341. Also tourist information kiosk at the airport.
Lagos Nigeria Tourist Board, 44 Norman William Street, Ikoyi.

Sarah Elder '95

NIGERIAN PETROL

Anyone driving from Nigeria to the border with Cameroon should fill up with cheap petrol well before the border town of Ikon. One set of travellers who waited until the last minute to fill up completely had to drive back 100km from Ikon to Ogoja before they found petrol.

Beware of overloading. The same people filled every tank and jerrican, including their water jerricans which they were unlikely to need again, to maximise the amount of cheap petrol they could take across the border. On their first day in Cameroon they experienced a real downpour on some steeply cambered mud roads and ended up on their side in a ditch. The driving conditions were treacherous, but they felt being heavily loaded with petrol contributed to going over. Fortunately a passing lorry gave them a nerve-racking but successful pull back upright.

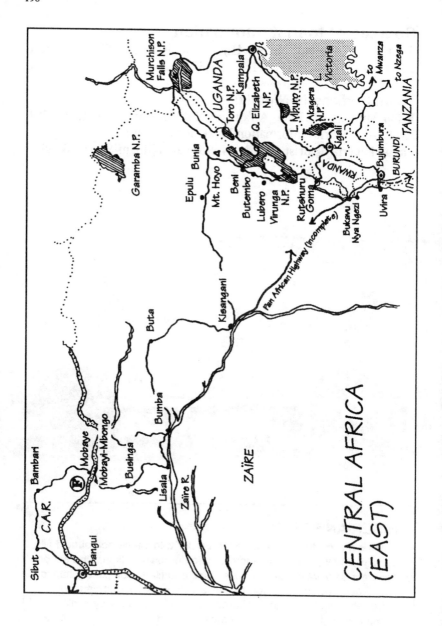

CENTRAL AFRICA
(EAST)

Chapter Seven

Central Africa

This is the real heart of Africa. Travelling through the rain-forests and along the narrow slippery mudslides they call roads, most travellers start to feel they belong at last — and can cope with the worst the continent can throw at them.

But central areas have much more to offer than hard driving, heavy rain and bananas. Few will come away without being infected with the area's enthusiasm for music, fun and life.

ROUTE GUIDE

The options are fairly limited in Central Africa. Many roads marked on maps are effectively impassable — or would take a very long time with the need constantly to clear a way through. Civil war in Angola for the past 20 years has also closed this option off as an avenue south (although things are now looking brighter for opening up than they have for many years).

Zaïre is at the very heart of Africa and it is through this great country (the third biggest in the continent after Sudan and Algeria) that most people must pass at some time or another on an overland trip — although the political instability of recent years means it is currently best to avoid larger towns.

One option is to head south from Cameroon along what is the only main route through Gabon and Congo. A ferry will take you across from Brazzaville to Kinshasa where you can join the Zaïre river steamer to sail all the way up to Kisangani, right into the interior of Africa (this is the journey of Joseph Conrad's *Heart Of Darkness*). This route is not often taken because of the poor roads in Gabon and Congo and the high cost of visas required by these countries.

By far the most common route is via CAR. Kinshasa and Kisangani have also been among the more difficult places in Zaïre

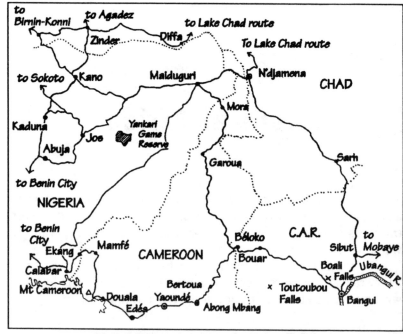

CENTRAL AFRICA (WEST)

recently. Entering CAR either from Chad or (far more frequently) from Cameroon, routes converge on Bangui — which is worth missing out if you don't have any visas to collect, as it doesn't have much to offer apart from bureaucratic problems and petty theft. If you do want to avoid the town, don't cross the PK12 checkpoint, which is just beyond the junction of the main roads from Bossanbélé and Sibut.

From Bangui take the road to Sibut, Bambari and Bangassou, which is the best place to cross the Oubangui River into Zaïre. By this point, vehicles which have taken the hard route across from Sudan, will have joined the main central route. The preferred route since Zaïre became more difficult is the northern one through Monga, Bondo, Buta, Bambesa, Poko, Isiro, Epulu and Bunia.

Following the war in Rwanda, it looks unlikely that the route south from here via Rwanda and Burundi will be open for quite some time. Until then, the only reasonable route from here will be through Uganda — either crossing in the north at Mahagi or heading south to Beni and across the border into the Queen Elizabeth

National Park.

Once the situation improves, you will again be able to go down the length of the beautiful Eastern Highlands of Zaïre to Rwanda and Burundi and then either on into Tanzania or taking to the water again for the trip down Lake Tanganyika into Zambia.

The pan-African highway from Kisangani to Bukavu is still under construction, and has been for many years — so it will be no great surprise if there are yet further delays. But if this section ever does open it will create an expressway across Africa, removing some of the most difficult sections.

CAMEROON

Area: 465,458km²

Population: 13.1 million

Capital: Yaoundé

Languages: French and English are the official languages.

Climate: The north is hot and dry with a long rainy season from May to October. The south is hot and humid (average temperature about 26°C) with a long dry season from November to February, with rains from March until June and then a heavy rainy season from July until October.

Visas: Required by most travellers, except Germans. Can be exceptionally difficult to get en route, with demands for letters of introduction or telexes to the embassy in your country of residence. If at all possible, it is best to get a Cameroon visa before you set out. This is the case even if your visa is likely to expire before you need to use it, as having one already makes getting another much easier. The London embassy is generally good.

Foreign embassies and consulates in Yaoundé: Canada (Immeduble Stamatiades, Rue de l'Hotel de Ville; Tel: 230203); **CAR** (off Rue Albert Ateba Ebé; Tel: 225155); **Chad** (Rue Mballa Eloumden; Tel: 230624); **Congo** (Tel: 232458); **Equatorial Guinea** (Tel: 224149); **France** (Rue Joseph Atemengué; Tel: 234013); **Gabon** (off Boulevard de l'URSS; Tel: 222966); **Liberia** (Rue Mballa Eloumden; Tel: 231296); **Morocco** (Tel: 225092); **Nigeria** (off Rue Monsieur Vogt; Tel: 223455); **Senegal** (Boulevard de l'URSS; Tel: 220308); **UK** (Avenue Winston Churchill; Tel: 220545); **USA** (Rue Nachtigal; Tel: 234014); **Zaïre** (Boulevard de l'URSS; Tel: 225103).

Other red tape: Standard motoring documents and vaccination certificates are required. Motoring insurance can be bought to cover the whole CFA (central) zone — although it is probably cheaper to buy insurance across the border in Nigeria.

Banks and money: Unit of currency is the CFA (central). Banks in main towns.

Public holidays: Independence Day (January 1), Youth Day (February 1), Good Friday, Labour Day (May 1), National Day (May 20), Reunification Day (December 10), Christmas Day (December 25). The Islamic holidays of Lailat el-Miraj, Aid el-Fitr,

Aid el-Adha, Hejri, el-Ashura and Mouloud are also observed, on dates varying from year to year.

Fuel: Available in main towns; not as expensive as CAR but costs far more than Nigeria.

Roads: Drive on the right. Mostly fairly poor although there are a lot of new road building projects, so the situation is improving all the time.

Routes: Either straight down from Mora and into CAR at Béloko or enter in the west and explore a little. A good route from Mamfé is to head south to Mount Cameroon, Douala, Edéa and then on down to Kribi. Southern Cameroon offers some of the most interesting rain-forest areas in Africa — although the entire route out to the port at Kribi is covered with convoys of logging lorries in the dry season. The best routes to CAR from Yaoundé are to the south of the main route, going via Abong Mbang. Foreign registered vehicles are supposed to register with the police at Bertoua (there are frequent police stops around this town); the road from Bertoua to the border is pretty awful.

Places to visit
Bamenda: A lovely highland area in the old English part of Cameroon.

Kribi: Absolutely beautiful area of white sandy beaches; a great place to relax.

Maroua: This quiet capital of the northern region presents a good contrast to the bustling south.

Mount Cameroon: Extremely good hiking excursions on the mountain, but you will have to pay for a guided trip to the top.

Places to stay
Generally hard to get off the road to bush camp, but there are no problems if you stop and talk to the head of a village for permission to camp. In cities it tends to be a lot safer to stay in hotels. We heard of two separate sets of people who lost everything they had in Yaoundé.

Bamenda: The *Presbyterian Mission* is run by a German who is happy for overlanders to stay.

Kribi: Good free camping and waterfalls along the superb white sands of Kribi Beach, south of the town. Local fishermen will stop by to offer fish, lobsters, crabs and palm wine!

Limbe: Six Mile Beach, to the north of the town, does have facilities although it is not an official campsite. Beware of thieves.

Mamfé: Campsite with rooms, advertised as a motel; food available.

Ngaoundéré: The *Ranch de Ngaoundéré* is 3 miles out of town down a dirt track. This old hunting lodge is not cheap but is a lovely place for a break with friendly staff and good food.

Yaoundé: No official campsite. Most people stay at the *Presbyterian Mission* in the Djoungolo district to the north of town. Theft is a major problem here.

Sources of Tourist information
Tourist office in Cameroon:
Yaoundé Délégation Générale au Tourisme, Avenue Vogt; Tel: 22 44 11.

GABON

Area: 267,667km²

Population: 1.1 million

Capital: Libreville

Languages: French is the official language; Fang is the main national language.

Climate: Equatorial; average temperature 30°C.

Visas: Required by all apart from citizens of France or Germany. They tend to be very expensive.

Foreign embassies and consulates in Libreville: Benin (Boulevard Léon Mba; Tel: 737692); **Cameroon** (Boulevard Léon Mba); **CAR** (Tel: 737761); **Cote d'Ivoire** (Barclays Bank Building, Boulevard de l'Independence; Tel: 720596); **Nigeria** (Boulevard Léon Mba; Tel: 732201); **Canada** (PO Box 4037; Tel: 743464/5); **USA** (Boulevard de la Mer; Tel: 762003).

Other red tape: Vaccination certificates are required for yellow fever. Standard motoring documents and insurance are required.

Banks and money: The unit of currency is the CFA (central).

Public holidays: New Year's Day, Renovation Day (March 12), Good Friday, Easter Monday, Labour Day (May 1), Ascension Day, Pentecost, Independence Day (August 17), All Saints' Day (November 1), Christmas Day (December 25). Some Islamic holidays are also observed.

Roads: Poor. Drive on the right.

Routes: There is effectively only one route through the country, from Ebor at the Cameroon border to Ndendé on the way out to Congo. There is a main road linking this route with Libreville on the coast.

Places to stay
Bush camping and stopping in villages provide the only options (apart from the expensive international hotels in Libreville).

Sources of tourist information
Tourist office in Gabon:
Libreville Office national gabonais au tourisme, BP 403; Tel: 72 42 29.

CONGO

Area: 342,000km²

Population: 2.5 million

Capital: Brazzaville

Languages: French is the official language; Kongo, Teke and Boutangui are the main national languages.

Climate: Equatorial — hot, humid and wet. The dry seasons are from May to September and from mid-December to mid-January.

Visas: Required by all apart from citizens of France and French-speaking African countries. 1995 charges were £25 (15 days single entry) to £100 (90 days multiple entry).

Foreign embassies and consulates in Brazzaville: Angola (Tel: 836565); **Cameroon** (Rue Général Bayardelle; Tel: 833404); **CAR** (Rue Fourneau; Tel: 834014); **Chad** (22 Rue des Ecoles; Tel: 832222); **France** (Avenue Alfassa; Tel: 831086); **Gabon** (Rue Fourneau; Tel: 830590); **Guinea** (Avenue Maréchal Foch; Tel: 832466); **Nigeria** (11 Boulevard du Maréchal Lyautey; Tel: 831316); **USA** (Avenue Amilcar Cabral; Tel: 832070); **Zaïre** (130 Avenue de l'Indépendance; Tel: 832938).

Other red tape: International motoring documents and vaccination certificate for yellow fever are required. Constant police stops along the road will check all documents in minute detail. Register with immigration at Loubomo.

Banks and money: The unit of currency is the CFA (central). Do not count on changing money outside of Brazzaville and Pointe-Noire. Banking hours are 6.30am to 1.00pm, Monday to Saturday.

Public holidays: New Year's Day, Labour Day (May 1), Readjustment of Revolution (July 31); Les Trois Glorieuses (August 13 to 15), All Saints' Day (November 1), Children's Day (December 25), Foundation Day (December 31).

Roads: Very poor. Drive on the right.

Routes: Few will contemplate anything other than the road from the Gabon border at Moussogo to Brazzaville — and then across the Zaïre river on the ferry to Kinshasa. Even this road is difficult. Much of the interior is inaccessible by road.

Places to stay
Bush camping in the country; hotels in the towns are expensive.

Sources of tourist information
Tourist office in Congo:
Brazzaville Syndicat d'Initiative, opposite the Post Office.

CENTRAL AFRICAN REPUBLIC (CAR)

Area: 622,436km²

Population: 3.1 million

Capital: Bangui

Languages: French is the official language; the main national language is Sango.

Climate: Hot and humid in the south, drier in the north. Rainy season in the south is from May until October, starting later and finishing earlier the further north you go.

Visas: Required by all except French, German and Swiss travellers and those from French-speaking African countries. They can be obtained from French embassies where there is no CAR consular office — including London. It is important to note, however, that there have been times when you need to get telex clearance from Bangui before a visa is issued. This can mean a long wait — as much as two months in London.

Foreign embassies and consulates in Bangui: Cameroon (Avenue de la France; Tel: 611687); **Chad** (Avenue Colonel Conus; Tel: 614677); **Congo** (Avenue Boganda; Tel: 611877); **Egypt** (Rue de la Corse Derriers, Bamag Avenue B Boganda; Tel: 614688); **France** (Boulevard Général de Gaulle; Tel: 613000); **Germany** (Tel: 610746); **Nigeria** (Avenue des Martyrs; Tel: 610744); **Sudan** (Avenue de l'Indépendence); **UK** (Consul, c/o SOCACIG, off Avenue Barthélémy Boganda); **USA** (Avenue David Dacko; Tel: 610200); **Zaïre** (Gama Abdel Nasser; Tel: 613344).

Other red tape: CAR can be a tough and unpredictable country to enter with new regulations being imposed from time to time. Check on the latest requirements before setting out. Standard motoring documents and vaccination certificate for yellow fever are required. Countless police checks will scrutinise your vehicle closely and fine you if anything is out of order. Check your lights, spare tyres, anything and everything. Make sure you can produce two warning triangles and a fire extinguisher. People have also been fined for not wearing seatbelts! The police check is at PK12, which is 12 kilometres north of Bangui. Passports are now stamped in Bangui rather than at PK12. You will be given an immigration slip which you must have on the way out — lose it and you're in trouble.

Banks and money: Unit of currency is the CFA (central). There are several banks in Bangui (which will mostly give hard currency on a credit card).

Public holidays: New Year's Day, Anniversary of the death of Boganda (March 29), Labour Day (May 1), Liberation of African Continent (May 25), Ascension, Whit Monday, Proclamation of the Republic (November 28), National Day (December 1), Christmas Day (December 25).

Fuel: Easy enough to get in Bangui but expensive. Best to stock up in Nigeria.

Roads: Drive on the right. Good roads have been built to the northeast and northwest of Bangui. The roads beyond Sibut (to the east) and Bossambélé (to the west) are not too bad, but closer to the Cameroon, Chad and Sudan borders they are very poor. You can be held up for long periods during the rainy season at rain barriers, which are intended to stop the roads being further damaged.

Routes: The main crossing from Cameroon is at Béloko (although there are fewer police checks within Cameroon on the road to Gamboula). Entry from Chad at Kabo is reasonably straightforward. All routes then converge on Bangui. There are three ferries across the Oubangui River into Zaïre: Bangui, Mobaye, Bangassou. The Bangui crossing is hardly ever used by overland vehicles because of persistent problems across the river in Zongo — if you do choose to go this way, make sure you cross early in the day and go at least 50km from Zongo before stopping. The previously preferred crossing at Mobaye has been out of action for the past few years — because of its proximity to the Zairois presidential palace in Gbadolite — so currently Bangassou is the best option for entry into Zaïre.

Places to stay
It can be difficult to find a place to camp, with the population heavily concentrated along the main routes.

Bangui: *Centre d'Accueil Touristique* — 7km from the centre, straight out along Avenue Boganda to the market and then continue along the dirt road. This site has one of the worst reputations for theft in Africa. You should be extra vigilant. The Peace Corps has room for one vehicle.

Boale Falls: Not an official campsite but this is a handy place to stay close to Bangui.

WATCH OUT FOR THEFT

Vigilance at all times is the golden rule for security — particularly when you are in the centre of a large town. Every city is a danger spot for petty theft — so watch out. But certain cities do seem to get a worse reputation than others. Among these, one of the worst is Bangui — a town that very few trans-African travellers will manage to avoid. Robberies at the campsite are a regular occurrence and our Land Rover was broken into at midday right outside the central immigration office.

But however much security you have, you can never be absolutely sure. One truck operator says his truck was parked outside the Bangui post office one day with no fewer than six people guarding it. Suddenly they heard a thump and saw a bag fall to the ground. Someone had climbed into a tree with a fishing line and was fishing for booty on the truck! Luckily the line was not up to the strain.

Kembé Falls: This is a pleasant place to camp, about 60 kilometres past the turning down to Mobaye (it is worth the detour). Avoid the obvious camping area by the road and go down the track to the side instead.

Sibut: The people running the *Auberge* are very friendly. They allow camping or will rent you a hut.

Toutoubou Falls: On the minor road from Berébati to Carnot, near the Cameroon border, this camping place can be difficult to find but is a lovely spot once you get there. Search through the mango trees and you will find a small space that is suitable for camping.

Sources of tourist information
Tourist office in CAR:
Bangui Avenue Bartélémy Boganda.

ZAÏRE

Area: 2,345,095km²

Population: 42.7 million

Capital: Kinshasa

Languages: French is the official language; the main national languages are Lingala, Kiswahili, Tshilubu and Kikongo.

Climate: A huge country straddling the equator, it is not possible to summarise the climate of the whole of Zaïre. Most of the country is hot, humid and wet — although the eastern highlands are extremely pleasant, being both drier and cooler. Along the northern route taken by most travellers, the only time of year when you can be fairly sure of dry weather is from December to February. There is also a 'less wet' season from June to July. In the south of the country the dry season is from May to October.

Visas: All visitors require a visa.

Foreign embassies and consulates in Kinshasa: Algeria (50 Avenue Colonel Ebeya; Tel: 22470); **Angola** (12 Avenue de l'Action); **Belgium** (Boulevard du 30 Juin; Tel: 25525); **Burundi** (4687 Avenue de la Gombe; Tel: 33353 — there is also a consulate in Bukavu); **Cameroon** (Boulevard du 30 Juin; Tel: 34787); **Canada** (c/o US Embassy); **CAR** (Avenue Pumbu 11); **Congo** (Boulevard du 30 Juin; **Cote d'Ivoire** (68 Avenue de la Justice; Tel: 30440); tel. 34028); **France** (Avenue de la République du Tchad; Tel: 22669); **Gabon** (Avenue du 30 Juin; Tel: 50206); **Germany** (Avenue des Troiz Z; tel. 27720); **Kenya** 5002 Avenue Ouganda; Tel: 33205); **Nigeria** (Boulevard du 30 Juin; Tel: 33343); **Rwanda** (50 Avenue de la Justice; Tel: 33080; you can also get a transit visa for Rwanda at the border); **Tanzania** (142 Boulevard 30 Juin; Tel: 34364); **UK** (Avenue de Troiz Z; Tel: 34775); **USA** (310 Avenue des Aviateurs; Tel: 21532/21628); **Zambia** (54-58 Avenue de l'Ecole; Tel: 23038; there is also a consulate in Lubumbashi).

Other red tape: Motoring documents and vaccination certificate for yellow fever are required. In theory local third party motor insurance is required but it would be difficult to track down on the overland route. Despite a bad reputation for corruption, we have found officials in Zaïre to be among the friendliest in Africa. With the right approach, you need have no problems. Land borders have been closed from time to time because of rebel activity in both the north and south of the country. Make sure you check on the latest situation.

Banks and money: Unit of currency is the zaïre.

Public holidays: New Year's Day, Martyrs of Independence (January 4), Labour Day (May 1), Anniversary of the MPR (May 20), Fishermen's Day (June 24), Independence Day (June 30), Parents' Day (August 1), Youth Day and Birthday of President Mobutu (October 14), Anniversary of the naming of Zaïre (October 27), National Army Day (November 17), Anniversary of the Regime (November 24), Christmas Day (December 25).

Fuel: Supplies can be erratic and will often only be available from unofficial sources. You may sometimes have to wait a few days for deliveries but you will ultimately get hold of some in all the main centres. Prices vary but are generally on the high side.

Roads: There are not many stretches of road in Zaïre that could be described as good. Very little is surfaced so the effects of the weather are extreme — roads which are fine in the dry season will become a sea of mud when it is wet. Conditions are at their worst east of Kisangani, where freight carried on the river up until here takes to the road. As a result convoys of trucks constantly get stuck and badly chew up the roads.

Routes: Few travellers will take anything other than the main route across the north of Zaïre, linking CAR and the eastern highlands. The best entry point at the moment is at Bangassou. The most common route is to go via Monga and Bondo to Buta, with a choice then of the northern route through Isiro or the southern one through Kisangani. These roads converge again at Nia Nia. An alternative is to take the track from Monga across two ferries to Yakoma and then down to Bumba, where it is possible to take the river steamer as far as Kisangani. After Nia Nia, the road goes through Epulu to Komanda. At the moment the only option is then to cross into Uganda — either via Bunia and Mahagi or further south from Beni into the Queen Elizabeth National Park. If the political situation improves, it may once again be possible to continue down through the extremely beautiful eastern highlands of Zaïre and through Rwanda and Burundi into Tanzania. The only way into Burundi without entering Rwanda is by the difficult but spectacular route via Nya-Ngezi down to Uvira; large sections of this have been compared with driving in the Hoggar mountains in Algeria!

Places to visit

Zaïre has become a much more difficult place to travel in recent years — largely as a result of political instability and raging inflation. Nevertheless, the country's exuberant sense of life still makes it a highlight of any trip.

Bukavu: Extremely pleasant town, just across the border from Rwanda and situated on the shores of Lake Kivu. There are a lot of good bars and restaurants and an excellent (and cheap) source of genuine local crafts. All in all, it's a good place to spend a day waiting for a Burundi visa to be processed.

Epulu: The only area in the world where you can see the okapi in its natural habitat. They are caught at the *Station de Capture* for research. Trips into the bush will also take you to nearby pygmy villages.

Garamba: An interesting game park in the north, for those with enough time to explore off the beaten track. This is the only place in the area where the white rhinoceros can still be seen in the wild.

Goma: Once the huge influx of refugees from Rwanda has been resolved, this will presumably once again be the place to come in order to book to visit the gorillas. You can also try going directly to the Rumangabo viewing area, just off the main Rutshuru-Goma road. There is another gorilla reserve at Djumba and a new chimpanzee reserve at Tonga.

The Highlands: The entire eastern highlands of Zaïre are utterly beautiful — and a real relief after the humid jungle. Look out for the wonderful Alpine-style cheese and selections of vegetables for sale by the side of the road.

Mount Hoyo: Beautiful walking area with many local pygmy villages at the end of a tough 13km track up from the main road. There is a whole local industry up here devoted to the tourists — with guides to the mountain, caves and villages cooking traditional dishes and selling local crafts. It can be a bit over the top but a good place to stop off nonetheless.

Nyiragongo and Nyamulagira: There are guided treks up these active volcanoes. The three day trip up Nyamulagira is said to be the more interesting of the two.

The Ruwenzori Mountains: This whole region offers wonderful hiking and climbing opportunities (see *Backpacker's Africa* by

Hilary Bradt for details).

Virunga National Park: As long as you stay on the main road, you can drive through this game park for free. You can see quite a few animals if you take your time — there are always plenty of hippos lounging about. The Ruwenzori Mountains serve as a spectacular backdrop.

The Zaïre River: Load your vehicle on the riverboat and see Zaïre from its very heart.

Places to stay

Zaïre is the land of the gravel pit. With the jungle hugging the edges of narrow tracks, there is often little opportunity to pull over to camp for the night. Where there is a clearing, it is generally for a village. Some long stretches are practically continuous villages — from Gbadolite to Businga, the first 100km from Lisala to Bumba and along most of the route from Mobayi to Bumba via Yakoma. Throughout most of this vast country there are basically, therefore, only two options for places to stay — asking permission from the head man to stay in a village or making use of one of the many 'gravel pits' you will see — open excavated areas formed by digging out materials to surface the roads. Here are a few further suggestions.

Bambesa: The hotel here has camping and workshops.

Bukavu: *Hotel Belle Vue* is a very comfortable mid-range hotel with safe parking just along the road from the Burundi consulate.

Bumba: Look for a walled freight compound near the ferry, where two old Portuguese colonials are quite happy for you to stay, although immigration officials may insist you find an official hotel.

Bunia: There is a big *American Mission Hospital* where you can stay; it is also good for treatment of anyone who is very ill.

Businga: *Camping Picnique* is an excellent stopover by the river between Gbadolite and Lisala. Food is available.

Buta: The *Protestant Mission* will allow you to camp.

Butembo: You can camp in the grounds of the modern hotel just off the main road. The restaurant is quite amazing (can you believe *escargots* and *steak au poivre* out here?).

Epulu: The *Station de Capture* provides an excellent and restful camping stop — right next to picturesque rapids. One of the few chances of a real break on the long haul across Zaïre.

Goma: Was already difficult for overlanders before the Rwandan refugee crisis. It has been a no go zone for some time now. When things start to improve again there are several missions down by the lake which may put up travellers. Alternatively there is a large quarry about 7km beyond the airport to the north of town.

Kisangani: *Hotel Olympia* used to be one of the key stopping off points for overlanders in the whole of Africa, making it an excellent place to catch up on the latest news from the route up ahead. It is a good site with lots of room, a restaurant and a bar. There have been problems here including a robbery and attack on the owners. Check with other travellers to see if things have settled down again.

Lisala: The mission is a good place to stop but it does suffer from thefts and enormous mosquitoes. Immigration officials will probably insist you stay in an official hotel. There is a motel in the town with safe camping in the grounds.

Lubero: There is a deserted ranch on the right as you drop down towards the town. There is no roof but you can drive in and park there. Also in this region of the eastern highlands, there are several farms that provide camping. Ask the locals selling cheese by the side of the road or look out for signs.

Mount Hoyo: You can camp in the grounds of the hotel complex. The hotel itself is quite expensive; but if you camp you will be given access to a room anyway so you can use the shower.

Nyabibwe: About halfway between Goma and Bukavu there is an old tin mine — the sign says *Société Minière de Goma*. When the mine is not operating, the friendly maintenance team allows overlanders to stay in the dormitories.

Nya-Ngezi: There is a large Catholic seminary here on the track avoiding Rwanda from Bukavu to Uvira.

Oysha: The *American Protestant Mission Hospital* is a good place to stop. It has an area specifically for camping, at a nominal charge. Extra facilities added in recent years make it look as if it is being specifically developed for camping. Hospital facilities are available for those who are sick.

Rutshuru: *Hotel Grafende* is a very pleasant local hotel; parking is inside the compound behind locked gates. Also, about 2km south of town there is a track leading off to a grass clearing; there is a good camping spot here by the falls.

Virunga: *Rwindi Lodge* is very expensive but it is the only place you are allowed to stay within the park. There is a small and basic campsite just outside the southern gate which is a bit of a rip off; better to bush camp just beyond.

Yaligimba: About 50 kilometres east of Bumba, there is a track leading off into the plantations. There is a large *Catholic Mission Hospital* here, just a few kilometres off the road. The Italian sisters there do not get too many visitors as it is off the beaten track.

Sources of tourist information
Bureau du tourisme, Rue du Card Mercier 35, 1000 Bruxelles, Belgium.

Tourist office in Zaïre:
Kinshasa Boulevard 30 Juin, BP 9502; Tel: 9502.

Guide books: *Zaïre Africa Handbook*, Christa Mang (Bradt).

By boat on the Zaïre
The Zaïre river steamer between Kinshasa and Kisangani is quite justifiably reckoned to be one of the classic journeys of the world. Problems in larger towns and the switch to a more easterly crossing point from CAR, mean that few are currently taking advantage of it. But it should still be possible to take the river from Bumba to Kisangani.

The first thing to make clear is that, despite being referred to as a steamer, the form of transport involved is not a single boat at all — more of a floating village. A number of barges are linked together and nudged up and down the river, getting stuck on sandbanks, floating with the tides, drifting apart, breaking down and bit by bit inching their way through the jungle canopy to their final destination.

The decks are a colourful sea of people, goats, chickens and much more. This is home for many days (allow a fortnight for the full trip going upstream) so this is the space where people live, cook, eat and sleep. Cabins are available at a price but if you load your own vehicle on to the boat you are better off staying with it and sleeping inside.

Every inch of space is taken up by people and their goods — trading takes place all along the river as *pirogues* come out to meet the boats and exchange local produce. One traveller tells of the time he managed to track down a welcome crate of beer. Carrying it back to base he found that the only way through was to walk straight down the back of a tethered crocodile!

Cyclists and motorcyclists can join either at Lisala or Bumba, but those with larger vehicles will need to make use of the lifting gear which is only available at Bumba. It is important to keep a careful eye on the loading and unloading at Bumba and Kisangani — it is a precarious process and accidents have been known to happen. Your vehicle falling in the river could mean the end of your whole trip.

RWANDA

Area: 26,338km²

Population: 8.4 million

Capital: Kigali

Languages: Kinyawanda and French are the official languages; Kiswahili is also spoken.

Climate: Its high altitude gives Rwanda a pleasant year-round temperature averaging 23°C. The rainy seasons are in mid-January to May and October to mid-December.

Visas: Required by all except German citizens. Transit visas are available at the border.

Foreign embassies and consulates in Kigali: Burundi; **Germany** (Tel: 5222); **Tanzania** (PO Box 669; Tel: 76074); **Uganda** (Rue d'Epargne; Tel: 6495/6); **UK** (Tel: 5905); **USA** (Boulevard de la Révolution; Tel: 75601); **Zaïre** (504 Rue Longue; Tel: 5026).

Other red tape: Vaccination certificate for yellow fever and standard motoring documents are required.

Banks and money: Unit of currency is the Rwanda franc.

Public holidays: New Year's Day, Easter Thursday, Good Friday, Easter Monday, Labour Day (May 1), Whit Monday, National Holiday (July 1), The Assumption, Government Holiday (October 26), All Saints' Day (November 1), Justice's Holiday (November 24), Christmas Day (December 25).

Fuel: Available in Kigali.

Roads: Drive on the right. Very good roads throughout; mostly surfaced.

Routes: The main through route is from Goma to Kigali and on towards the southeast and the Tanzanian border. You can also head north from Kigali into Uganda. Driving from Bukavu in Zaïre to Bujumbura in Burundi it is also necessary to cut across Rwandan territory.

Places to stay

Rwanda was very difficult for travellers even before the war, with no campsites, little open land and an official policy against bush camping. If you do bush camp, be prepared for the police to come and move you along and even fine you. You are unlikely to stay long in the country — the best bets as long as you are here will be small hotels and the many Catholic missions.

Butare: The mission here has been recommended.

Sources of tourist information
Tourist office in Rwanda:
Kigali Office Rwandais du Tourisme et des Parc Nationaux, Boulevard de la Révolution, BP 905; Tel: 6512.

BURUNDI

Area: 27,834km²

Population: 6.1 million

Capital: Bujumbura

Languages: French and Kirundi are the official languages; Swahili is also spoken.

Climate: Mild and pleasant over most of the country but hot and humid near Lake Tanganyika. Rainy seasons are from October to mid-December and from mid-January to May.

Visas: Visas are required by all. South African citizens are not admitted.

Foreign embassies and consulates in Bujumbura: Belgium (Avenue de l'Industrie; Tel: 3676); **France** (Tel: 3176); **Germany** (Tel: 3211); **Rwanda; Tanzania** (Chaussée Prince Louis Rwagasore); **USA** (Avenue des Etats-Unis; Tel 223 454); **Zaïre**.

Other red tape: Vaccination certificate for yellow fever and standard motoring documents are required.

Banks and money: Unit of currency is the Burundi franc. Most banks will give cash advances and sell travellers cheques on a credit card.

Public holidays: New Year's Day, Easter Monday, Labour Day (May 1), Ascension Day, Whit Monday, Independence Day (July 1), The Assumption, UPRONA Day (September 18), Rwagasore Day (October 13), All Saints' Day (November 1), Christmas Day (December 25).

Fuel: Available in Bujumbura and some other towns; prices are reasonable.

Roads: Mostly very good. Drive on the right.

Routes: The two main routes converge on Bujumbura from Bukavu and Kigali. The best route into Tanzania is via Kayanza (the *Auberge Kayanza* is a great place for lunch), Ngozi, Muyinga, Kabanga and Rulengé. A wonderful and cost-effective route down to Zambia is to take your vehicle on the river steamer down the length of Lake Tanganyika from Bujumbura.

Places to visit
Bujumbura: A pleasant town with good beaches along the shores of Lake Tanganyika.

Gitega: Has the national museum and is also the home of the world famous Burundi drummers (there are regular performances).

Places to stay
Bush camping is possible — although the density of population can make it difficult.

Bujumbura: The *Viguzu Mission*, which is run by Americans, is recommended by many travellers. The university has a residential compound which generally has rooms to spare if you manage to make contact with any of the Western teaching staff. *Hotel Résidence* is a reasonably priced hotel near to the centre with large rooms and a car park.

Gitega: Try the *Catholic Mission*.

Sources of tourist information
Tourist office in Burundi:
Bujumbura Office National de Tourisme, BP 902; Tel: 2023/30 84.

THE LAKE TANGANYIKA STEAMER
The best route south from Burundi to Zambia is to load your vehicle on to the boat in Bujumbura and enjoy the four-day cruise down Lake Tanganyika to Mpulungu.

Arrangements should be made at the shipping office in Bujumbura. You will need to reserve a cabin in advance, but do make sure you get on the boat early as they go on a first come first served basis and the ones at the front of the deck are infinitely preferable to the ones below deck.

There are beautiful views all the way down the Tanzanian coastline. The ship anchors off a series of small coves, where *pirogues* swarm out to meet it. All in all, it is a colourful, relaxing and economic way of heading south.

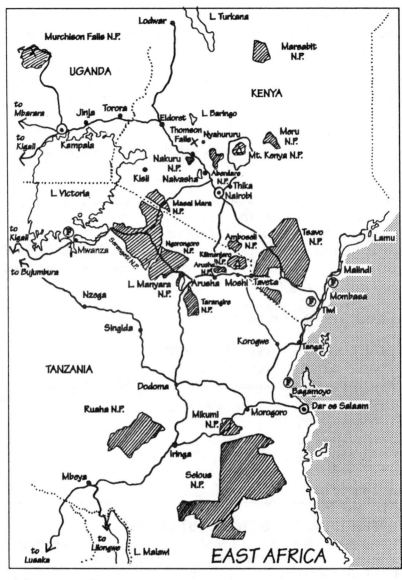

EAST AFRICA

Chapter Eight

East Africa

It is a wonderful feeling to break through into the cool highlands of East Africa after the sweat and grime of the steamy central jungle. Not only can you start to choose your own routes again but simple things like picking up supplies suddenly seem so easy. Then you finally arrive at the beautiful clear blue Indian Ocean, with its long beaches, coral reefs and cool breezes.

Eastern and southern areas are much easier to travel in than any of the areas covered by previous sections. If you have chosen a trans-African route, this is where you can finally allow yourself a holiday. If you have come up from the south, this is where the rest of Africa begins. Most overlanders laze on the beach for a while, take in a few game parks and eat massive quantities of the excellent food — Indian cooking in particular is both of good quality and available everywhere.

The east is also an ideal area to fly into direct and hire a car locally. Two-wheel drive will be fine in most places but if you want to get off the beaten track, four-wheel drive vehicles are available from all the main hire companies in the bigger towns.

ROUTE GUIDE

There are basically two ways into East Africa from the west — passing one side or the other of Lake Victoria. To the north of Lake Victoria, the most interesting route passes through the beautiful Ruwenzori Mountains into Uganda, across to Kampala and into Kenya just below Mount Elgon.

To the south, you can enter Tanzania either from Burundi or Rwanda — once this area is again open to travellers. Nearly all roads in the west and north of Tanzania are very bad indeed (with the exception of the beginnings of a new road leading from Rwanda, which is ultimately planned to link Kigali and Dar es Salaam).

From this northwestern corner of the country you can head for Kenya, via Mwanza, Serengeti and Arusha. The alternative is to head southeast to Nzega, Singida and Dodoma. From Dodoma you can either follow the good new road to Morogoro and Dar es Salaam or take the dirt road south to Iringa and then on to Mbeya. This is also the point of entry for all those coming from the south.

Roads within Kenya are generally very good and your route will be determined by what you want to see, rather than ease of communications.

To the north, it is now possible to enter Ethiopia at Moyale — although be sure to check on convoys as a protection from bandits between Isiolo and Moyale. There is a good direct road from here to Addis Ababa. The best route then goes via Lake Tana and Gondar north into Eritrea. Cross into Sudan at Kasala.

TANZANIA

Area: 945,037km²

Population: 28 million

Capital: Dar es Salaam — although some offices have moved to Dodoma, which is planned as the new capital by the end of the 1990s.

Languages: The national language is Kiswahili; English is also widely spoken.

Climate: Hot and humid along the coast (particularly from December to March); rains come from April to May and in November. On the central plateau covering most of the country it is warm and dry (average 27°C); it is a little cooler in the highlands.

Visas: Visas are required by all apart from citizens of the Commonwealth, Ireland and Scandinavian countries. In 1993 UK citizens were required to have a visa, so check in advance. Exceptions require a visitor's permit — but this is not always insisted on at quieter borders.

Foreign embassies and consulates in Dar es Salaam: Australia (IPS Building, Samora/Maktaba Street; Tel: 24292); **Burundi** (Lugalo Road; Tel: 29281); **Canada** (38 Mirambo at Garden Avenue; Tel: 46000/9); **Egypt** (24 Garden Avenue; Tel: 22857); **France** (Bagamoyo Road; Tel: 34961); **Germany** (NIC Investment House, Samora Avenue; Tel: 23286); **Kenya** (NIC Investment House, Samora Avenue; Tel: 31502); **Malawi** (IPS Building, 9th Floor); **Mozambique** (25 Garden Avenue, Upanga; Tel: 33062/8); **Rwanda** (32 Upanga Road; Tel: 46502); **Switzerland** (17 Kenyatta Drive; Tel: 66008); **Uganda** (Floor 10, IPS Building, Azikime Street; Tel: 46256); **UK** (Hifadhi House, Samora Avenue; Tel: 29601-5); **USA** (36 Laibon/Bagamoyo Road; Tel: 66010); **Zaïre** (438 Malik Road; Tel: 23452); **Zambia** (5-9 Ohio Street/Sokoine Drive, Upanga); **Zimbabwe** (Longido Street, Upango; Tel: 34896).

Other red tape: Standard motoring documents and vaccination certificate against yellow fever are required. Tanzania is the only country in east and southern Africa which requires a cholera certificate. On entry you pay US$90 for a vehicle plus $3 road tax. Road tolls inside the country have been abolished.

Banks and money: The unit of currency is the Tanzanian shilling. There is no longer a currency declaration on entry though it is still illegal to import or export Tanzanian currency. Banking hours are 8.30am-12.30am Mondays to Fridays and 8.30am-11.30am on Saturdays. In major towns some banks are also open in the afternoons. In Dar es Salaam the Forex Bureaux offer better exchange rates than banks. Upmarket hotels will expect to be paid in hard currency but most moderate and budget places prefer local currency.

Public holidays: New Year's Day; Zanzibar Revolution Day (January 12), CCM Day (February 5), Good Friday, Easter Monday, Union Day (April 26), Workers' Day (May 1), Farmers' Day (July 7), Independence Day (December 9), Christmas Day (December 25). The Islamic holidays of Aid el-Fitr, Aid el-Haj and Mouloud are also observed, on dates varying from year to year.

Fuel: Can be difficult to find in the huge remote west of the country. Price isn't bad — but is a little more than in either Kenya or Burundi.

Roads: Drive on the left. What were amongst the worst roads in Africa are now much improved. The road from Dar es Salaam to Arusha and on to Moshi is now finished. Even the Bagamoyo coast road has been repaired though beware of regular speed bumps.

Routes: From Rwanda you can drive south of Lake Victoria on the dreadful road to Mwanza, then on mostly good surfaced roads to Serengeti and through the park to Ngorongoro Crater and Lake Manyara. Continue on the main road to Arusha and up to Kenya. Alternatively, the more southerly road from Rwanda and Burundi has some excellent brand new sections, but then it takes you back onto bad potholed earth roads through Nzega and Singida to join the road either north to Arusha or south to Dodoma. From Dodoma you can head east on a good tar road to Dar es Salaam or south to Malawi and Zambia. One further option is to cross from Burundi at the Mugina-Manyovu border and head to Kasulu (fuel and change available), then take the poor road running parallel to Lake Tanganyika all the way to the south. This is a beautiful and remote route — but it would be just as cheap to take the boat from Bujumbura to Mpulungu.

Places to visit
Tanzania has some of the best game parks in Africa. Charges for foreign-registered vehicles are high — usually US$20 per head plus $150 for a truck. Camping is $20 per head. The game parks are very strict about timing your 24 hours — if you are half an hour

over you have to pay again. Because of these high charges most overland trucks use local operators for game park safaris.

Arusha: The main centre for organised tours to the surrounding game parks. This has traditionally been a key centre for selling vehicles and equipment — but the process is far from easy. The main problems encountered are with customs documents, currency declaration forms and bans on exporting hard currency. Security is a big problem in Arusha — people have been held up and vehicles broken into.

Bagamoyo: Excellent beaches and a faded colonial waterfront with some older buildings dating back to the Omani slave traders; fishing boats bob through the waves. There is an excellent museum in the Holy Ghost Mission, the oldest church on the East African mainland. The 12th century Shirazi ruins at Kaole, 5km from the modern town, are also worth a visit.

Dodoma: Officially the capital, Dodoma remains a sleepy and dusty town with a bustling central market.

Gombe National Park: Only accessible by boat from Lake Tanganyika so not many people make it here — but it is a magical place. You can see chimpanzees in the wild here but fees are high — it is cheaper to see chimps in Uganda. Boats leave from Kigoma town.

Kilimanjaro: The highest peak in Africa and quite a thrill to climb — it can be cheaper to make arrangements at the park gate rather than booking in Moshi though the risk of things going wrong is greater. Low cloud means you generally have a better chance of actually seeing the peak from the Kenyan side.

Kizimkozi: You can arrange to swim with dolphins here through local boat owners.

Mwanza: Tremendous bustling and colourful market town with a strong Asian influence. Centre of the cotton industry. The ferry service to Kenya was discontinued in 1993 with the completion of a good tar road between Mwanza and Kisumu.

Lake Natron: Away from the major tourist trails, this is a beautiful and remote place. Take the track that leads off the Makuyuni-Manyara road, just south of Mto Wa Mbu.

Ngorongoro Crater: Utterly unmissable — an amazing sight: the largest intact volcanic crater in the world (you could fit the entire city of Paris inside it). Once you drop down its steep walls, you are in one of the richest areas of game it is possible to imagine.

Olduvai Gorge: Between Ngorongoro and Serengeti, this is the site of Richard Leakey's most famous excavations, where some of the oldest remains have been found of the forerunners of the human race.

Serengeti: The best known game park in Africa and one you should not really miss. Apart from the great migrations of wildebeest and zebra in May or June, it is also excellent for lion, other big cats and most game.

Tarangire National Park: Hailed as the best Tanzanian park for elephants and the worst for tsetse fly. Basic camping facilities.

Zanzibar: There are three ways to reach one of the most beautiful islands in the world — local ferry (2-4 hours), hydrofoil (1 hour) and plane (20 minutes). The ferry has gone up to US$30 + $5 departure tax both ways so it's worth checking out flight prices, especially for a group as you can negotiate discounts. Make sure you find secure parking for your vehicle at the airport or at an hotel.

Places to stay

Larger hotels are ridiculously expensive and not particularly good. They must be paid for in hard currency. Campsites in the game parks are also expensive and require hard currency. Small local hotels and campsites are the best bets. Free camping is generally safe apart from the stretch between Korogwe and Moshi.

Arusha: The best place to stay is at the *Masai Camp*, 2 miles out of town on the old road to Moshi. It has workshop facilities, good security, a restaurant and bar. The *Arusha Vision Campsite* next to the Equator Hotel on Boma Road has also been highly recommended. Also camping at Lake Duluti, 12km along the main road to Moshi.

Bagamoyo: The *Badeco Beach Hotel* has camping facilities.

Dar es Salaam: There is nothing in the city itself but 20km north along the Bagamoyo Road at Kunduchi Beach there are two sites to choose from. The *Rungwe Oceanic* is used by overlanders despite increasing reports of theft. The *Silver Sands* is a beach hotel owned by the university but it also has a small expensive camping area. If you do need to stop the night in the city itself, the *Hotel Kilimanjaro* does have secure parking — but it is difficult to square the expensive prices with the facilities.

Dodoma: The *Dodoma Inn* is an exceptionally good hotel by Tanzanian standards and has safe parking. Not as expensive as it looks.

Game parks: All game parks have camping areas but they are incredibly expensive with few facilities.

Iringa The *Hotel Isimila* is a cheap local hotel with guarded parking.

Korogwe: The *Korogwe Travellers' Inn* is a cheap local hotel with safe parking.

Lake Manyara: Camp at the *Karatu Safari Camp* in Mtowa Mbu, a small town just outside the park gate (lots of space, showers, bar, restaurant). You can book trips by jeep around Ngorongoro Crater here for around US$100 a day.

Mbeya: The last 100km before you reach the Malawi border has villages all the way, so bush camping can be difficult. There are several hotels in Mbeya itself and the Langiboss Hotel in Tukuyu has been recommended as a base to explore the region.

Mbuyuni: There is a hilly area near here with a forest of baobab trees and a waterfall. It is a good place to camp.

Moshi: You can camp behind the *Keys Hotel* for US$5 per head and behind the *Golden Shower* restaurant for $2-3. The *Moshi Hotel* is one of the better hotels in Tanzania and is not as expensive as many that are of a far lower standard.

Mwanza: No camping. But to the south there is an old mission signposted as you come off the ferry from Buisisi. You can camp on the lawns.

Ngorongoro Crater: The only reasonable options in the park are the basic campsite at *Simba Camp* (US$20 per person) or the institutional but fairly expensive *Rhino Lodge*. If you do want a treat, it is much better to stay the night at *Gibbs Farm*, along the road between Lake Manyara and Ngorongoro, near Karatu. Run by an English couple, the place offers the most wonderful food you can imagine in a very British style. There are several cheaper places to stay around Karatu such as *Safari Junction Campsite*.

Sources of tourist information
Tourist offices in Tanzania:
Dar es Salaam Maktaba Street.
Zanzibar Creek Road.

Guide books: *Guide to Tanzania*, Philip Briggs (Bradt); *Visitors' Guide to Kenya and East Africa*, Philip Briggs (Southern Books, RSA); *Kenya and Northern Tanzania, a travellers' guide*, Richard Cox (Kenway Publications); *Kenya, Tanzania and Seychelles* (Fodor); *Guide to Zanzibar*, David Else (Bradt).

KENYA

Area: 582,646km²

Population: 28.2 million

Capital: Nairobi

Languages: English is the official language and Kiswahili is the national language; many other African languages are spoken according to region.

Climate: Coastal areas are tropical and hot but tempered by monsoon winds. The wettest months are April, May and November; the hottest are February and March; the coolest are June and July. The lowlands are hot and dry. Much of Kenya, however, stands at over 5,000 feet and has a more temperate climate with four seasons. There is a warm and dry season from January to March; a rainy season from March to June; a cool, cloudy and dry season from June to October and a rainy season from November to December.

Visas: Visas are required by all apart from citizens of the UK and other Commonwealth countries (with the exception of Australia, Canada, India, New Zealand, Namibia, Nigeria and Sri Lanka), Denmark, Ethiopia, Finland, Germany, Italy, Norway, San Marino, Spain, Sweden, Turkey and Uruguay. Visas are normally obtained at point of entry but it is wise to check in advance as some nationalities may be refused visas at the border. The standard fee was £18 at the end of 1994.

Foreign embassies and consulates in Nairobi: Australia (Riverside Drive; Tel: 445034/39); **Burundi** (Development House, Moi Avenue); **Canada** (Comcraft House, Haile Selassie Avenue; Tel: 214804); **Eritrea** (New Woumin House, 4th floor, West Janols; Tel: 443164); **Ethiopia** (State House Avenue; Tel: 723027); **France** (Embassy House, Harambee Avenue; Tel: 339783; will issue visas for many of the French-speaking African countries not represented in Nairobi); **Germany** (Williamson House, Ngong Avenue; Tel: 712527); **Italy** (International Life House, Mama Ngina Street; Tel 337356); **Malawi** (Standard Street; Tel: 221174); **Netherlands** (6th Floor, Uchumi House, Nkrumah Avenue); **New Zealand** (Minet ICDC Insurance, 3rd Floor, Minet House, Nyerere Road; Tel: 722467); **Nigeria** (Kencom House, Moi Avenue); **Rwanda** (International Life House, Mama Ngina Street; Tel: 334341); **Sudan** (ICDC House, Moi Avenue); **Tanzania** (Continental House, Harambee Avenue; Tel: 331056/7); **Uganda** (4th Floor, Cooperative

Building, Haile Selassie Avenue; Tel: 330801); **UK** (13th Floor, Bruce House, Standard Street; Tel: 335944); **USA** (Corner of Moi and Haile Selassie Avenues; Tel: 334141); **Zaïre** (Electricity House, Harambee Avenue; Tel: 229771); **Zambia** (City Hall Annex, PO Box 48741); **Zimbabwe** (6th Floor, Minet ICDC Building, Mamlaka Road; Tel: 721071).

Other red tape: Standard motoring documents are required. You must also have vaccination certificates for yellow fever and cholera if travelling from an infected area.

Kenya has some of the toughest regulations against the sale of vehicles in Africa (safeguarding its own manufacturing base); Kenyan levels of duty greatly increase the cost of your carnet. On arrival it is necessary to buy local motor insurance. Within one week of arrival you need to get a temporary road licence from the ground floor of Nyayo House at the junction of Kenyatta Avenue and Uhurn Highway. This is free but you need to show your insurance in order to get it. You will need to show the licence when you leave or ship your vehicle out. Despite rumours to the contrary there are no problems taking foreign registered private vehicles into the game parks.

At the end of 1994 an Australian citizen working in Lamu was expelled for being a homosexual. Homosexuality is prohibited under Kenyan law.

Banks and money: The unit of currency is the Kenyan shilling. Banking hours are 9.00am-2.00pm Monday to Friday. Outside these hours you can change money at hotels and lodges. It is an offence to export Kenyan currency.

Public holidays: New Year's Day, Good Friday, Easter Monday, May Day (May 1), Madaraka Day (June 1), Kenyatta Day (October 20), Independence Day (December 12), Christmas Day (December 25), Boxing Day (December 26). The Islamic holiday of Ai el-Fitr is also observed, with the date varying from year to year.

Fuel: Readily available, except in the more remote areas. Reasonable price, slightly cheaper than in Tanzania.

Roads: Drive on the left. The main roads are excellent. Many of the minor roads are also good. You are unlikely to need four-wheel drive except in the game parks and remote northern areas. Both two-wheel and four-wheel drive vehicles are available for hire from the main centres.

Routes: Entry and exit will almost certainly be on the main roads leading in from Arusha or Tanga in Tanzania, Tororo in Uganda, or Moyale in Ethiopia. All roads converge on Nairobi. An excellent road then leads to the coast at Mombasa — which is a popular port for shipping vehicles. Those considering a trans-African trip in reverse or wishing to concentrate on east and southern Africa could ship their vehicle from Europe to Mombasa to begin there.

Motoring organisations: AA of Kenya, PO Box 40087, Nairobi.

Spare parts: Rufiki's, on the main Thika road out of Nairobi, is one of the best places in Africa to pick up second-hand parts for any vehicle.

Places to visit

Game Parks: A visit to a few game parks will be a must for most people while in Kenya. Although Kenya has done a great deal to make the most of the tourist potential of its wildlife, this has meant that some areas are saturated with visitors. The parks are therefore not always as interesting as in some less developed countries, but they are easily accessible. Admission costs are lower in Kenya than in Tanzania. For full details of the parks and where to stay in them, see *Camping Guide To Kenya* by David Else (Bradt).

Lake Borgoria: A good place to see flamingos. Camping is possible but there are no facilities.

Mount Kenya: The second highest peak in Africa and a great mountain to trek; although the lower slopes are safe for walking you should take a guide if you are planning a serious trek as it is easy to get lost with potentially fatal consequences in bad weather.

Kisii: The best place to go for supplies of soapstone sculptures. At the quarries in Tabaka Village they are a fraction of the price you will pay in Nairobi.

Lamu: Driving north from Malindi to visit this beautiful old Swahili island town is no longer a safe option. Quite a few vehicles have been held up.

Malindi: An old town with beautiful beaches, coral reef and sailing *dhows* bobbing in the water. Off-shore is the Marine National Park, with its incredibly rich variety of marine life.

Masai Mara: This is probably one of the best national reserves anywhere for seeing game.

Meru National Park: Easily accessible in your own vehicle with a good network of roads within the park itself. Despite this it sees very little tourism.

Mombasa: A beautiful old city bringing together African, Asian and Arabic influences — plus idyllic beaches stretching away to both north and south. The old quarter and the old harbour are essential to visit; Fort Jesus is the main tourist attraction.

Nairobi: The luxuries of eating and drinking in this highly developed city are very tempting for a while for those who have arrived overland. Nairobi has all the attractions of a lively big city, featuring the Nairobi National Park, a wonderful railway museum, an arboretum and much more besides. A free monthly listings magazine gives details of what's on. Also check posters for details of live music, theatre and dance. Be particularly vigilant about security and personal safety as mugging is a real problem.

Lake Nakuru National Park: Famous for its magnificent flock of flamingos, this small park also presents a chance to see other game such as warthog, waterbuck, water buffalo, impala, gazelle and giraffe.

Samburu National Reserve: Set in a beautiful range of fertile hills north of Mount Kenya, this is a good park for unusual species such as Grevy's zebra and reticulated giraffe. There is a well-equipped hostel and campsite about 4km south of Maralal.

Lake Turkana: A wonderful trip into the remote and ancient world in the north of the country. Four-wheel drive is recommended.

Places to stay

There are no restrictions on bush camping away from towns (except in national parks). For those planning a lengthy stay in Kenya, David Else's *Camping Guide to Kenya* (Bradt) lists all campsites in the country. It is available in Nairobi.

Lake Baringo: *Robert's Camping* is a good campsite by the lake with excellent facilities.

Eldoret: The *Naiberi River Camp* has a bar, meals and showers. It is 20km outside the town — coming from Nakuru the road is signposted about 2km before Eldoret. Campsite with good facilities

14km north of Eldoret. Take the Murram Road towards Soy and turn right after Kiplombe Primary School.

Kericho: You can camp in the beer garden of the *TAS Lodge* next to the Tea Hotel, and use the facilities. The new *TAS Hotel* on the edge of town also caters for campers.

Kisii: The *Kisii Hotel* is a nice old run-down kind of place.

Kisumu: There is camping in the gardens of *Dunga Refreshments*, a restaurant on the shores of Lake Victoria, 3km from the town centre.

Kitale *Sirikwa Safaris* about 10-12km north of town is a beautiful clean site in a garden with hot showers.

Malindi: The *Silver Sands* campsite is right next to the sea at the southern end of town. It is a pleasant place with a selection of hotel bars just along the beach.

Mombasa (Tiwi and Diani Beaches): The *Twiga Lodge* campsite at Tiwi Beach is an attractive site with good facilities, restaurant and bar, set right on a perfect beach with a coral reef stretching out before you. This is the place where overlanders have for many years rested after their long journey.

Lake Naivasha: *Safariland Lodge*, along the road to the south of the lake, is an excellent and comfortable place in a peaceful setting. It has a campsite. About five kilometres further round the lake is *Fisherman's Camp*, which also has a good campsite. You can visit Elsamere, the home of Joy Adamson, which has a troop of black and white colobus monkeys in the garden.

Nairobi: The *Kamuka* campsite opposite the west gate of Nairobi National Park has a workshop and tools available. There is also room for a few vehicles in *Ma Roche's* overcrowded and over-rated garden at 3rd Parklands (opposite the Aga Khan Hospital). The *Scout Camp* at Jamhuri Park (out along Ngong Road to the Jamhuri Park showground and follow the signs) is a good alternative with much more space and reasonable facilities (even a swimming pool), but it is well out of town and is sometimes over-used. The *Tea Zone Hotel*, Ngara Road (take the Limuru exit at the roundabout north of Moi Avenue, then second left) has a walled compound with 24-hour guard, friendly staff, lively bar and restaurant. Rooms are good value. 35km from Nairobi on the Kiserian to Isinya road the *Whistling Thorns* ranch has camping (US$10 per person in 1995). Swimming pool and cottage accommodation. Runs safaris and game and bird walks.

National Parks: All national parks have camping areas; see *Camping Guide To Kenya* by David Else for details.

Nyahururu: There is camping at the *Thomson's Falls Lodge* — which is right next to the falls themselves. The lodge is a wonderful old colonial style place with a bar that is just like an English pub — it even has a log fire in the grate.

Taveta: Just inside Kenya on the Tsavo road. Outside of the town is Lake Chala, a beautiful volcanic lake which is a good spot to camp. The lake is in the foothills of Mount Kilimanjaro and offers amazing views in the morning.

Sources of tourist information
Kenya National Tourist Office, 25 Brook's Mews, London W1Y 1LG; Tel: 0171 355 3144.
The Chief Tourist Officer, Ministry of Tourism, PO Box 54666, Nairobi.

Tourist offices in Kenya:
Mombasa Kilindini Road.
Nairobi Junction of Moi Avenue and City Hall Way (make sure you pick up copies of *Nairobi — things to see and do* and *Tourist's Kenya*).

Guide books: *Visitors' Guide to Kenya and East Africa,* Philip Briggs (Southern Books, RSA); *Rough Guide to Kenya*; *Kenya* (Lonely Planet); *Globetrotter Guide to Kenya,* Dave and Val Richards; *Insight Guide to Kenya* (APA Productions); *Kenya and Northern Tanzania, a travellers' guide* Richard Cox (Kenway Publications); *Kenya, Tanzania and Seychelles* (Fodor).

Bicycles and black cotton mud in the Masai Mara
by Christian and Gilly Lee
We stopped together at the point where a little track left the main road. As usual there were no signposts. Nairobi was 500 miles away, across the vast plains of the Masai Mara, some of the last

remaining wilds of Africa, and our track was swallowed by the bush after only 500 yards.

We had been advised not to tackle this route until the rains were over. But we had cycled right around Lake Victoria through the rainy season and hadn't got wet for over a week so we figured they must be over now. 'Goodbye tarmac, hello dirt track,' we sang as we turned our bikes onto the deep red soil. It seemed pretty well baked by the sun and we made good progress, though our appearance frightened small herds of impala who leapt gracefully into the safety of the bush.

But the rainy season had not ended. That night, camping in the bush and cocooned in our tiny tent, the rain cascaded down without mercy. Panic! The whole bottom half of our tent was afloat. There was a stream bubbling up beneath us. Should we get out and try to move and be half drowned or stay and suffer a little dampness inside?

We decided to stay where we were and slept with our legs tucked up under our chins as the river continued to gurgle a few inches away from our toes. Next morning the sun was shining again. We crawled out stiffly, stretched our cramped limbs and stood with sinking hearts as we looked at what had become of the track. Nothing was going to get through.

We were stuck in the middle of a quagmire of black cotton mud, which has the consistency of dough with the sticking powers of superglue. It was horrific. It wrapped itself around our wheels, which then become solidly stuck against our mud guards. The only solution when this happened was to push the bikes over on their sides, take off the wheels and laboriously pick out all the mud.

We seemed to be walking around on six inch platforms of mud, stuck to the soles of our shoes. Our hands became unrecognisable under an almost unnatural growth of the stuff. We would slide from one quagmire to another; we were losing the battle. It took us five hours to go 10 miles and things were looking desperate. We stopped for a rest and should have called it a day but we doggedly continued hoping that around each corner it might get better. But it got worse — it was a muddy sticky river where no traffic had passed for a long time.

The stress of it all brought on an almighty row, which marked the start of 36 hours of silence between us. Humour had long since sunk in the mud along with patience and civility. It was desperately hard and frustrating work. We tried dragging our bikes through the semi marsh and grass along the sides — but it wasn't much better and there was the added danger of snakes. We battled on in total silence.

We were actually riding along the borders of the Masai Mara National Park. There are no fences and plenty of game spills out onto this huge area of land. All day we passed herds of zebra and wildebeest, and saw the Thomson's gazelles grazing peacefully, lifting their heads suddenly with noses twitching as they smelt us approaching. Troops of baboons would bark a warning and scatter ahead of us; the little vervet monkeys kept giving us cheeky glances and disappearing up the trees to peer down at us safely from above. Two elephants foraged with their agile trunks pulling up long strands of succulent bush to eat; they just watched us carefully as we struggled slowly and silently past.

As the sun began to dip towards the endless African horizon, we came to the edge of an escarpment and looked down on views that made us and our quarrel feel small compared with their magnificence. The Masai Mara plains with their golden grasses and acacia trees shimmering in the distance gave a wonderful feeling of space. We sucked in the beauty of it all and descended exhausted down the winding track.

As we bumped our way down, large ominous clouds with spectacular lightening displays came crackling towards us. We could see them jettisoning their loads of rain over 20 miles away.

While bicycling through these areas we were concerned about the wildlife. Buffalo and rhinoceros, for example, are unpredictable. But the rhinos are now so rare it would almost be a miracle to come across one. We always found that as soon as the animals smelt or saw us, they would stir uneasily, stamp, break out and gallop away to safety. We always kept our distance, especially with elephants. As long as we gave no reason to appear threatening, they would always move away or pretend to ignore us while really watching us very carefully.

There on our bicycles in the middle of all this, moving so slowly, hearing every rustle in the bush, smelling every smell and feeling each breeze, we felt so much a part of it all. Our senses, like those of the animals around us, were constantly aware and alert — completely different to the sterile confines inside a car. People can become bored by watching an elephant from inside a car — you are not really a part of its world. But on a bicycle you have a one to one relationship with your surroundings.

We continued across the plains of savannah land towards the mountains in the distance. No longer muddy, the road had become hard and rocky. Although we bumped viciously along its path, it was a blessing in comparison with black cotton glue.

We were trying to make for a village to stock up on food again.

We were empty and hungry. The roads were not impossible but they had become dried out scars — the aftermath of the rainy season. At times we were performing perilous balancing acts along a foot-wide plinth in the centre of the road with three-foot trenches on either side, where trucks had gouged their way through. One mistake could mean the end of the trip, with a bent wheel or frame. Perhaps we should have walked but we were so hungry that our stomachs led the way.

Gilly stopped suddenly to say that she had heard a strange rattle. As she spoke, the whole front rack of her bike collapsed, wrapped itself around the wheel and finished up looking like a piece of modern art. It could have been disastrous if it had happened at speed. We took the whole thing off and shared her front load between us. Bumping along, we willed the road to end so that we could eat and rest ourselves and our poor bikes.

Eventually, with a final burst of strength that came from nowhere, we sped up to a dusty square. The villagers ran out and surrounded us. Nobody believed where we had come from and we didn't care. They showed us to their little café in a hut and we dived in. The Masai queued outside to take their turn to come in and inspect the two *Wazungu*. The owner was completely run off his feet, bewildered at how his quiet morning had come to such an abrupt end and his café suddenly turned into a cabaret act.

While a young Masai boy quietly took on the role of guarding our bikes outside for us, inside we were surrounded by at least 50 Masai, crammed into every possible space. We set the café alive as we went through our routine of pointing and basic Swahili to order some food. They all watched as, oblivious of our surroundings, we devoured goat stew and potatoes, two chapattis, one loaf of bread, four cups of tea and one huge sticky bun. The owner came up with questioning eyes, smiling at our empty plates.

'Same again, please!'

UGANDA

Area: 241,040km²

Population: 19.1 million

Capital: Kampala

Languages: English is the official language; a simplified form of Kiswahili is spoken as a second language, mostly in rural areas.

Climate: Uganda's position on the equator is tempered by its high altitude, giving it a very pleasant climate. The average temperature is 23°C. The rainy seasons are from March to June and October to December.

Visas: Required by all apart from citizens of the UK and Commonwealth and the EU, Iceland, Turkey, and the USA. In 1994 single entry visas were £10.00.

Foreign embassies and consulates in Kampala: Burundi (Nehru Avenue); **Egypt** (Plot No 33, Kololo Hill Drive; Tel: 61122); **Kenya** (60 Kira Road; Tel: 231861); **Rwanda** (2 Nakaima Road); **Tanzania** (6 Kagera Road; Tel: 257357); **UK** (10-12 Parliament Avenue; Tel: 257054/9 and 257301/4); **USA** (Parliament Avenue, Tel: 25972/3/5); **Zaïre** (20 Philip Road, Kalolo; Tel: 233777).

Other red tape: Standard motoring documents and vaccination certificate for yellow fever are required. Foreign registered vehicles must buy a 30-day temporary road licence on entry (US$20-100 depending on the weight of the vehicle).

Banks and money: The unit of currency is the Uganda shilling. There are no restrictions on importing foreign currency. Banking hours are 8.30am to 2pm, Monday to Friday.

Public holidays: New Year's Day, Liberation Day (January 26), International Women's Day (March 8), Good Friday, Easter Monday, Labour Day (May 1), Uganda Martyrs' Day (June 3), National Heroes' Day (June 9), Christmas Day (December 25), Boxing Day (December 26). The Islamic holidays of Aid el-Fitr and Idd Aduah are also observed, with their dates varying from year to year.

Fuel: Supplies variable.

Roads: There are no problems with main routes as the roads have been much improved. Drive on the left.

Routes: Uganda is currently the main route between east and west — it is also one of the most beautiful parts of Africa. The most common route is from Bunia and Mahagi in Zaïre, via Murchison Falls National Park and then south to Kampala. But it is also possible to go along the roads from Beni or Rutshuru to Fort Portal and then straight through to Kampala and Eldoret. The roads in the east follow some stunning scenery but are slow going The road from the Kenyan border at Malaba to Kampala is excellent.

Places to visit

Bwindi Impenetrable Forest National Park: Situated in southern Uganda, this is the richest forest in terms of different plant species, and one of the richest faunal communities in East Africa. There are two groups of habituated gorillas you can visit. It is advisable to book in Kampala. Charges are the same as for the Zaïre gorillas but without the additional cost of visas.

Jinja: A bustling market town with an attractive lakeside setting. The main market is on Saturdays.

Kampala: A pleasant town set in hills; a good place to meet up with other travellers.

Kibale Forest: This is the place to see chimpanzees in the wild plus ten other primate species and other mammals.

Kisoro: Right on the border with Zaïre, this is the base for visits to the gorillas in the Virungas. In 1994 trips cost US$120 plus $5 tax. Lodges are $5 a night with your own tent. It will cost you US$50-70 extra if you don't have a Zaïre visa, then $20 to re-enter Uganda.

Mount Elgon: Volcanic mountain rising to 4,322 metres, on the border with Kenya.

Murchison Falls National Park: This northern park is the site of the spectacular Murchison Falls — where the waters of the Nile force themselves between a gap of under seven metres and drop to the rocks 45 metres below. Hippos, crocodiles and birds are prolific and elephant are often seen along the river.

Queen Elizabeth (or Ruwenzori) National Park: Game park on the route into Uganda from the east, joining Zaïre's Virunga National Park.

Places to stay

There are lots of cheaper hotels but hardly any with secure parking. However, few people have security problems in Uganda. It should be safe enough to camp practically anywhere.

Entebbe: You can camp down at the lake.

Fort Portal: A new campsite with all facilities has opened on the edge of the golf course near the police station.

Jinja: You can camp at the yacht club.

Kabale: Most overlanders stay at *Sky Blue Julieta* or *Sky Blue Romeo* on the main road. The *Victoria Inn* has safe parking in a compound.

Kampala: Camping and rooms are available at the *Natete Backpackers' Hostel*, three miles west of town. You can also camp at the *Athena Club* though this is a bit dirty.

Lake Mburo: There is a rest camp with bandas and camping at this national park about four hours from Kampala on the Mbarara road.

Semliki Valley: VSO has set up a small campsite near Ntandi village.

Tororo: There is a seedy little motel here with safe parking.

Sources of tourist information
Tourist offices in Uganda:

Kampala Parliament Avenue; also try the Uganda Tourist Board, PO Box 7211; Tel: 232971/2. Maps are available from the Department of Lands and Surveys in Entebbe.

Guide books: *Guide to Uganda,* Philip Briggs (Bradt); *Visitors' Guide to Kenya and East Africa*, Philip Briggs (Southern Books, RSA).

ERITREA

Area: 124,320km²

Population: 2.5 million

Capital: Asmara

Languages: The main working languages are Tigrinya and Arabic. Italian is also still spoken by many of the older generation in Asmara, and to a lesser extent in Keren and Massawa. English is also widely spoken in the towns.

Climate: Eritrea has a varied topography so the climate is different in each of the three main zones. In the highlands, the hottest month is usually May with highs of around 30°C. Winter is from December to February, with lows at night that can be near freezing point. Asmara's climate is pleasant all year round. Short rains are in March and April, the main rains from late June to early September. On the coast, travel is not recommended between June and September when daily temperatures range from 40-50°C (and considerably hotter in the Danakil Desert). In winter months the temperature ranges from 21-35°C. Rain is rare, and occurs only in winter. In the western lowlands the rainy seasons are the same as the highlands; the temperature pattern is the same as that of the coast.

Visas: Required by all and available in advance from an Eritrean Embassy or Consulate. If travelling north through Africa, visas are available at the embassy in Addis Ababa. Proof of 'sufficient funds' is generally required (in the UK Consulate this is currently set at US$400 per person). Visas are issued for any duration up to a maximum of three months. Overland entry is permitted.

Foreign embassies and consulates in Asmara: Ethiopia (Franklin D Roosevelt Street; Tel: 116144); **Italy** (45 Shemelis Habte Street; Tel: 120774; Fax: 121115); **UK** (PO Box 5584; Tel: 120145; Fax: 120104); **USA** (34 Zera Yacob Street, PO Box 211; Tel: 123720/123410; Fax: 127584). A great meany new embassies have opened recently. All are easily located in central Asmara.

Other red tape: Vaccination certificate for yellow fever required. Major electronic items, such as video cameras and personal computers, that could be sold for profit in Eritrea, may have to be registered on arrival. Currency declaration forms are no longer issued. Birr cannot be taken from Eritrea to Ethiopia and vice versa. For overland visitors, the latest information is that carnets are not required, but you may be required to show some other proof that you intend to re-export the vehicle. Road licences should be obtained from the Road Transport Authority in Asmara (opposite St Mary's Cathedral). This is a swift and cheap process, and they can offer helpful advice on any other requirements. (As a general rule the bureaucratic quagmire that can engulf the overland traveller in Addis Ababa is not a feature in Asmara.)

Banks and money: The unit of currency is still the Ethiopian birr, but this may be changed in time. Currency can be changed in government-run hotels, at branches of the Commercial Bank of Eritrea, or the Red Sea Corporation in Asmara. Rates are better at the latter.

Public holidays: New Year's Day, Orthodox Christmas (January 7), Timket (January 19), Women's Day (March 8), Eid el-Fitr, Easter, Liberation Day (May 24), Martyrs' Day (June 20), Eid el-Adha, Start of the Armed Struggle (September 1), Orthodox New Year (September 11), Meskel (September 27), Eid Milad el-Nabi, and Christmas are among the major public holidays. The festivals of all major religions and interest groups are observed. It is not possible to give dates for the major Muslim festivals as these are determined by the lunar calendar.

Roads: A substantial road building project is underway. There are good tarmac roads between Asmara and Massawa, Keren and the towns to the south of the capital. The main road through the western lowlands (Agordat-Barentu-Tessenei) is currently being improved. Off the beaten track, particularly in the Denakil Desert, the going can be very tough. Eritrea is safe. Theft, for example, is not yet a feature of Eritrean life. There are only two security considerations at the moment: the border with Sudan is closed, so there may be areas close to the border where, for your own safety, you may be prohibited from travelling; in addition mines remain a problem, although not on main routes. If in doubt, ask at the local administration office and always stick to routes clearly used by others. Do not travel off the beaten track in the Danakil Desert, where you are always advised to find a guide.

Routes: As and when the border with Sudan opens, access to Eritrea is through Tessenei in the west, or Karora in the north. The main border crossing with Ethiopia is just south of Senafe. It may be possible to cross the border south of Tessenei, at Humera, but no foreigner has been known to take this route as yet. Access to Djibouti is possible, south of Assab. Petrol and diesel (gasoil) are readily available in major towns, but it is always as well to travel with adequate supplies. Although there are both Land Rover and Land Cruiser agents in Asmara, do not rely on major work being undertaken there. Spare tyres, mostly Korean or Chinese, can be bought in Asmara, Massawa and Assab.

Places to visit
Archaeological sites: To the south of Asmara are various remains from the Axumite period, the main ones being Qohaito and Metara. The ancient Axumite port of Adulis is one hour south of Massawa.

Asmara: One of the most beautiful capital cities in Africa, and certainly the safest. Many churches and markets and an interesting architectural mix. The centre of town is the long tree-lined Liberty Avenue.

Danakil Desert: Only to be visited with a guide as there is a danger of mines and the route changes constantly. Consult local authorities as you go if you intend to travel close to the border with Ethiopia. (There is as yet no up-to-date map of Eritrea. The track through the Danakil does not run along the coast as shown on most versions.)

Keren: The gateway to the rugged landscape of the mountains of northern Sahel, Keren is a quiet, pleasant town with much more of a Muslim atmosphere than Asmara. Interesting markets, and well-tended cemeteries for those killed in World War II.

Massawa: The port is reached via a spectacular three hour drive from Asmara, during which you descend some 2,500m. There is ample evidence of its history under Turks, Egyptians, Massawa is the start point for visits to some of the 209 Dahlak Islands.

Sahel Hills: North of Keren, this remote part of the country was the only area not occupied by Ethiopia during the long war for independence.

Places to stay
There is a wide range of accommodation in the major cities (Asamara, Massawa, Assab, Keren) from basic to comfortable hotels. Camping presents no problems.

Sources of tourist information
Guide book: *Guide to Eritrea*, Edward Paice (Bradt).

ETHIOPIA

Area: 1,104,200km²

Population: 54.9 million

Capital: Addis Ababa

Languages: The Oromo who speak Orominya are by far the most numerous ethnic group. Amharinya is the main spoken language in and around the capital. Tigrinya and English are also spoken.

Climate: The main rainy season is from June to September with lighter rains from February to April. The lowlands are very hot from April to June.

Visas: Required by all except citizens of Kenya and Sudan. Visas have been for entry only by air as overland entry to Ethiopia is not officially allowed — although overlanders have nonetheless found it possible to enter. See section *Driving through Ethiopia: 1994* by Edward Paice.

Foreign embassies and consulates in Addis Ababa: Canada (Higher 23, Kebele 12, House No 122, Old Airport Area; Tel: 71 30 22); **Cote d'Ivoire** (PO Box 3668; Tel: 20 12 12/20 12 14); **Egypt** (PO Box 1611, Tel: 11 31 63/06); **Eritrea** (PO Box 2175; Tel: 514302/2692); **Malawi** (Higher 21, Kebele 01, House No 377); **Mozambique** (Makamisa Road, PO Box 5671; Tel: 71 29 05/71 00 21); **Namibia** (Higher 17, Kebele 19, House No 002; Tel: 61 19 66/61 20 55); **Tanzania** (PO Box 1077; Tel: 51 81 55); **UK** (Fikre Mariam Abatechab Street; Tel: 161 2354); **USA** (Entoto Street; Tel: 55 06 66); **Zaïre** (Makanissa Road; Tel: 71 01 11); **Zambia** (PO

HISTORIC NOTE

Eritreans fought for 30 years to gain independence and in the process their country was severely damaged and tens of thousands lost their lives. Hundreds of thousands were driven from their homes. They are fiercely proud of their achievement, but at the same time bear no grudge against Ethiopia. The regime there has changed as well, and relations with the new government are good. It is as well to be sensitive to their recent history, and to respect the fact that there have been few tourists in the last 15 years. The people are very friendly, generous and helpful, disarmingly so in the countryside, and travellers should be aware that they are even more ambassadors of their respective countries than usual.

NORTHEAST AFRICA

Above: Eritrea, Africa's newest nation (E Paice)

Below: Lalibela, Ethiopia (G Roy)

EAST AFRICA
Above: Tanzania (H Bradt)
Below left: Samburu warrior, Kenya (H Bradt)
Below right: Local architecture, Rwanda (H Bradt)

SOUTHERN AFRICA
Above: Lake Malawi (P Cook)
Below: Hout Bay, South Africa (H Bradt)

NAMIBIA
Photos by N Dunnington-Jefferson

Box 1909, Old Airport Area); **Zimbabwe** (Higher 17, Kebele 19, House No 007; Tel: 61 38 72/7).

Other red tape: There is no limit on currency imported but currency must be declared on entry. Bank receipts are checked when you leave. See section *Driving through Ethiopia 1994* by Edward Paice.

Banks and money: The unit of currency is the birr. Changing money is straightforward in Addis Ababa. It is not normally a problem in other major towns, though the process may be tedious.

Public holidays: Ethiopian Christmas (January 7), Ethiopian Epiphany (January 19), St Michael's Day (January 20), Battle of Adowa (March 2), Good Friday and Easter Sunday (one week after the Gregorian Easter), May 1, Ethiopian New Year (September 11), Feast of the Founding of the Cross (September 27), St Gabriel's Day (December 28). The main Islamic holidays are also observed on dates varying from year to year.

Fuel: Can be hard to find and generally poor quality. Particularly difficult to find in the north, where you may have to pay two or three times the normal price for black market supplies.

Roads: Mostly poor but with some new tarred sections.

Routes: The best route through the country is from Moyale to Addis, Lake Tana, Gondar and Axum into Eritrea.

Places to visit
Ethiopia is one of the most culturally diverse and historically fascinating countries in Africa. Much of the country is mountaineous, fertile and breathtakingly scenic.

Awash National Park: Antelope, gazelles, baboons and monkeys but best for bird watching — in the wet season you are supposed to be able to see over 150 species in a day.

Axum: Was the capital of an empire which covered much of northern Ethiopia and beyond for over 1,000 years and the spiritual home of the 1,600 year old Ethiopian Orthodox Church. Archaeological sites dotted around the modern town include the highest obelisk erected in ancient times and a multitude of subterranean stone tombs and ruined palaces.

Bahir Dahr: The largest town on the shores of Lake Tana is the base for visits to the Blue Nile Falls (one hour's drive). The genuine island monasteries can only be visited by boat but in the dry season you can drive to within 2km of the island monastery on the Zege peninsula and walk the rest.

Bale Mountains National Park: Ethiopia's second highest mountain range is the place to see rare endemic mammals such as Simien fox and mountain nyala, as well as 16 endemic bird species. The road which crosses the national park between Goba and Dola Mena via the 4,000m high Saneti Plateau is the highest all-weather road in Africa and spectacularly scenic.

Gambela: A lazy fading colonial port on the banks of the Baro River, a tributary of the Nile that is navigable to Khartoum. Beyond Gambela is the attractive but little visited Gambela National Park.

Gonder: The 16th century capital of Christian Ethiopia has several castles enclosed in the Royal Compound. Outside the town the Church of Debre Birhan Selasie is magnificent with painted interior walls depicting biblical stories and Ethiopian saints.

Harer: Old walled city near the Somali border which is the spiritual centre of Ethiopia's Muslims. It has been described as atmospheric and friendly, possibly because activity centres around chewing mildly narcotic *quat* leaves.

Lalibela: The medieval churches of Lalibela, carved from solid rock, are considered by many to be one of the wonders of the ancient world. Unmissable.

Omo Valley: The wilderness areas of the Omo and Mago National Parks are home to some of the most remarkable ethnic peoples in Africa — it is said that until a few years ago most people in this region had never even heard of Ethiopia. The best bases for visits are Konso, where you can camp at a mission, and Jinka.

Rift Valley Lakes: The string of lakes that runs through the southern Rift Valley offers great birdwatching, particularly at Zwai. The scenic Nechisar National Park is near Arba Minch.

Simien Mountains: Breathtaking scenery with the mountain roads following the contours through a series of hairpin bends, sweeping along ridges and winding their way along the edges of valleys.

Places to stay

Arba Minch: Camping in the grounds of the *Bekele Mola Hotel*, and also in nearby Nechisar National Park.

Awash National Park: Camping beside the river with tap and long-drop toilets. Accommodation at the Kereyo Lodge in 'oven-hot caravans' is incredibly expensive.

Axum: Camping in the car park of the Hotel Axum. The *Kaleb Hotel* has inexpensive self-contained rooms and safe parking.

Bahir Dar: Camping at the hotel *Ghion* which also has cheap meals. 185km from Nifas.

Bale Mountains: Camping at the *Dinsho Lodge*. No food available.

Dila: You can camp at the *Italian mission* just past the barrier on the north side of town.

Gonder: Camping in the car park of the *Terara Hotel*.

Harer: The *Theodros Hotel* has inexpensive self-contained rooms and safe parking.

Lake Langano: Camping at the *Bekele Mola Hotel* which also has reasonably priced rooms.

Lalibela: The *7 Olives Hotel* has expensive rooms but you can pay to camp in the car park. Other hotels are cheaper but there is no safe parking.

Mekele: The *Green Hotel* has cheap rooms.

Nifassmewchja: The *New House* hotel has a locked compound, at this village 146km from Dilb along the new Chinese built road from Weldiya to Bahir Dar.

Wondo Genet: The *Wabe Shebele Hotel* next to the springs has rooms and allows camping. In nearby Shashemene the *Bekele Mola Hotel* is better value for money and has safer parking.

Sources of tourist information

Guide book: *Guide To Ethiopia*, Philip Briggs (Bradt).

Ethiopia — a drive into the unknown

by Gavin and Val Thomson

A week later than planned we left Nairobi to join the convoys heading to the Ethiopian border from Isiolo. Next morning we arrived at the police checkpoint at 7.15am to see the 7.30am convoy disappear in a cloud of dust. As it had no escort anyway, was very quickly spread out and we'd been assured that there was no danger from the Somali bandits in this part of northern Kenya, we headed off on our own along the atrocious corrugated road through semi-desert scrub.

We stayed that night in an Ethiopian-run 'hotel' in Marsabit — a town perched in incredibly green hills which are often mist-enshrouded in the mornings even though the desert is only half an hour away. The local police had said a convoy with armed police would leave from the village of Turbi, some 80km from Marsabit. The road turned out to be 130km and ran across an enormous barren rocky plain — obviously a safe route as nothing broke the skyline except the occasional camel-train.

At Turbi we joined an 8-truck convoy with several armed police riding shotgun on top of a truck or two and set off at 1.30pm amid great clouds of dust. Although the border town of Moyale was only 120km away it was 7.15pm before we arrived, having waited for 50 minutes in a village for no apparent reason and then twice for 45 minutes while drivers mended punctures.

We decided to ask the police for a suitable hotel and were taken to the Hotel Minden with a sign on the stairs reading: 'The Management Prohibits Prankerdness, Chewing Miram, Prostuitior, Lateness and Reserves the Right to Wake Up at 2.00am, No Untidness'. A bucket of water to sluice some of the dust off completed the extensive amenities.

This was Val's birthday and her birthday spread, a meal of lumpy rice and nameless stew, cost 40p for two. This was our first sample of the Ethiopian national dish of wat and injera — a bread of sour millet paste made into a thin pancake about 2 feet in diameter and bearing an uncanny resemblance to a sheet of thin grey foam-rubber! This is used for scooping up the wat, a thin stew of tough beef, chick peas or whatever.

On crossing the border into Ethiopia a few changes were immediately apparent. Firstly the language and alphabet were Amharic and completely incomprehensible — this was not too important, however, as there were no road signs. Secondly we were now labelled 'ferenji' not 'msungu'. The bank was unable to change money, having run out of official receipts, though the manager offered to change on the black market for us. We declined.

In no time we felt we'd left Africa behind as so many things were different. The land was very green, the whole feel of the villages and fields was of medieval Europe. A visit to Shashemane revealed this was the first country in our travels where it was possible to buy a good cup of coffee. Obviously it wasn't just the driving they learnt from the Italians. Every village seemed to have a 'Pastery' with an espresso machine — appropriate, really, as Ethiopia is probably the original home of the coffee bean.

At last on the Monday morning we were able to change money and full of birr (pronounced beer!) we headed for the Bale Mountains. Vast state farms spread over rolling plains, *tukuls* (huts) gathered behind neat reed fences, horse and mule riders muffled in cloaks herded goats. These scenes gave way to foothills, juniper and hagenia forests and the climb up to 3,500m where the park had a choice of a self-catering guesthouse or a campsite. We chose the former bearing in mind the temperature — the Swedes who built the pleasant guesthouse must have had this in mind too as they had included a sauna!

Unfortunately, the first manifestation of the legendary Ethiopian bureaucracy crept into our lives as we not only had to pay for using the sauna, we also had to pay separately for the wood it used. There were separate charges for using the kitchen (no choice), us entering the park, our car entering the park, staying in the guesthouse, our car not staying in the guesthouse or using the loo.

We were fascinated on our descent when we passed through a stream of locals returning from a market. Weather-beaten faces peered from under wide-brimmed hats, becloaked horsemen cantered by in the rain, loads of thatch or produce bent the walkers' backs - it was like driving through a scene in *Henry V*!

The campsites in the southern sector of Awash National Park are beautifully situated under huge fig and acacia trees on the banks of the Awash river. Nearby we saw a colourful collection of birds including the bluest of blue Abyssinian Rollers and the very red Blackbilled Barbet.

In the northern sector of the park we drove to Filwoha Hot Springs which featured thousands of palm trees, millions of biting sand-flies and very little else. We'd just erected our side-awning against the fierce sun when rain started lashing down — it's been used as an umbrella far more often than as a sunshade!

By morning the hoped-for Hamadryas baboons had not made an appearance so we headed off towards the hot springs resort at Sodere. On the way kids held up guinea fowl for sale — at other times we'd been offered tortoises, porcupines and an owl. Coupled with the widespread deforestation it was clear the conservation message is tragically late getting to Ethiopia.

Then came Addis... Our intended three-day stay became 12 and we loathed almost every minute of it! On the very first afternoon the Landie was broken into via two padlocks and a door lock. A basket of belongings including our binoculars was stolen. To put it mildly the police were unhelpful in the extreme. We'd been parked outside the Department of Road Transport where we were beginning an epic attempt to obtain compulsory Ethiopian driving licences and number plates for the car.

We found it impossible to obtain any information about shipping the car from anywhere to anywhere so we decided on a re-route through Sudan and Egypt to Suez. This meant four days hanging around waiting for visas.

We finally left Addis for a town called Dese. It was 425km away along a road that if it wasn't potholed was unnervingly undulating, making all nine hours of driving very tiring. Between Dese and Weldiya there were numerous wrecked tanks, trucks and missile launchers. These became all-too-common sights, uglifying the truly breathtaking mountain scenery which Ethiopia has in abundance. At Weldiya we turned onto the superb Chinese-built road which climbs and climbs in a series of hairpin bends until it reaches a plateau.

Lalibela and its 11th century rock-hewn churches are extraordinary — one of the little-known wonders of the world. Some had been completely separated from the surrounding rock before having their interiors beautifully carved. Others were caves, still part of the solid rock although you could walk right round them. Still others were carved from a wall of rock and several of them were attached by one wall. All were of soft red rock, many with pillars and shaped windows, and all had legends attached to their building. They were as impressive an achievement in their own right as the pyramids — well worth the six hour's rough drive!

Back to the Chinese road and the spelling conundrum of Nifassmeowtchja, where a room in the local hostelry cost all of $1! The next morning we passed through the enchantingly named GobGob before passing through another obvious tank battleground. Our next stop was in Bahir Dar on the shores of Lake Tana — the third source of the Nile we had seen.

We managed to take in some of the sights of Gonder which are not inconsiderable. The royal castle compound consists of a range of grand walls, keeps, towers and other structures. The church of Debre Birhan Selasse (Holy Trinity) was tiny inside but magnificent, the walls entirely covered in vivid paintings.

We headed north through the Simien Mountains — yet another range of utterly spectacular peaks, chasms, cliffs and hair-raising roads. Whole ridges of peaks like church spires dominated the horizon each time we climbed tortuously up the side of another ridge to be met with an unending vista of foothills rising to mountains in the distance.

In Axum we were stunned to be asked for $18 for camping in the hotel car park — wearily we bargained down to $6 before embarking on a search for the Eritrean representative. We eventually tracked him down only to be told he could only give permits to locals — which meant we would have to try the same exercise again in Mekele, the capital of Tigre and some 250km in the wrong direction.

The next day we were not at all surprised to find there was no petrol available throughout Tigre — by this time we had realised that whatever could go wrong would. On arrival in Mekele on a Saturday lunchtime we naturally found the Eritrean office shut but a very kind guy took us to the house of the secretary. But he refused to help, saying that the Chairman was in Eritrea for the long weekend and nothing could happen until Tuesday — two days after the expiry of our Ethiopian visas.

Three hours later we decided to head back to Addis where it didn't take long to decide that enough was enough. We were both very tired, physically from the arduous driving of the past week and mentally and emotionally from all the frustrations. So we decided to return to Kenya and unwind on the coast for a while before shipping back to England from Mombasa.

The first hurdle was getting an exit visa to leave via Moyale — our point of entry from Kenya. Remember that nothing is simple in Ethiopia — including getting out of the place. 'It is impossible to go out through Moyale,' was the bureaucratic reply, despite the fact we had entered the country there.

We had to produce a letter from the Ethiopian government (giving us permission to enter through Moyale) and our vehicle permit before we could collect our duly stamped passports the next day. Try not to get involved in Ethiopian bureaucracy — they make up the rules as they go along.

Driving through Ethiopia: 1994
by Edward Paice

Red tape: Although technically overland travel across the Ethiopian borders is still not allowed it is, in practice, perfectly possible, entering the country either at Senafe (border with Eritrea), or Moyale (border with Kenya). Carnets do not seem to be required, and border formalities are straightforward providing your visas are in order. Visas issued in Eritrea are very expensive (US$63), so obtain them in advance in your country of origin.

It was clear to me that nobody in Ethiopia, outside Addis Ababa, is clear about just what the regulations for overland travel are, and with rather more momentous issues to be decided by the new government it is likely to remain that way for some time. In Addis Ababa the civil service is still suffering from the conditions imposed upon it by the previous regime; asking someone what rules apply can unnecessarily set you off on a path of almost Herculean trials. As a general rule, being armed with confidence, politeness and an array of standard papers (carnet, insurance, driving licences, registration documents etc) will appease any official even if you are stopped in downtown Addis, and should be sufficient to show that you mean no wrong. Internal travel was virtually forbidden for 15 years so it is no wonder that you may be regarded with some suspicion.

My journey, taking six weeks from Senafe to Moyale, was from an administrative point of view relatively trouble-free. There was no bother at the borders. My main mistake was in Addis, trying to play things by a non-existent book. As nobody knows what the rules are this is a big mistake and can easily involve two or three weeks in offices in the capital. To dispel the two commonly accepted theories which had me caught up with relevant authorities: you do not need to register for Ethiopian plates, although some form of domestic licence is worth getting from the Road Transport Authority (allow a week!); and you do not need special permission to exit overland, although you do need standard exit visas (these can be obtained in a day).

Until the law is actually clearly defined, my advice would be that if you run into difficulties with paperwork, move on. Government is still devolved, and communication between the various parts of the country is minimal. For example, I was lucky enough to receive a promise from a senior immigration official that he would ensure smooth passage at the border post at Moyale, and I watched as he wrote the appropriate letter and despatched it. Three weeks later when I arrived there, they'd never heard of me, not that it mattered. I never had papers checked anywhere in the country, except at borders; only once was I stopped, without problems arising, in downtown Addis.

There is obviously one major exception to this rule: if you are not just going about your business as a tourist, but have committed some crime or misdemeanour, it goes without saying that they'll find you wherever you are, so do not expect release from custody to be swift or easy.

Practicalities: Both petrol and diesel are readily available within about 100 kilometres of Addis. Elsewhere there is obviously a severe problem, particularly on the route north. Your only option may be the black market. It is advisable to travel with as much fuel as you can carry. Once over the borders, fuel of both types is available immediately inside Kenya and Eritrea. While there are workshops in Addis, do not expect any major work to be undertaken. Tyres are also in short supply, especially in 4WD sizes, outside Addis, although as with fuel I found the situation better south of Addis than north.

Security: Although there are no areas currently billed as 'no-go', and escorts are not required anywhere, the following rules apply. Do not drive after dark on any account. You should treat the whole country as if there is a risk of banditry. In 1994 the Simien Mountains and the whole region east of Bale National Park were not safe. You will find it hard to find anyone who will tell you about the security situation in the regions, and even your own embassies may not have reliable information. The closer you are to the main arterial route though (Moyale-Addis-Senafe) the safer you are; proximity to the Sudanese border or, even worse, Somalia, makes the risk greater.

You should never leave your vehicle unattended, particularly in Addis where almost every overlander I have ever met has had their vehicle broken into (my advice: park it in a major hotel car park, and leave someone with it while doing whatever you have to do downtown).

General observations: I have met very few people before, during, or since who could claim to have enjoyed driving through Ethiopia. This has nothing to do with the condition of the roads. In travellers' parlance it is more of an experience. The sights, historic and natural, are magnificent but there is a price to pay. The level of hassle is almost intolerable even for the most thick-skinned; hotels and the food served therein are appalling. Most important of all, I found that there is an all-pervasive atmosphere of aggression.

While the tragic recent history of the country can be partly blamed, as can intense poverty and mass unemployment, it is striking that the atmosphere changes the minute you cross the border into Eritrea which has suffered exactly the same privations. In the towns to the north of Addis, on the historic route, the car was stoned, spat at, and one's unassuming presence was generally greeted with expletives. The car was shot at twice (I didn't wait to find out by whom).

The friendly face of Ethiopia
by Philip Briggs

In 1994 I spent four months travelling through Ethiopia gathering information for Bradt's recently published *Guide to Ethiopia*. I arrived in Addis Ababa with some trepidation, having read the sort of comments contained in the above letters.

I left besotted and enraptured with a country that is the most fascinating, warm and bizarre I have ever visited. Yes, once or twice I was frustrated by petty bureaucracy, but it was nothing serious. And on the credit side are the countless occasions when, as a visitor, I was pushed to the front of the queue, be it on buses, in post offices, in shops or in government departments.

I thought the budget hotels, when judged by African standards, were exceptional value for money. Ethiopian food, stewed in spicy *kai wat* sauce, is by far the most consistently tasty of any African country I have visited.

And sure, Ethiopians, particularly children and teenagers, can be massively irritating, but the endless yelling and performing is not, in my opinion, indicative of anything more than curiosity and insensitivity. Only rarely did I encounter unambiguous aggression. Far more often I found Ethiopian adults to be charming, dignified, friendly, humorous and overwhelmingly responsive to minor cultural adjustments on my part (like eating with my hands, drinking in local bars rather than government hotels and making the odd fumbling attempt at speaking Amharinya).

In many respects Ethiopia is a more difficult country to adapt to than most. It is certainly a country that evokes extreme positive and negative reactions — sometimes in the same individual in the same day (I can vouch for that). It is also, of all the countries I have visited, the one I miss the most — and many other people who have travelled in Ethiopia have the same feeling. I recently met two Israeli travellers who said it had become like a second home to them and whenever I meet other travellers who have been to Ethiopia we end up talking about it for hours.

The key to enjoying Ethiopia is, in my opinion, to accept it and to absorb yourself in it.

Chapter Nine

Southern Africa

There are many good roads throughout Southern Africa, with only some tracks in Botswana presenting any real problems. In South Africa itself, you will have the most comprehensive communications network in the continent to choose from.

The political transformation of South Africa has had a huge impact on overland travel. The local tourist industry has greatly benefited from a big increase in visitors and South Africans themselves now have the opportunity to travel north and explore the rest of the continent. South Africa must now be regarded as one of the best starting and finishing points for an overland journey — as well as providing some excellent shorter trips around the region.

ROUTE GUIDE

The excellent network of roads in South Africa means the entire country is accessible to travellers in two-wheel drive vehicles. However, many of the mountain tracks in Lesotho are difficult without four-wheel drive.

Routes out of South Africa depend on your destination — north from Cape Town into the magnificent desert landscapes of Namibia, from Mafeking up into Botswana and the Kalahari, across Beitbridge into the green highlands of Zimbabwe or east to Komatipoort and the relatively unexplored riches of Mozambique — cut off until recently by 16 years of war.

A particularly interesting route taking in the best of the region starts by heading north into Namibia and Fish River Canyon, along the minor but excellent dirt road via Helmeringhausen and Sesriem to Swakopmund. The whole region to the north of Swakopmund is worth exploring before heading through Etosha National Park and along the Cubango river to enter Botswana at Shakawe. Once improvements are complete, the road from here to Maun will be excellent. Continue north from Maun into Chobe National Park, where the soft sandy tracks make four-wheel drive a must. This takes you into Zimbabwe close to Victoria Falls. From here there is a good tar road to Bulawayo, Beitbridge and back into South Africa. Alternatively, the road network in Zimbabwe is excellent and the country is well worth taking time to explore.

From Zimbabwe there are also good road links into Mozambique or north to Zambia. The Tete corridor, linking Harare with Malawi across a narrow strip of Mozambique, was the only road that remained open during the Mozambique war, with Zimbabwean troops escorting convoys through the danger zone.

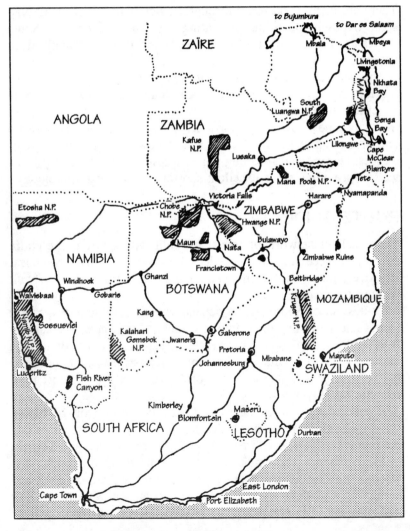

SOUTHERN AFRICA

Now that peace has come to Mozambique, this is the quickest route between Zimbabwe and Malawi.

Harare to Dar es Salaam by motorbike
by Wally Wilde

Many bikers dream of travelling through Africa on their machine. Only a few actually achieve it. On planning my trip I got a mixed reaction — either I was very brave or just plain stupid. Perhaps I was a little of both!

I started planning when I got an old 1982 R80 G/S BMW scrambler. I fitted track tyres and imported a 43 litre Paris le Cap tank from Germany for 2,100 South African rand. I made aluminium panniers and a carrier over the handle bars and made sure the bike was mechanically sound.

Then the red tape started. I had to join the South African AA to enable me to get a carnet for Zimbabwe, Malawi and Tanzania. Normally a *triptyque* would suffice for Zimbabwe and Zambia. A carnet is not valid in Zambia so we had to get a permit at the border at no cost.

In the past in South Africa you were required to deposit R6,000 with your bank as security for the AA but this has now changed. A small deposit of R500 is all that is required. In total the cost of joining the AA, the cost of the permit and a small medical insurance cost me R1,000.

I finally loaded my gear, tent, spares and first aid kit and set off with my wife by train from Durban station to Harare — which took 33 hours and cost R399. In Harare customs had to check the bike, logbook and third party insurance for Zimbabwe before the carnet could be stamped.

We headed straight for Kariba Dam, 379km away in terrific heat — at 50°C it was the hottest place of our entire trip. If you don't die of heat exhaustion, the mosquitoes will eat you alive anyway!

The real Africa starts as you cross into Zambia, winding down the valley below the dam wall and up the other side to a border post where a mass of travellers and migrant workers try to push their way through. The first 35km is a brand new road through scrub bushveld. At this stage the bike started missing and spluttering. With our hearts in our mouths we stopped a couple of times to check what was causing this, cursing the dirty fuel we must have picked up at Kariba, only to discover the tank bag was squashing the breather pipe on the fuel cap which was causing fuel starvation!

The road from Lusaka to Petauke must be one of the worst roads in Africa, with potholes in patches right across the road, so you can't weave around them. We met the most road blocks along this stretch of road and had to produce our log book, passports and vehicle permit each time — be warned!

175km from the Malawi border we discovered to our horror that the bag carrying our clothing was sitting too close to the exhaust which had burnt a hole through the bag. Most of my wife's clothing, wet suit and swimming costume were burnt beyond repair.

We crossed the border into Malawi at Mchinji and found the roads to be excellent. We were warned to get fuel at the border, but being the optimist that I am, we rode on — Lilongwe was only 125km from the border. But I had forgotten to fill up in Petauke. With many villages but absolutely no fuel available on this stretch of road, the inevitable had to happen. Fortunately Muzi, a local lad, happened to be walking along.

He first ran to the nearest village 500m away to ask if the local agent had any fuel. He returned to explain there was no fuel there but he would catch a bus to the next village, 7km away. He assured us he would return in an hour. We watched him stop a friend on his bicycle, pay him a fee and off he went down the road with a plastic 5 litre can which he fetched from home.

An hour on the dot and Muzi appeared carrying the 5 litre can filled with a substance which resembled fuel. By this time quite a crowd had gathered to watch the proceedings. We quickly filled the tank and made our getaway without properly remunerating Muzi for his trouble. We couldn't open our money belt among the crowd and only had enough local currency to pay for the fuel. We gave our address to Muzi and are hoping he will write giving us his address so we can reimburse him in some small way. The 5 litres of fuel was enough to get us to Lilongwe, only 25km away.

There are quite a number of traders on the road from Senga Bay to Salima, selling exquisite wood carvings and curios. You won't believe the prices and you can mail your purchases home. The vendors will pack it for you. Postage is apparently only Kw100 (R25) anywhere in the world.

There is a very scenic drive along Lake Malawi to Nkhotakota Bay on a really good road which takes you down a mountain pass of 21 hairpin bends to Livingstonia. The views of the lake are incredible. However, on reaching the bottom you will hit 100km of the worst road imaginable — this is a no-go stretch of road for a motor car. The entire road is breaking up and there is no alternative but to travel at breakneck speed so that you virtually fly over the bumps.

After the Tanzanian border control post at Vesamulu you will find the most incredible scenery with miles of banana and tea plantations.

We spent Christmas Eve in Iringa and were invited to a special dinner laid on in the restaurant of the Isimila Hotel where we witnessed the meat being brought in — a goat in a metal bucket, head and all, followed by a swarm of flies and a stench to match. We declined the offer of dinner and chose to see Christmas in with a packet of biscuits, biltong and peanuts in our room. Needless to say, we had an early night.

The next day the main road took us through the Mikumi Nature Reserve, which was alive with a huge variety of game — elephant, buck, giraffe, zebra, warthog, buffalo, birds and baboons, all in abundance. We were a little worried about travelling through by bike but luckily the five lions spotted lounging on the main road the day before had moved by then.

We arrived in Dar as Salaam just after mid-day on Christmas Day. It was incredibly humid with a mass of people swarming around. Constant police road blocks did nothing to relieve the traffic congestion. We found great difficulty occupying our days over the Christmas period as everything shut down for four days. To make matters worse, there was no electricity or water during the day from 6.00am to 9.00pm. Fortunately we discovered non-residents could use the pool at the Hotel Kilimanjaro for R6 a day, including a towel.

Once business reopened after the Christmas shutdown, we decided to ship the bike back to Durban. But be warned — this is an expensive option. Here is an indication of what this little exercise will cost you.

Shipping agent's fees (for the paper work)	R270
Harbour freight charges	R35
Shipping	R713
Road transport (from agent's offices to ship)	R110
Carpenter to build the crate	R135
Bill of lading	R40
Harbour fees	R75
Insurance — couldn't afford it!	
Unloading in Durban — wharfage fees	R167
Sub-total	R1,545
2 airfares from Dar Es Salaam to Harare (to catch our train)	R2,240
Total cost	R3,785

We definitely plan to do another trip with a small select group of true bikers in 1996 or 1997. If you are interested, write to Wally at PO Box 51200, Musgrave Road, 4062, South Africa.

SOUTH AFRICA

Area: 1,123,226km²

Population: 43.9 million

Capital: Pretoria (executive), Bloemfontein (judicial) and Cape Town (legislative).

Languages: There are 11 official languages including English, Zulu, Xhosa, Sotho, Tswana, Shangaan, Ndebele, Swazi, Venda and Afrikaans.

Climate: Most of the country enjoys a temperate climate, with warm summers and cool winters. The Natal coast can be extremely hot and humid in summer — at its height in February. The Western Cape has a Mediterranean climate with dry summers and temperatures of around 20°C from October to March.

Visas: Required by all apart from citizens of Australia, Botswana, Brazil, Canada, the EU, Israel, Japan, Lesotho, Namibia, New Zealand, Norway, Singapore, Swaziland, Switzerland, the USA and Uruguay. Visas are issued free of charge.

Foreign embassies and consulates in Pretoria: Australia (4th Floor, Mutual and Federal Building, 220 Vermuelen Street; Tel: 342 3740); **Canada** (the High Commission is in Johannesburg at Cradock Place, 1st Floor, 10 Arnold Street, Rosebank; Tel: 442 3130); **France** (807 George Avenue, Arcadia); **Germany** (180 Blackwood Street); **Lesotho** (343 Pretorius Street, 6th Floor West Tower, Momentum Centre; Tel: 322 6090-2); **Malawi** (First Floor, Delta Building, 471 Monica Road, Lynwood); **Netherlands** (First Floor, Netherlands Bank Building, Church Street); **Namibia** (Tulbagh Park, Eikendal Flat Suite 2, 1234 Church Street, Colbyn; Tel: 342 3520); **Switzerland** (818 George Avenue, Arcadia); **UK** (the Embassy is in Cape Town — 12th Floor, Southern Life Centre, 8 Riebeeck Street; Tel: 253 670; there are also consulates in Johannesburg, 19th Floor, Saulam Centre, Corner Jeppe/von Wielligh Street; Tel: 337 9420; and in Durban on the 10th Floor, Fedlife House, 320 Smith Street; Tel: 305 3060); **USA** (877 Pretorius Street; Tel: 342 1048; also consulates in Cape Town, Durban and Johannesburg).

Other red tape: Carnet and standard motoring documents are required. South Africa is part of a single customs unit, together with Botswana, Lesotho and Swaziland — so you should only need to get your carnet stamped on entering or leaving the area as a whole.

THE AUTOMOBILE ASSOCIATION OF SOUTH AFRICA

The AASA (or AA) provides the same services as the AA in Britain or AAA in the USA. They have a reciprocal arrangement with AA members in Britain allowing them to have roadside repairs, accommodation advice, route planning (including into the neighbouring countries), technical and legal services and so on. If you are planning to buy a vehicle or drive in southern Africa it would be well worth taking out membership. If joining in South Africa this costs R190 per year. For membership information phone 0800 010 101; for touring information (South Africa) phone 0800 111 999, and in neighbouring countries, 0800 010 7000.

Vaccination certificate against yellow fever required if travelling from an infected area.

Banks and money: Unit of currency is the Rand. There are banks in all centres of population.

Public holidays: New Year's Day, Good Friday, Family Day (the Monday following Easter Sunday), Constitution Day (April 27), Workers' Day (May 1), Youth Day (June 16), National Women's Day (August 9), Heritage Day (September 24), Day of Reconciliation (December 16), Christmas Day, Goodwill Day (December 26).

Fuel: Readily available at reasonable prices.

Roads: Excellent. Two-wheel drive is perfectly adequate — flying in and exploring with a hired car is a good option. Drive on the left.

Routes: The main points of entry are from Zimbabwe at Belt Bridge, from Botswana at Ramatlabama or from Namibia at Vioolsdrif or Nakop. After that you have the most comprehensive network of surfaced roads in Africa at your disposal. Cape Town is a popular port for shipping vehicles both in and out.

Motoring organisations: See box above.

Places to visit

South Africa has more than 300 game and nature reserves, 2,000km of coastline and extraordinary scenic variety.

Cape Town: South Africa's oldest settlement founded by the Dutch in 1652 is among the most beautiful cities in the world — a breathtaking combination of sea, sand and mountains, dominated by Table Mountain.

Cape Winelands: Not far from Cape Town, Stellenbosch is South Africa's second oldest city and one of its most atmospheric. It is also the heart of its main wine growing region. The surrounding mountains and wine estates are extremely beautiful.

Drakenberg Mountains: This extensive range of mountains extends into three of South Africa's provinces as well as occupying the entire highland plateau of Lesotho. The most beautiful part of the range stretches along the western border of Kwazulu-Natal and offers excellent hiking and walking particularly around the Royal Natal Park. Further south Giant's Castle reserve is recommended for large mammals and rock paintings.

Garden route: The stretch of coastline between Mossel Bay and Cape Saint Francis offers an endless succession of unspoilt beaches, lush coastal forests and scenic lagoons. Don't miss Knysna and the Storms River mouth in Tsitsikama National Park. The campsite at Nature's Valley is arguably the most beautiful in South Africa.

Johannesburg: The economic capital of South Africa and reputedly one of the most dangerous cities in the world offers little in the way of organised sightseeing, but as the country's most dynamic city it shouldn't be missed. The most attractive area to visitors is Yeoville, a suburb that is rich in bohemian nightlife and is a genuine cultural melting pot. Wherever you are, be careful — armed mugging and carjacking are everyday occurrences.

Kalahari Gemsbok National Park: The remote red dunes of the Kalahari offer some of the best predator viewing in Africa. Out of the way but a place you will never forget; it is accessible with two wheel drive.

Kruger National Park: One of Africa's largest and best stocked reserves with 150 mammal and over 500 bird species recorded. Facilities include a vast network of well-maintained internal roads, self-catering accommodation and campsites.

Kwazulu-Natal coastal belt: Steeped in Zulu history with some of

South Africa's finest game reserves (Hluhluwe, Umfolozi, Mkuzi and the wonderful Saint Lucia estuary), excellent bird watching, off-shore scuba diving at Sodwana Bay and several hiking trails.

Places to stay

Accommodation is rarely a problem in South Africa. There are over 1,000 campsites in the country with prices generally around US$5 per person. A good list of campsites is available from any Satour office. In most large towns there are now several backpackers' hostels with camping facilities and in some cases secure parking. A full and regularly updated list of hostels is available from the Hostels Association of South Africa, 101 Boston Road, Strand Street, Cape Town 8001; Tel. 021 419 1853. If you are starting your travels in Johannesburg rather than Cape Town, a recommended hostel is Rockey Street Backpackers, 34 Regent Street, Yeoville; Tel. 648 8786 — this is conveniently situated in Yeoville, has secure parking and can supply information about hostels countrywide.

Sources of tourist information

Tourist guides, maps and information are available free at borders. **South African Tourism Board**, 5-6 Alt Grove, London SW19 4DZ; Tel: 0181 944 8080.

Tourist offices in South Africa:

Bloemfontein Ground Floor, FVB Centre, Maitland Street.
Cape Town 3rd Floor, Broadway Centre, Heerengracht; Tel: 021 216274.
Durban 3rd Floor, 320 West Street.
Johannesburg Suite 4611, Carlton Centre.
Kimberley City Hall, Market Square.
Port Elizabeth Library Building, Market Square.
Pretoria 3rd Floor, Frans du Toit Building, Schoeman Street.

Guide books: *Guide to South Africa,* Philip Briggs (Bradt); *Travel Guide to South Africa* (Hildebrand); *The Rand-Wise Guide to South Africa,* Glynis van Rooyen (Don Nelson, Cape Town). *Guide to Southern African Game and Nature Reserves,* Chris and Tilde Staurt (Struik, Cape Town); *South Africa, Lesotho and Swaziland* (Lonely Planet); *South Africa, Swaziland and Lesotho,* Rupert Isaacson (Cadogan Books).

LESOTHO

Area: 30,355km²

Population: 1.9 million

Capital: Maseru

Languages: English and Sesotho.

Climate: The high altitude of this mountain kingdom is a dominant factor in its climate, making winters very cold (May to September). Most rain falls between October and April.

Visas: Visas are no longer required for tourist visits of less than 30 days. For longer visits, visas are available from UK consulates where there is no Lesotho representation. In 1994 visas cost £5 for a three month single entry and £10 for a six month multiple entry.

Foreign embassies in consulates in Maseru: Germany (Tel: 22750); **Swaziland; UK** (Tel: 313061); **USA** (PO Box 333; Tel: 312666).

Other red tape: Lesotho is part of a single customs unit together with South Africa, Swaziland and Botswana — so you only need to get your carnet stamped on entering or leaving the area as a whole. Standard motoring documents are required. You can be fined for not wearing seat belts.

Banks and money: The unit of currency is the loti, equivalent to the South African rand. All foreign currency transactions must be conducted in Maseru. Banking hours are 8.30am-1.00pm Mondays to Fridays and 8.30am-11.00am on Saturdays.

Public holidays: New Year's Day, Moshoeshoe's Day (March 12), National Tree Planting Day (March 21), Good Friday, Easter Monday, Ascension Day, Family Day (first Monday in July), King's Birthday (July 17), Independence Day (October 4), National Sports Day (first Monday in October), Christmas Day (December 25), Boxing Day (December 26).

Fuel: No problems in Maseru.

Roads: Drive on the left. There are some good surfaced roads along the border; a more basic road leads up into the mountains. Many of these roads are impassable during the rainy summer season. Much of the country is accessible only by bridle paths (this is great walking and riding country).

Places to visit

Lesotho differs from most African countries since it has no game parks. Its attractions lie in the magnificent mountain scenery and friendly people.

Places to stay

Bush camping in the mountains — but be prepared for cold nights, even in the summer, and frost and snow in the winter. Talk to the village headman if you want to camp in the area.

The *Malealea Lodge* in the Maluti Mountains, 84km from Maseru, has secure parking. In 1994 prices ranged from 30 rand for dormitory accommodation to 60 rand for bedrooms with shower and toilet. The lodge organises treks on horseback from one hour to six days, staying in local Basotho village huts.

Sources of tourist information
Tourist office in Lesotho:

Maseru Lesotho Tourist Board, PO Box 1378, Maseru 100; Tel: 312896/323760.

Guide books: *Visitors' Guide to Lesotho*, Marco Turco (Southern Books); *Guide to Lesotho,* David Ambrose (Winchester Press); *Guide to Southern African Game and Nature Reserves*, Chris and Tilde Staurt (Struik, Cape Town); *South Africa, Lesotho and Swaziland* (Lonely Planet); *South Africa, Swaziland and Lesotho*, Rupert Isaacson (Cadogan Books).

SWAZILAND

Area: 17,364km²

Population: 936,400

Capital: Mbabane

Languages: SiSwati and English.

Climate: Very changeable according to altitude, mostly ranging from 32°C to 0°C. Rain falls mainly between October and March.

Visas: You only need a visa if you are not a citizen of the UK, the Commonwealth, Australia, Belgium, Canada, Denmark, Finland, France, Greece, Iceland, Ireland, Italy, Israel, Luxembourg, Netherlands, New Zealand, Norway, Portugal, South Africa, Sweden, Switzerland, Uruguay or the USA. Single entry visas cost £8 in 1994.

Foreign embassies and consulates in Mbabane: Mozambique (Highlands View, Princess Drive Road, PO Box 1212; Tel: 43700); **UK** (Allister Miller Street; Tel: 42581); **USA** (Central Bank Building, Warner Street; Tel: 46441).

Other red tape: Vaccination certificate required for yellow fever if arriving within 6 days from an infected area. Swaziland is treated as part of a single customs unit, together with South Africa, Lesotho and Botswana — so you only need to get your carnet stamped on entering or leaving the area as a whole. Road tax is payable on entry.

Banks and money: The unit of currency is the lilangeni, which is tied to the South African rand. Banking hours are 08.30am-1.00pm Mondays to Fridays and 08.30am-11.00am on Saturdays.

Public holidays: New Year's Day, Good Friday, Easter Monday, King's Birthday (April 19), National Flag Day (April 25), Ascension Day, Commonwealth Day (June 11), Umhlanga Day (in August or September), Independence Day (September 6), Christmas Day (December 25), Boxing Day (December 26), Ncwala Day (in December or January).

Fuel: No problems in Mbabane.

Roads: Apart from the road from Oshoek to Lomahasha which is tarmac, roads are gravel but of a reasonable standard. Drive on the left.

Places to stay

Always ask permission before you bush camp as you may be on sacred ground. Otherwise you can camp at the *Timbali Caravan Park* at Ezulwini, *Mlilwane Wildlife Sanctuary*, *Malalotje Nature Reserve*, *Hlane National Park* and *Mlawula Nature Reserve*.

Sources of tourist information

Southern Africa Regional Tourism Council, PO Box 675, Gerrards Cross, Bucks, SL9 8YS.

Tourist office in Swaziland:

Mbabane Gilfillan Street.

Guide books: *Visitors' Guide to Swaziland to Swaziland*, Marco Turco (Southern Books); *Guide to Southern African Game and Nature Reserves*, Chris and Tilde Staurt (Struik, Cape Town); *South Africa, Swaziland and Lesotho,* Rupert Isaacson (Cadogan Books); *South Africa, Lesotho and Swaziland* (Lonely Planet).

MOZAMBIQUE

Area: 799,380km²

Population: 17.3 million

Capital: Maputo

Languages: The official language is Portuguese. The four main African languages are Tsonga, Sena, Nyanja and Makua-Lomwe. English is spoken by very few people outside Maputo apart from near the Malawi and Zimbabwe borders.

Climate: Tropical and sub-tropical with three climatic zones: rainy in the north and centre, drier in the southern half of the country, and a cooler rainy zone in the plateaux and mountain regions of Namaacha, Manica, Maravia-Angonia, Gurue and Lichinga. In Maputo, average rainfall is lowest in July and August (13mm) and highest in January (130mm). The dry season is from April to September when it is cooler and less humid. Rains are frequent from November to January.

Visas: Required by all. Available from embassies in London, Brussels, Lilongwe, Dar es Salaam, Lusaka, Harare, Johannesburg and Mbabane (Swaziland). Entry visas are valid for 30 days, renewable for two further periods of 30 days each. You can also get a multiple visa for up to 180 days, but only after you arrive in the country. At the end of 1994 visas in London cost £20 if processed in five days and £35 if processed in 24 hours.

Foreign embassies and consulates in Maputo: Egypt (Avenida Mao Tse Tung, 851; Tel: 49 23 65); **Malawi** (Avenida Kenneth Kaunda No 750 P4148); **Swaziland** (Avenida do Zimbabwe 608); **Tanzania** (Ujamaa House, PO Box 4515; Tel: 49 01 10/12/13); **UK** (Avenida Vladimir I Lenine 310, Caixa Postal 55; Tel: 42 01 11/2 and 42 01 15-7); **USA** (Avenida Kenneth Kaunda 193; Tel: 49 27 97); **Zaïre** (385 Avenida dos Martires de Machava; Tel: 74 23 54) **Zambia** (Avenida Kenneth Kaunda 1286 CP 4655); **Zimbabwe** (Avenue Kenneth Kaunda 816/820, Caixa Postal 743; Tel: 49 94 04).

Other red tape: Standard motoring documents are required. Reasonably priced insurance is available at the border. Yellow fever vaccination certificate required if travelling from an affected area. Government office hours are 7.30am-12.30am and 2.00pm-5.30pm Mondays to Fridays.

OVERLANDING SAFELY IN MOZAMBIQUE

After a 16-year war which claimed a million lives, Mozambique is at last at peace and held the country's first ever elections in October 1994. The poorest country in the world has also opened up for overland travel.

However, mines continue to be a real problem — mine clearing contractors are only clearing roads, not verges. Two commonly travelled roads — Milange to Quelimane and Dondo to Inhaminga — were heavily mined along the verges. These are roads every traveller will use but you shouldn't get off the road even to have a pee. If you break down just stay where you are. Don't let anybody else force you off the road to overtake — it's safer just to back off. Because of mines you shouldn't use roads that are not regularly travelled unless you take someone local who knows the road. Don't suddenly decide to take a track to the beach without asking. Lots of people want to hitch lifts which can be useful as they know the roads better than you do. There is no set of conventions on lifts — a lot of Mozambicans give lifts for money, even picking people up from taxi ranks — but as an overlander it would only be fair to swap a lift for local knowledge that keeps you out of trouble.

Another big problem is the hundreds of trenches which were dug across roads to prevent troop movements — especially from Quelimane to the Zambezi River. They have been roughly filled but not paved and can still cause damage at speed. You get used to looking out for them. There are lots of bridges down from war damage especially in Zambezia. At the end of 1993 it was reported that half the bridges in rural Mozambique had been destroyed.

There is armed banditry but the reason you should not drive at night has less to do with bandits than the fact people drive around without headlights and sometimes without brakes as well. You are more likely to have a road accident than to be held up. There have been one or two armed hijackings in Maputo — mainly kids reaching in to take stuff. So don't leave your vehicle unattended, though outside of big cities this is less of an issue. Also watch out as theft of car parts is a very real issue — tail lights, windscreen, headlights, anything that can be removed.

Roadside culture is not as well developed as other countries which means there can be hygiene problems, though this is likely to improve. There are very few medical facilities as these were a favourite target of the Renamo rebels (because they were seen as a victory for the Frelimo government). The Blue Cross (Cruz Azul) is a large private clinic in Maputo which is expensive but OK. Within the state health service there is immediate private consultation for foreigners (you pay in hard currency) which is fine for basic problems like broken bones or malaria.

Banks and money: Currency is the metical (plural meticais). Prices are often quoted in contos (1 conto = 1,000 meticais). There is a legal secondary market which pays a rate about halfway between the official rate and the rate you get changing unofficially on the street — look for signs at travel agents etc. Generally only two currencies are accepted — US dollars and South African rand. It's harder to change travellers cheques than cash except at banks that do foreign exchange. Credit cards are not much use. Banking hours are 8.00am-12.00 noon Mondays to Fridays. Shops are open from 8.30am-12.30pm and 2.00pm-6.00pm Mondays to Fridays and 8.30am-1.30pm on Saturdays.

Public holidays: New Year's Day, Heroes' Day (February 3), Women's Day (April 7), Worker's Day (May 1), Independence Day (June 25), Victory Day (September 7), Armed Forces and Revolution Day (September 25), Family Day (25 December).

Fuel: Only really available in cities, there are few supplies in rural areas. Petrol is average and fairly constant in price. Diesel tends to be more available than petrol in rural areas but mainly from local traders selling their own supply so it will have a high mark-up.

Roads: Mines are a major problem (see box). They are being cleared but only from roads and not from verges. This means you should never take roads that aren't regularly travelled without someone local to advise you and should never come off the road except in villages or towns. Main roads are tarmac with some potholes but are reasonably well maintained. Elsewhere roads are dirt or gravel.

Routes: The easiest entry points are Milange (from Malawi), at Chandia on the road from Zambia that leads to Tete, on the road from Mutare (in Zimbabwe), Ressano Garcia (from South Africa) and at Namaacha from Swaziland. If you are coming from Malawi the post at Nsanje is now also open, as is the post at Mandimba though the roads are much worse. There are only two crossings of the Zambezi - the bridge at Tete and the ferry at Caia (there are no others in the entire country that will take vehicles).

Places to visit
Maputo: It's worth visiting the Museum of the Revolution on Avenida de Julho. Other museums are Natural History, the National Coin Museum at Casa Amarela, the National Art Museum and the Museum of Colonial Occupation. There is a lively market on Avenida 25 de Setembro near the railway station.

Places to stay

Because of mines bush camping is genuinely dangerous and will be for some years to come. Camping in villages is possible, but ask first and watch out for petty theft. It's generally all right to camp on the edge of bigger towns. There are also hotels in the bigger towns but they tend to be expensive.

Sources of tourist information

A local guide, *Time Out in Maputo*, also covering Beira, is available in English from PO Box 2242 Maputo; Tel: 33445/33456 (send US$5).

Guide books: *Guide to Mozambique*, Bernhard Skrodzki (Bradt); *Guide to Mozambique,* Mike Slater (Struik Publishers, 80 McKenzie Street, Cape Town, South Africa).

NAMIBIA

Area: 823,144km²

Population: 1.6 million

Capital: Windhoek

Languages: English is the official language.

Climate: Hot in summer (as high as 40°C plus) but cool in the evenings and cold in winter. Rainfall is mainly from October until April, with more falling in the north than the south. The coastal strip of the Namib Desert is cool, damp and rainless with mist for much of the year.

Visas: Not required by citizens of the Commonwealth, the EU, Angola, Australia, Botswana, Canada, Iceland, Japan, Mozambique, New Zealand, Norway, South Africa, Swaziland, Switzerland, Tanzania, USA, Zambia and Zimbabwe.

Foreign embassies and consulates in Windhoek: Angola (3rd Floor, Angola House; Tel: 22 03 02); **Botswana** (22 Curt von Francois Street; Tel: 22 19 41); **Egypt** (10 Berg Street, Klein; Tel: 22 15 01-3); **France** (1 Goeth Street; Tel: 22 90 21); **Germany** (11 Uhland Street; Tel: 22 92 17); **Kenya** (Leutwein Street; Tel: 22 68 36); **Malawi** (56 Bismarck Street); **Nigeria** (4 Omuramba Road); **UK** (116 Robert Mugabe Avenue; Tel: 22 30 22); **USA** (Ausplan Building, 14 Lossen Street; Tel: 22 16 01); **Zambia** (22 Curt von Francois Street); **Zimbabwe** (Gamsberg Building, Independence Way; Tel: 22 77 38).

Banks and money: In 1993 Namibia's currency was changed from the South African rand to the Namibian dollar, currently fixed at the same value. Both dollar and rand are legal tender in Namibia, though you cannot use Namibian dollars in South Africa. Credit cards are widely accepted and most major towns have Bank Windhoek ATMs where you can withdraw cash with Visa or Mastercard. Banking hours are 9.00am to 3.30pm Monday to Friday and 8.30am to 11.00am on Saturday.

Public holidays: New Year's Day, Public Holiday (January 2), Independence Day (March 21); Good Friday, Easter Monday, Workers' Day (May 1), Cassinga Day (May 4), Ascension Day, Africa Day (May 25), Heroes' Day (August 26); Human Rights Day (December 10), Public Holiday (December 11), Christmas Day and Boxing Day.

Roads: Drive on the left. The roads are good. Two-wheel drive is sufficient, except for parts of the Namib Desert, Kaudom Reserve and Kaokoland.

Routes: It is possible to enter Namibia from Zambia or Botswana and drive through the Caprivi strip along a good dirt road or from Botswana at Mahongo, which is also a good road. Alternatively, if you have a four-wheel drive vehicle, it is possible to enter from Botswana across the Kalahari Desert. The easiest entry is on the good surfaced roads from South Africa or by flying to Windhoek and hiring a car there.

The most interesting route is to leave the main roads from South Africa where they converge at Corunan. After a detour to Fish River Canyon, take the minor roads north to Helmeringhausen, Sesriem, Solitaire and Swakopmund. Take the minor roads via The White Lady, Brandberg, Twyfelfontein, Rock Finger and Outjo to Etosha National Park. Then on the main road to Tsumeb, Grootfontein and the Cubango River, leaving Namibia into Botswana and the Okavango Delta or along the Caprivi Strip.

Motoring organisations: The Automobile Association of Namibia, Carl List Haus, corner of Independence Avenue and Peter Müller Streets, Windhoek; Tel: 2-4201.

Places to visit
The tourist potential of Namibia is very high and previously relatively untapped. Already popular with South African travellers, this huge, empty and beautiful country — Namibia literally means 'nothing' — is poised to become a major travel destination. One sure sign of this is that game park fees were doubled at the beginning of 1995.

Brandberg and the White Lady Rock Painting: Spectacular desert mountain area with beautiful places to camp. It's worth the 45 minute walk there and back to see the impressive White Lady Rock Painting.

Cape Cross Seal Reserve: All-year colony of between 80,000 and 100,000 cape fur seal (be warned — the smell can be overpowering). November to January is the best time to see pups. From mid-October to January adult males come ashore to breed.

Daan Viljoen National Park: Small park about 20km from Windhoek which is a good place to camp. No cats, elephant or buffalo so you can walk the game trails to see zebra, klipspringer, wildebeest and hartebeest. Temperatures at night can fall below freezing between June and August.

Damaraland: Beautiful rugged semi-desert area with springbok, giraffe, zebra and desert elephants often seen near the Palmwag Lodge trying to dig up the water pipes.

Etosha National Park: Based around a huge salt pan this is incredibly rich in game particularly just before the rains when water is scarce. The floodlit waterhole at Okaukuejo is an excellent place to see rhino, elephant, lion and all sorts of antelope.

Fish River Canyon: The second biggest canyon in the world after the Grand Canyon. A spectacular view from the top. Hikes down the canyon and back are possible but it's hard work. In summer the best time to walk down is late afternoon. Four hours should get you down and back in time to see the sunset.

Kaudom Game Reserve: Flat sand veld reserve in northeastern Namibia. Access by four-wheel drive only and the authorities insist you travel with a minimum of two vehicles. Booking at the Nature Conservation Office in Windhoek is essential.

Kolmanskop: Spooky desert ghost town just outside Luderitz which was once a diamond mining centre. Guided tours available or you can clamber over the sand-filled ruins and imagine how rough it must have been to live here. One house is completely restored and there is a museum and coffee shop.

Luderitz: The port of the old diamond mining area, buried among the sand dunes on the coast. A quirky little town with strong German influences. Can be one of the windiest places on earth. The Kapps Hotel has excellent crayfish at affordable prices and good draught beer.

Namib Desert: A strange place. For most of the year the coastal belt is engulfed in sea mist — but 200 yards inland it is one of the driest deserts in the world. You will need a permit to enter the northern area, obtainable either in Windhoek or from the Department of Nature Conservation at Swakopmund. This is where you can see the strange desert plant, the Wilwitchia.

Rock Finger: Worth the detour off the road from Khorixas to Outjo to see this strange massive finger of rock jutting out of the landscape.

Skeleton Coast: A barren windswept area often engulfed in a cold sea mist which is the only source of moisture for fauna and flora. Permits available at the park gates to travel through the southern section of the reserve (approximately 145km).

Sossusvlei: Said to be the tallest sand dunes in the world, these are one of the most spectacular sights in Africa. They can be reached in a two-wheel drive vehicle followed by a 45 minute walk. Or you can go all the way to the main dunes with four-wheel drive. The only base for a trip to Sossusvlei is the campsite at Sesriem, 50km away. No camping is allowed any closer than this.

Swakopmund: Has a distinct German flavour in both architecture and food. The much-used town launderette has a bar, snack machines and 'casino' with gaming machines.

Twyfelfontein: Site of the famous bushman rock etchings and paintings.

Windhoek: A pleasant enough town. Visit the Nature Conservation Office on the corner of Independence Avenue and John Meinert Street for detailed information on travel throughout Namibia. You can book campsites and lodges from here and hire camping equipment.

Places to stay

There are campsites with good facilities at main tourist attractions. Outside of desert areas it can sometimes be difficult to bush camp as much of the land beside main roads is fenced off. The Nature Conservation Office in Windhoek issues a booklet called *Accommodation Guide for Tourists*.

Damaraland: The somewhat pricey *Palmwag Lodge* has camping, chalets and bar.

Etosha National Park: Camping and accommodation at all three rest camps.

Fish River Canyon: The *Hobas Campsite* at the north end of the canyon has very good facilities. Camping also at Ai-Ais hot springs at the bottom end of the canyon.

Kaudom Game Reserve: Camping facilities available at both rest camps. Booking essential, through the Nature Conservation Office in Windhoek.

Khorixas: A rest camp 2km out of town (about 40km from Twyfelfontein) has excellent facilities including chalets, camping, bar and restaurant.

Luderitz: The campsite is on a promontory so if you are here in the windy season make sure your tent is secure. On the road that leads to the campsite you will see the legendary sign: 'This is government property. It is not a race track or drinking place. Respect the town and the tourists and they will respect you.'

Namib-Naukluft: There are various isolated campsites with long-drop toilets and no water in the northern section of the park.

Orange River: About 2km after the South African border on the main road north take a left turn on the D212 dirt road towards Poskantoor to reach the *Felix White Provenance Camp*. Run by a helpful Portuguese called Carlos, this is in a beautiful setting on the Orange River. You can book canoe trips on the river here (50 rand for a full day and 25 rand for half a day in December 1994).

Rundu: The *Sarasungu River Lodge* on the Kavango River has camping with barbecue facilities, bungalows, bar and restaurant.

Sesriem: There are walled-off camping spots at the *Karos Lodge* 50km from the dunes at Sossusvlei. It is almost always full, so booking is advisable though there is an 'emergency' area with no facilities outside for people without reservations. You can book in Windhoek.

Skeleton Coast: Camping at Torra Bay is only open from 1 December to 31 January. Huts available at Terrace Bay. Book for both through the Nature Conservation Office in Windhoek.

Swakopmund: Camping at Mile 4 is not recommended, but there are cheap municipal chalets available here. You can also bush camp on the beach further north though this is very exposed to the road.

Twyfelfontein: Municipal campsite nearby has basic facilities and bar.

Walvis Bay: There is a municipal campsite.

Windhoek: Camping and chalets at *Arabbusch Travel Lodge* on the outskirts of town. Also at *Daan Viljoen Park* 20 km away.

Sources of tourist information

Nature Conservation Office, PO Box 13267, Windhoek 9000 (at the corner of Independence Avenue and John Meinert Street); Tel: 061 29251.

Guide books: *Guide to Namibia and Botswana* Chris McIntyre, and Simon Atkins (Bradt); *Guide to Southern African Game and Nature Reserves*, Chris and Tilde Staurt (Struk, Cape Town); *Zimbabwe, Botswana and Namibia* (Lonely Planet); *Globetrotter Guide to Namibia*, Bill and Andrea Revilio (New Holland); *Insight Guide to Namibia*.

A taste of Namibia
by Luc Lebeau

Windhoek is an extraordinary town surrounded by mountains and with a wide central street full of colour and life. There are even parking meters! We disappear into the shops where I buy four different kinds of chocolate! The officials in the Nature Conservation Office give us maps and documents for the rest of our journey. Tomorrow we will spend the morning with them booking campsites and entry to the parks on their computer and getting the various passes for protected zones.

When we arrive in the park we are welcomed in an impeccable building which houses the reception and maintenance staff. A black Namibian kindly shows us the layout and facilities of the camp. He speaks perfect English, Afrikaans, some German and his own local language. You can even pay with credit cards!

The campsite is on a little plateau in the middle of mountains overhanging a plain and a lake where game strolls idly by. The grass is incredibly green and as well tended as a golf course. Each camping spot has a place to park, a splendid barbecue, a tap and an electric socket. Close by, Nicole and Hélène find a room where there are electric cookers, a sink to wash dishes and even a fridge. Everything is spotlessly clean. The toilets, showers and bath are also spotless and the hot water is incredibly hot. We look at each other in disbelief.

The evening ends with a barbecue washed down by South African wine. A family of foxes is attracted by the smell. We can hear them approach in the dry grass to catch the scraps of meat we throw to them. It's tough getting up the next day, though. We are not only still exhausted but after a freezing night there is frost on the windscreens of the vehicles.

That morning we are kept busy sorting out the documents for the rest of the trip before we visit the park which is like an open-air zoo without barriers. In the evening we plan the coming week by reading our guide books and comparing information on our various maps. The children don't have to be asked to go to bed and with a dinner of seasoned pork chops and some more South African wine it's like being in an open-air restaurant in the desert. The manager talks to us enthusiastically about his country. We could happily stay here for weeks, or even months.

In the morning our grey and yellow tent sifts the first rays of the sun. It's absolutely freezing! The condensation has frozen on the walls of the tent. I get out to make a hot drink and discover our 10 litre jerrican of water has turned into a block of ice. The campers next to us show us their hair, stiffened under a fine layer of white ice. Pol and I light the fire surrounded by a light fog. We estimate the temperature must have fallen to -10°C and regret not having brought our polar sleeping bags — absurd in Africa!

We finally warm ourselves up and get on the road. It's a long way to the sea — 400km, of which 200km will be in the famous Namibian desert. We reach a beautiful chain of mountains. Amongst the stones there are a few dry bushes and stunted yellow trees with no leaves. The landscape is stunning because there's practically nothing there, except the barren mountains clothed in reds and browns of every shade. We cross several roads leading to isolated farms, their windmills visible in the distance. At 3.00pm we stop in this magical land, our stomachs grumbling.

Pol and Hélène have brought a whole stock of supplies from Zaïre for us to use. We end up with an incredible mixture which is talked about for a long time afterwards: beef curry accompanied by chicken in a cream sauce, pre-cooked carrots and a cocktail of Chinese vegetables. All four tins are simply emptied into a big pot. It's just as well we are hungry!

Half an hour later we are at the edge of the desert. We leave the main 'road' for a piste which takes off to the right. Bizarre plants with thick leaves and solitary trees suddenly appear here and there under a sky of intense blue. In the distance we can see two zebras and a few gazelles.

Then the sun starts to set and a light mist appears, lending a fairy-like atmosphere to the empty space which surrounds us. It would be wonderful just to stay here for hours without moving, just looking at the spectacle. The lunar landscape which stretches out before our eyes surpasses anything you could possibly imagine. The dying rays of the sun exaggerate the magic of the place.

The following day we arrive at the seal reserve at Cape Cross and get out of our comfortable air-conditioned cars to find ourselves surrounded by a heavy suffocating stench. It is impossible to breathe without feeling sick from the smell of decomposing bodies. At first we can't see anything but a low wall, and then there they are — the famous seals. There are supposed to be 200,000 of them and we are ready to believe it. It is incredible to see such a concentration of them in just a few hundred metres.

Apart from this mountain of seals, the Natural West Coast Tourist Recreation Area is a little monotonous. Of course, it's wonderful to arrive at the top of a dune and see the sea sparkling into infinity at the bottom of mountains of sand. But you drive for hours on an interminable road without any change of scenery. It is only when we leave the Skeleton Coast Park for Khorixas that we enter a more interesting region where the vehicles strain up mountains covered with red gravel.

During this section Kim takes it into her head to burst into tears for no apparent reason. Pol and Hélène have trouble hearing what we are saying through her strident cries. The piste is full of holes which our suspension and the top of our heads will remember for years. No wonder we feel euphoric when we pull into Khorixas at nightfall.

We put up our tent on a fine stretch of grass and light a fire to cook something to eat. Just then Morgane, tired of being told to stop quarrelling with Nicolas, throws a stone which hits him right in the head, blood spurting from the wound. The gash is deep but we dress it with a 'steri-strip', a marvellous invention which avoids the need for stitches. Half an hour later Nicolas is back to normal, demanding to know why Morgane won't play with him.

This extract is taken from Un Peu Plus Loin *by Luc Lebeau — a self-published account of his 6,000km trip through Zambia, Zimbabwe, Botswana and Namibia with Nicole Moens and their children Kim (9 months) and Morgane (4½) and their friends Pol and Hélène and their son Nicolas (3½).*

BOTSWANA

Area: 581,730km²

Population: 1.4 million

Capital: Gaborone

Languages: English is the official language; Setswana is the national language.

Climate: Much of the country is desert with the most habitable areas in the north and east. It is hot throughout the year — but particularly from October to April. The main rainy season is from December to April.

Visas: Required by all apart from citizens of Australia, Austria, Belgium, Canada, Caribbean States, Cyprus, Denmark, Finland, France, Gambia, Greece, Guyana, Hong Kong, Iceland, Ireland, Italy, Kenya, Lesotho, Luxembourg, Malawi, Malaysia, Malta, Netherlands, New Zealand, Norway, Sierra Leone, Singapore, South Africa, South Korea, Sweden, Switzerland, Tanzania, Uganda, UK, USA, Zambia and Zimbabwe.

Foreign embassies and consulates in Gaberone: **France** (761 Robinson Road; Tel: 35 36 83); **Germany** (2nd Floor, IGI House; Tel: 35 31 43); **Nigeria** (The Mall; Tel: 31 35 61); **UK** (Queen's Road; Tel: 35 28 41-3); **USA** (Badiredi House, The Mall; Tel: 35 39 82); **Zambia** (The Mall, Queen's Road; Tel: 35 19 51); **Zimbabwe** (The Mall; Tel: 31 44 95/7).

Other red tape: Standard motoring documents are required. Botswana is treated as part of a single customs unit with South Africa, Lesotho, Namibia and Swaziland — so you only need to get your carnet stamped on entering or leaving the area as a whole. You sometimes need special internal visas for game reserves and the desert. You are not allowed to import meat or dairy products from Namibia, Zambia or Victoria Falls.

Banks and money: The unit of currency is the pula, which is a hard currency. This has made Botswana a favourite place in the past for selling vehicles (particularly in Maun). Banking hours are 8.15am-12.45pm Monday to Friday and 8.15am-10.45am on Saturday.

Public holidays: New Year's Day, Public Holiday (January 2), Good Friday, Easter Saturday, Easter Monday, Ascension Day, President's Day (third Monday in July), Botswana Day (September 30), Public Holiday (October 1), Christmas Day and Boxing Day.

Fuel: You will be taxed on any fuel imported in jerricans. It should generally be available in main centres but make sure you have plenty to spare if travelling in remote areas as it can sometimes be hard to find.

Roads: Drive on the left. There are some good surfaced main roads but the rest are tracks and pistes.

Routes: Entering in the north, you can drive straight down through Gaberone and into South Africa or head through the Chobe National Park (or via Nata) on a sandy track to Maun and the Okavango delta. It is possible to go beyond this on sandy tracks southwest to Namibia. The road around the west of the Okavango is now surfaced as far north as Gumare and there is an improved dirt road beyond. A track also cuts across the Kalahari from north to south, via Kang. It is very rough with deep sand and some deep ruts. Good maps of the country are available at the border.

Places to visit
Chobe National Park: A good park with a lot of elephant and antelope, but a bit on the expensive side.

Gaberone: There is a very good museum in the centre, at the junction between Independence Avenue and Queen's Road.

Jwaneng: This is where the surfaced roads finish south of the desert. It has some of the most productive diamond mines in the world.

The Kalahari Desert: A quiet and featureless wasteland.

Moremi Wildlife Reserve: Includes the eastern edge of the Okavango Delta. You can take short trips into the delta from here.

Okavango Delta: One of the great wonders of Africa — a visit into this vast inland delta is an absolute must. Most interesting wildlife are the birds and crocodiles. Trips into the delta can be arranged from Maun. It is possible to leave your vehicle behind in safety and head off in small boats into this wildlife haven.

Places to stay
Chobe National Park: The campsite at Savuti has been destroyed by elephants. There are good places to bush camp where Chobe borders with Moreni Wildlife Reserve.

Francistown: You can camp in the grounds of the *Marang Hotel*. It has a swimming pool. This is the biggest town in Botswana and one of the best places to fill up with supplies — it offers the best stocked shelves you are likely to come across.

Gaberone: There is nowhere to stay in the town but there are a lot of hotels between Gaborone and the border with South Africa.

Ghanzi: There is camping at the *Kalahari Hotel*.

Maun: The *Island Safari Lodge* has camping. This is a good place to hire boats for the trip into the delta. Also camping at *Sitatunga Camp*, 12km south of Maun.

Nata: There is camping at the *Nata Lodge* with a pool, bar and expensive food.

Sources of tourist information
Tourist literature is available at the border.

Tourist office in Botswana:
Gaborone P Bag 0047, BBS Building, Broadhurst Mall; Tel: 353024.

Guide books: *Guide to Namibia and Botswana*, Chris McIntyre and Simon Atkins (Bradt); *No frills guide to Zimbabwe and Botswana*, David Else (Bradt); *Guide to Southern African Game and Nature Reserves,* Chris and Tilde Staurt (Struik, Cape Town); *Rough Guide to Zimbabwe and Botswana*; *Zimbabwe, Botswana and Namibia* (Lonely Planet).

Durban to Kampala by Motorbike
by Jocelyn Phillips
Planning a journey through Africa is like a game of snakes and ladders. Three days before 'Go' we had been looking forward to a trans-Saharan start, passing through Algeria on our two XT350s before travelling south towards Uganda, Botswana and, finally, South Africa. But now the label on the XTs' packing case read 'To Durban, South Africa'. I could have sworn that was nowhere near the Sahara.

It was just three days before the off that we discovered the Algerian border had been closed to British overland travellers. A rapid change of plan was required. Our own answer was to turn the map upsidedown and start again.

So it was that two weeks later we found ourselves unpacking the bikes in the sticky heat of South Africa's largest port. They fired up with little persuasion as we set off to explore the wide open roads ahead. We cruised along under azure blue skies past some of the most dramatic scenery in Africa — the Garden Route along the wild coast and the Drakensberg mountains — and headed northwest towards Botswana. We rode through the hot plains with the wind whistling in our helmets and grit peppering our sunburnt faces — keeping up our speed in an effort to keep cool. But cruising along those Botswanan roads we suddenly had to brake for what was our first, best and cheapest experience of wildlife in Africa. A giraffe strode elegantly across the road in front of us, head rocking gracefully as it went.

With the bikes behaving themselves, we headed north through Zimbabwe, Malawi and Zambia to Lake Tanganyika, where we paid for a three-day passage to Burundi and Zaïre. With the bikes safely stored among the freight, it was time to relax and watch the shores of Zaïre and Tanzania slip past.

To motorcycle adventurers, Zaïre means mud — and plenty of it. Stories circulate of trucks slipping into muddy ruts in the rainy season and being marooned there until the next dry season. So it was with some trepidation that we swapped to mud tyres and entered Zaïre. First we skirted the eastern edge of the country, following the lakes of the rift valley. We tried to do most of our riding in the mornings, before the rains started. If we failed, we would get caught in a downpour with tyres churning uselessly in a sea of wet mud.

Our next destination was Uganda and, in particular, the Ruwenzori mountains, where we decided to take a short cut to the Ruwenzoris. The red dirt road snaked through lush countryside as we eagerly looked forward to our first glimpse of the mountains. But the best laid plans in Africa have a habit of being changed — turning a corner, my front wheel lodged in a rut and I suddenly had a worm's eye view of the road. A broken collar bone meant that this was one fall too many and it was time for a bumpy pillion ride back to Kampala.

After three months and 6,000 miles we were therefore forced to sell the bikes and head back home. Cape to Cairo it may not have been but Cape to Kampala had been just as much fun. I had still seen, absorbed and become intoxicated by the sheer size and space of Africa.

A longer account of Jocelyn Phillips' journey was published in Bike *magazine.*

ZIMBABWE

Area: 390,759km²

Population: 11 million

Capital: Harare

Languages: English is the official language; Shona and Ndebele are the national languages.

Climate: A temperate climate due to the country's high altitude. Highland temperatures range from 22°C in October to 13°C in July; in the Zambezi valley it ranges from 30°C to 20°C. Rainy season is December to March. Cool season is May to September.

Visas: Not required by citizens of the UK, the Commonwealth, the EU, Iceland, Norway, Switzerland and the USA.

Foreign embassies and consulates in Harare: Australia (4th Floor, Karigamombe Centre, Samora Machel Avenue/Julius Nyerere Way; Tel: 794591); **Botswana** (Southern Life Building, Jason Moyo Avenue; Tel: 729551); **Canada** (45 Baines Avenue; Tel: 733881); **Egypt** (7 Aberdeen Road, Avondale; Tel: 303445); **France** (2nd Floor, RAL House, Samora Machel Avenue); **Germany** (14 Samora Machel Avenue); **Kenya** (95 Park Lane); **Malawi** (42-44 Harare Street); **Mozambique** (152 Herbert Chitepo Avenue, PO Box 4608; Tel: 790837/9); **New Zealand** (6th Floor, Batanai Gardens, 57 Jason Moyo Avenue; Tel: 728681-6); **South Africa** (Temple Bar House, 39 Baker Avenue); **Switzerland** (9th Floor, Southampton House, Union Avenue); **Tanzania** (Ujamaa House, 23 Baines Avenue; Tel: 721870); **UK** (Stanley House, Jason Moyo Avenue; Tel: 793781); **USA** (172 Herbert Chitepo Avenue, PO Box 3340; Tel: 794521); **Zaïre** (24 Van Praagh Avenue; Tel: 724494); **Zambia** (Zambia House, Union Avenue).

Other red tape: Standard motoring documents and certificate of vaccination for yellow fever are required. A temporary import permit will be issued free of charge to those without a carnet. Zimnat Insurance in Harare can issue a 'yellow insurance card' providing third party cover for Zimbabwe, Malawi, Tanzania, Kenya and Uganda. South African driving licences are valid.

Banks and money: Unit of currency is the Zimbabwe dollar. There are no foreign currency restrictions but you cannot take more than 100Z$ in or out of the country. More expensive hotels and tour operators will expect you to pay in hard currency — travellers cheques and credit cards are accepted and in some cases will mean a better rate because you avoid paying sales tax. Banking hours are 8.00am-3.00pm Monday, Tuesday, Thursday and Friday; 8.00am-1.00pm Wednesday and 8.00am-11.30am Saturday.

Public holidays: New Year's Day, Good Friday, Easter Monday, Public Holiday (April 2), Independence Day (April 18), Workers' Day (May 1), Africa Day (May 25), Heroes' Day (August 11), Defence Forces Day (August 12), Christmas Day (December 25), Boxing Day (December 26).

Fuel: Despite a recent hike in price Zimbabwe is one of the best places in Africa to buy fuel. Quality is no problem.

Roads: Excellent. Drive on the left.

Routes: Most will be satisfied with the main routes linking Victoria Falls, Bulawayo, Harare and the Botswana or South Africa borders. All roads are very good. Maps are available at the border.

Motoring organisations: Automobile Association of Zimbabwe, Fanum House, Samora Machel Avenue, Harare.

Places to visit

Zimbabwe's importance as a centre for overland travel has increased over the past few years as more and more tour operators run out of Harare. Visits to game parks here are cheaper than in both Kenya and Tanzania, for independent travellers. Huge fees charged to foreign tour operators mean that the truck companies use local tours.

Bulawayo: There are good ethnographic and natural history museums plus an unmissable art museum at the corner of Main Street and Leopold Takawire Avenue, which is a great source of reasonably priced work by local artists.

Bvumba Botanical Gardens: Worth a visit. Well kept gardens and nature reserve 30km from Mutare.

Chimanimani National Park: Has a beautiful setting in the eastern highlands. You can walk in the hills — right up to the Mozambique border at Skeleton Pass.

Chinhoyi Caves Recreational Park: Caves to explore include the Dark Cave and Cave of the Bats. The famous Sleeping Pool is 46m below ground level.

THE ZIMBABWE BEAT

Anyone who claims there's little to do in Harare obviously isn't a night owl. After dark this is one of the most exciting music capitals in the world, with dozens of clubs presenting some of the most infectious dance beats you will ever come across.

Like most African musicians, bands tend to warm up slowly — they know there's a long night ahead of them. Typically they play for many hours with the hottest sounds coming after midnight. On the really big nights — the last weekend of the month when everyone has just been paid — the music rarely stops before dawn.

Apart from central hotel venues such as the Queen's and the Federal, there's plenty of music to be had at clubs throughout the suburbs — The Club Hide Out 99, the Skyline, the Red Lantern. Apart from the music, the other essential element at all of these places is a liberal supply of cold beer. Indeed, many of the main venues are billed as beer gardens.

The two best sources of information on what's on are the daily paper *The Herald* and the hundreds of posters that appear each day all over town. On a recent trip to Zimbabwe, we had a 'wish list' of six of the country's top bands. We would have been more than happy if just one of them was playing while we were staying in Harare. But on arrival we opened *The Herald* to see that all six were playing that very night. Decisions, decisions.

In the end we decided to go for Oliver Mtukudzi at the Federal. He has long been one of the top two musicians in Zimbabwe, alongside Thomas Mapfumo. Of the two, Mtukudzi (or Tuku as he is commonly known) is the most popular in Zimbabwe although Mapfumo is better known on the international circuit.

The evening built in intensity throughout his first two and a half hour set, as more and more singers arrived on stage and more and more people arrived at the club to dance the night away. And dance you must. This is no place to sit and watch. By the time the second set began at around 12.30am the joint was really jumping.

The main bands - such as Mtukudzi, Mapfumo, the Four Brothers, the Real Sounds of Africa, Leonard Dembo and John Chibadura — play the Harare clubs three or four nights every week. But they do also occasionally play elsewhere in the country. Bulawayo is the main other opportunity to pick up on them. This is also the centre of the Zimbabwean jazz scene, with an excellent club at the Bulawayo Sun Hotel.

Chipangali Animal Orphanage: Cares for abandoned and injured animals. A chance to see many animals rarely seen in the game parks. 23km from Bulawayo.

Great Zimbabwe Ruins: Built in the 12th to 15th centuries, these are the remains of the biggest pre-colonial structure south of the Sahara. Situated 30km south of Masvingo, they are not to be missed.

Hwange National Park: Has been badly degraded by elephants. Large trucks are now banned from the park. Walking tours are possible.

Kyle Recreation Park: Near the Great Zimbabwe Ruins and including the Kyle Dam. Game viewing tours on horseback and well known for walking.

Mana Pools National Park: Walking tours are no longer permitted.

Matobo (formerly Matopos) National Park: A good place to see rhino. The beautiful Matobo Hills are sacred to the Matabele. You can visit caves with rock paintings. This is the burial place of Cecil Rhodes. You can no longer camp here.

Mongwe Fishing Camps: In the Zambezi valley. Boats can be hired for fishing trips.

Nyanga National Park: This is a beautiful place in the eastern highlands with views across Mozambique and lots of waterfalls.

Victoria Falls: The best view of the falls is from the Zambian side. It's worth spending several days here if you are into trying white water rafting, bungee jumping, parachute jumps, etc. Otherwise see the falls and move on.

Places to stay

The standard of campsites is universally high. Bush camping is difficult as almost all land is fenced. Many game ranches will allow camping.

Bulawayo: There is a good campsite near the centre of town behind the botanical gardens. You should not walk back over the bridge in the park on your own at night. You can also camp at the *Country Rest Camp* 20km north on the Victoria Falls road. It is very pleasant with chalets, camping and a small pool

Bvumba Botanical Gardens: A beautiful campsite in a stunning setting. Facilities are fairly basic though there is a swimming pool.

Chimanimani National Park: Has a terraced campsite.

Chinhoyi Caves Recreational Park: Camping at *Orange Grove Motel*, including use of pool.

Great Zimbabwe Ruins: There is a campsite just outside the ruins. Or stay at the *Sekato Bay Campsite* in Lake Kyle Park which is very isolated and quiet.

Harare: The *Spaybay Campsite* 20km out on the Mutare Road has very good facilities and a workshop. The *municipal campsite* is at Coronation Park, 5km out on the Mutare road, but there have been reports of theft and tents being slashed during the night. Also camping and rooms at *71 Hillside Road*, 10 minutes from Mukuvisi Woodlands.

Hwange Game Park: You can camp at *Sinamatella Lodge*, *Main Camp* and *Robins Camp*. There are also cheap chalets.

Kariba: The *Moth Campsite* has a swimming pool and lots of vervet monkeys.

Kyle Recreational Park: There is a small campsite between the office and the rest camp, overlooking the lake.

Mana Pools National Park: If you book in Harare you may be told the site is full though this is rarely true. Campsite is unfenced and frequently visited by lion and hyena at night.

Mongwe Fishing Camp: Ten campsites with water and toilet facilities. No fuel or supplies available.

Nyanga National Park: There is a luxurious campsite in a pine forest just south of the park.

Victoria Falls: The municipal campsite has all the standard facilities but it can get crowded. There is also another site which tends not to be so busy out along the road to the west of the falls. Chalets available at both.

Sources of tourist information

Zimbabwe Tourist Office, 429 Strand, London WC2R; Tel: 0171 240 6169.

Tourist guides, maps and other information are handed out free at the border.

Tourist offices in Zimbabwe:

Bulawayo City Hall, Leopold Takawira Avenue and Fife Street.
Gweru Livingstone Avenue, PO Box 295; Tel: 2226.
Harare corner of Jason Moyo Avenue and Second Street at Africa Unity Square; Tel: 705085/6. Good maps for all of Zimbabwe from the Surveyor General's Office, Samora Machel Avenue.
Mutare Market Square, Milner.
Victoria Falls Just by the side entrance of the municipal campsite.

Guide books: *No frills guide to Zimbabwe and Botswana*, David Else (Bradt); *Rough guide to Zimbabwe and Botswana; Spectrum Guide to Zimbabwe. Guide to Southern African Game and Nature Reserves*, Chris and Tilde Staurt (Struik, Cape Town); *Zimbabwe, Botswana and Namibia* (Lonely Planet); *Discovery Guide to Zimbabwe*, Melissa Shabs (Immel); *Globetrotter Guide to Zimbabwe*, Paul Tingay (New Holland).

ZAMBIA

Area: 752,614km²

Population: 9.2 million

Capital: Lusaka

Languages: English is the official language; the main national languages are Bemba, Nyanja, Lozi and Tonga.

Climate: Sunny but cool from May to September; hot from October to November; rains from November until April.

Visas: Required by all apart from citizens of the UK, the Commonwealth, Ireland, Romania, Sweden and Pakistan. All visas are available at the border.

Foreign embassies and consulates in Lusaka: Australia (Ulendo House; Tel: 229371); **Botswana** (2647 Haile Selassie Avenue; Tel: 229371); **Canada** (5199 United Nations Avenue; Tel: 21532 ext. 2314); **Egypt** (United Nations Avenue; Tel: 250229); **France** (Unity House, Katunjila Road/Freedom Way; Tel: 212917); **Germany** (350 Independence Avenue; Tel: 227938); **Kenya** (Harambee House, United Nations Avenue; Tel: 212531); **Malawi** (5th Floor, Woodgate House, Cairo Road; Tel: 223750); **Mozambique** (Mulugushi Village, Kundalila Road, Villa 46; Tel: 253354); **Namibia** (6968 Kabanga Road, Addis Ababa Drive; Tel: 252250); **Tanzania** (Ujamaa House, United Nations Avenue; Tel: 227698); **Uganda** (Kulima Tower; Tel: 227916); **UK** (Independence Avenue; Tel: 228955); **USA** (Independence Avenue/United Nations Avenue; Tel: 228595); **Zaïre** (1124 Parirenyatwa Road; Tel: 614247; **Zimbabwe** (Memaco House, 4th Floor; Tel: 229382).

Other red tape: You can use your carnet but if you are worried about filling up your pages you can get a free temporary import permit instead. Cholera vaccination certificates are no longer required. Zambia is the cheapest place in eastern and southern Africa for postage.

Banks and money: The unit of currency is the kwacha. You must pay in hard currency for hotels. It is easy to get hold of US$ in Lusaka. No restrictions on importing foreign currency.

Public holidays: New Year's Day, Public Holiday (March 19), Good Friday, Easter Monday, Labour Day (May 1), African Freedom Day (May 25), Heroes' Day (first Monday in July), Unity Day (first Tuesday in July), Farmers' Day (first Monday in August),

Independence Day (October 24), Christmas Day (December 25).

Fuel: Widely available; below average prices for the region.

Roads: Have deteriorated, with the worst bitumen in the east and south. Mostly poor. Drive on the left.

Routes: Most travellers simply run along the main roads from the Malawi or Tanzanian borders (or from the boat at Mpulungu) to Lusaka and then on to Harare or Victoria Falls. No problems.

Motoring Organisations: Automobile Association, Dedan Kimathi Road; Tel: 75311.

Car hire: Eagle Travel, Findeco House, Lusaka; Tel: 214554/214916.

Places to visit
Kafue National Park: Severe poaching has reduced animal populations though you should see puku, oribi and elephant. A good park for birds. Night driving is permitted. Entry in 1995 was US$10 per person plus $15 for a vehicle.

Kundalila Falls: A spectacular 60 metre drop.

Nsalu Caves: Prehistoric rock paintings.

South Luangwa National Park: A stunning game park, home to a rich variety of wildlife — particularly elephants. One of the few parks where you can drive at night, for US$25 in 1995. Entry charges then were US$15 for a vehicle plus $5 per person.

Victoria Falls: Unmissable. The best white water rafting trips at the falls are from the Zambian side. Costs per head are lower if you book with a group.

Places to stay
Hotels are very expensive and must be paid for in hard currency. There are camping facilities at all the major tourist sights. There are also plenty of good opportunities for bush camping.

Kafue National Park: The pleasant *Chunga Campsite* is in North Kafue by the lake.

Livingstone: You can camp here at the *Rainbow Lodge*, but hard currency requirements now make it very expensive. There is a campsite at the backpackers' hostel. Some people cross over to the Zimbabwe side and stop there at Victoria Falls. It is easy enough to cross back during the day if you wish.

Livingstone Memorial: Camping at *Rainbow Lodge* is not secure. *Busiku Farm* 10km to the north has camping and chalets.

Lusaka: You can camp in the compound of the *Salvation Army Hostel* close to the centre. *Andrews Motel*, out on the edge of town, also offers camping facilities. 11km on the road to Kariba, *Eureka Farm* has camping in pleasant surroundings with clean facilities. Lusaka is very bad for theft so never leave your vehicle unguarded in the city.

South Luangwa: The old campsite was washed out by the floods but it is possible to camp at the crocodile farm by the entrance to the park.

Sources of tourist information
Zambia National Tourist Board 2 Palace Gate, London W8; Tel: 0171 589 6343

Tourist offices in Zambia:
Lusaka National Tourist Board, Century House, Cairo Road, PO Box 30017; Tel: 217761. Maps are available from the Department of Lands and Surveys, Malungushi House, Independence Avenue. **Livingstone** Musi-o-Tunya Road, PO Box 60342; Tel: 21404/5.

Guide books: *Visitors' Guide to Zambia*, Nicholas Plowman and Brendan Dooley (Southern Book Publishers, 1995); *Guide to Southern Africa Game and Nature Reserves*, Chris and Tilde Staurt (Struik, Cape Town).

MALAWI

Area: 118,484km²

Population: 9.8 million

Capital: Lilongwe

Languages: English is the official language; ChiChewa is the main national language.

Climate: Very pleasant. Cool in the highlands; warmer by the lake — but with cooling breezes along the lake shore. The rainy season is from November to March.

Visas: Not required by citizens of the UK and Commonwealth, Belgium, Denmark, Finland, Germany, Iceland, Ireland, Luxembourg, Madagascar, Netherlands, Norway, Portugal, South Africa, Sweden and the USA. You can no longer buy visas at the border. Visas cost £17.00 in 1995.

Foreign embassies and consulates in Lilongwe: Egypt (Tsoka Road, PO Box 30451; Tel: 44538); **Mozambique** (Commercial Bank Building; Tel: 733144 or 733803); **South Africa** (Impco Building, Lilongwe 3; Tel: 730888; Lilongwe is the best place to get South African visas as they can take weeks to come through in Harare); **UK** (PO Box 30042; Tel: 782400); **USA** (PO Box 30016; Tel: 783166); **Zambia** (Convention Drive, Lilongwe 3; Tel: 731911); **Zimbabwe** (7th Floor, Gemini House; Tel: 784988/784997).

Other red tape: Vaccination certificate for yellow fever required if travelling from an infected area.

Banks and money: The unit of currency is the kwacha. There is no longer a currency declaration form though you may be asked for a figure which is not normally checked. Banking hours are 8.00am to 1.00pm Monday to Friday.

Public holidays: New Year's Day, John Chilembwe Day (January 15), Martyrs' Day (March 3), Good Friday, Easter Monday, Labour Day (May 1), Freedom Day (June 14), Republic Day (July 6), August Holiday (first Monday), Mother's Day (second Monday in October), Christmas Day and Boxing Day (December 25 and 26).

Fuel: No problems.

Roads: Mostly good surfaced roads; a few more difficult dirt roads. Drive on the left.

Routes: The most attractive route is to follow the lake right the way down, including the section after Nkhata Bay which is now surfaced and excellent. The inland route is quicker but less scenic. The quickest route across to Zimbabwe is to go down to Blantyre and take the Tete corridor through Mozambique. The alternative is to head for Lilongwe and take the long detour through Zambia. If Mozambique is your destination, the best crossing is at Milange.

Motoring Organisation: Automobile Association, Box 333, Blantyre; Tel: 635451.

Car hire: Best to book in advance from the airports or major hotels in Blantyre, Mzuzu or Lilongwe. The best selection is in Blantyre. Insurance is not included in hire charge.

Places to visit

Kasungu National Park: In central Malawi, 165km from Lilongwe. Most famous for elephant. Has Stone and Iron Age sites which can be seen on a 10km walking trail. Best time for game is August to January. The only rest camp is being converted into a luxury lodge so if you're on a budget, plan to stay outside the park.

Livingstonia: This is probably the most beautiful place in Malawi. The road up the escarpment is not too bad despite a series of 21 hairpin bends.

Liwonde: Malawi is justly famous for the quality and reasonable prices of its wood carvings. A good tip for some of the very best is to try the ebony worker Ellard Chipojola, 8km out of Liwonde on the road to Zomba. He mostly works on commission to the big embassies, but personal callers can also buy.

Majete Game Reserve: Most of the game has been shot out but dramatic river scenery includes Mpatamanga Gorge, Kapichira Falls and Hamilton Falls. Best viewing of falls is February to July. Chalets and camping facilities at *Safari Camp* on the Shire River just south of the entrance to Majete. 67km from Blantyre. Roads closed in the rainy season.

Mulanje Plateau: Spectacular mountainous hiking area in the south of the country. Well-known for its cedar trees, you are also likely to come across rock hyrax, klipspringer and blue monkey.

Nkhotakota Wildlife Reserve: Woodland and rain forest dominate the oldest wildlife reserve in Malawi. 115km from Lilongwe. Guided walks must be arranged in advance. Camping at Chipata, Wodzi and Bua.

Nyika National Park: A cold highland area of tall grassland with patches of pine plantation and indigenous forest; good for walking. Mammals include roan antelope, reedbuck, bushbuck and zebra. Leopard sightings are regular. Best place in Africa to see rare wattled crane.

Zomba Plateau: Not as spectacular as nearby Mulanje but still an excellent hiking area.

Places to stay
The general standard of campsites in Malawi is very high. There are many to choose from, and also plenty of rest houses throughout the country, which are good cheap places to stay. It is no longer advisable to bush camp along the lake because of theft.

Blantyre: The best place to camp is *Doogall's* next to the bus station. There is a good campsite at the golf course. You can also stay at *St Michael's Mission* or camp on waste ground at the sports club.

Cape Maclear: *Stevens'* campsite is run by two brothers and is regarded as one of the best places to stop and put your feet up for a while; good food and good beer available. *Emanuelle's* is also recommended. Bilharzia has now been confirmed in Lake Malawi.

Chilumba and Chitimba: There are several private campsites on the lakeshore in this area.

Chintheche: There is an overland site at *Kande Beach*.

Dzalanyama: The *Forest Rest House* is signposted at the roundabout near the post office.

Karonga: You can camp in the grounds of the *Marina Hotel*.

Lilongwe: The official camping at the golf course has good facilities for US$4 per person. You can also camp at *The Gap* hostel 1km from the bus station.

Limbe: Camping at the *Limbe Country Club* where you can use the snooker room.

Livingstonia: The *Rest House* has excellent views and is a good place to camp.

Mulanje: The *Likumbhulu Forest Rest House*. Take the turn off near the PTC Supermarket in Mulanje village.

Mzimba: 10km from Mzimba is the *Luwawa Forest Reserve Rest House* with rooms and a communal dining area. Cook prepares your own food. Tranquil setting. There is also a rest house in the Viphya Hills about 3km south of Chikengawa about 300m of the main Mzuzu road, which has camping and cottages with hot showers.

Nkhata Bay: Rooms and camping at *Njaya Bay* and *Africa Bay*, both close to the village. The *Njaya Resort* 3km south on Chikale Bay has camping and cheap food.

Nyika National Park: The rest camp at Chelinda has chalets, standing tents and a campsite.

Senga Bay: The *Livingstonia Beach Hotel* has camping but it is very expensive. Most people prefer to camp at the nearby *Hippo Hide Resort*.

Zomba Plateau: There is a campsite here near the hotel — absolutely perfect, hot water, idyllic.

Sources of tourist information
Tourist office in Malawi:
Lilongwe Department of Tourism, PO Box 30366, Capital City; Tel: 731 711.

Guide books: *Guide to Malawi*, Philip Briggs (Bradt, 1996).

Chapter Ten

Culture and further reading

Wherever you may go, an understanding of local culture and history goes a long way to enrich your experience. Making an attempt to learn about the countries you visit is one of the main elements that distinguishes travellers from tourists.

In the case of Africa, there is such a rich cultural heritage to discover that most will only be able to scratch the surface. As you travel through Africa you will discover the diversity of this huge continent.

The visual arts are intimately tied to the craft traditions of carving and weaving. These will best be appreciated as you travel. It is easier, however, to build up a knowledge and enjoyment of music, literature and history before you leave.

MUSIC

One of the easiest and most enjoyable ways to start learning about Africa is through its music. The growing interest over recent years in modern African music is a refreshing development and means a vast catalogue of material is now available.

Most good record shops nowadays stock a reasonable selection of African records. But the very best specialist outlet remains Stern's Records (116 Whitfield Street, London W1P 5RW; Tel: 0171 387 5550). There is very little Stern's will not have in stock and the helpful staff are always ready to advise and give tips on the best selections.

Stern's publishes a monthly guide to new releases and African musicians currently on tour in Britain, called *Trade Winds*. It has also produced a book called *Stern's Guide To Contemporary African Music* (by Ronnie Graham, published by Pluto Press, ISBN 1-85305-005-9), which gives a regional guide to the music and provides detailed discographies. The most comprehensive guide to music in both Africa and many other parts of the world is *The Rough Guide to World Music* (ISBN 1-85828-017-6). Another very good guide is *African All Stars* by Chris Stapleton and Chris May (Paladin, ISBN 0-586-08781-8), which features interviews with many of the musicians concerned.

The variety and volume of African music available means that any guide to the highlights will necessarily be a partial and personal selection. This is ours.

Mali

The traditional music of Mali is dominated by the *griots* — the singers who have been charged through history with maintaining the oral literature of the area. Their pure voices typically combine with two beautiful instruments — the 21-stringed kora and the balafon (xylophone).

Since independence, Mali has also produced a number of tremendous and quite distinctive large bands. Its contemporary music typically integrates traditional patterns and styles with modern instruments. Quite a few former *griots* have made the transition.

One of the country's most successful musical exports has been Salif Keita, the singer with a voice of pure gold. If you are happy for the music to be filtered through modern Western pop, then solo albums like *Soro* and *Ko-Yan* are worth a listen. But if you want to hear Salif Keita at his best, look for the albums made between 1974 and 1984 with Les Ambassadeurs (the easiest to find is probably the 1984 release *Les Ambassadeurs Internationaux*).

One classic album from Mali that is reasonably easy to find is by Salif Keita's former group, The Super Rail Band. He left in 1973 but it was not until 1985 and the band's first UK release, *New Dimensions In Rail Culture*, that it achieved international success. This album features the voices of Sekou Kante and Lanfia Diabate.

The Super Rail Band is based in Bamako, but the second largest town of Segou boasts the excellent Super Biton Band. Their best album is simply called *Super Biton de Segou* (we bumped into the lead singer one day in a bar in the town).

When you are checking out the music of Mali, also make sure that you don't ignore the work of the magnificent Ali Farka Toure. His work is some of the most accessible to Western tastes, even though his music is based on traditional forms of the region. He reached an even wider audience with the 1994 release of *Talking Timbuktu*, recorded together with American guitarist Ry Cooder.

Guinea

Guinea shares the *griot* traditions of Mali and many musicians have moved between the two countries. Guinean *griot* Mory Kanté, for example, replaced Salif Keita in The Super Rail Band. He subsequently left and has released a number of excellent solo albums.

For many years, the national band of Guinea was the Beyla group Bembeya Jazz, which used modern electric instruments to interpret traditional themes. Although they have now disbanded, a large catalogue is available. Guinea's most popular performer of semi-acoustic Manding music is now former Bembeya Jazz singer Sekouba Bambina Diabaté. The all-woman equivalent band was Les Amazones (which was sponsored by the police force). Two of its members, Sona Diabate and M'Mah Sylla, released an excellent album in 1988, called *Sahel*, featuring acoustic instruments.

The best known musician from the country in the West is now Mory Kanté, a wonderful singer whose breakthrough album was *Akwaba Beach*. He also appears with Kanté Manfila and Balla Kalla on the rootsy *Kankan Blues* — a much more raw sound recorded at the Rubis Nightclub in Kankan, Guinea.

Ghana

The greatest musical contribution from Ghana is 'highlife' — the danceband music that has developed throughout this century with its synthesis of African and Western styles. The acknowledged king of highlife is E T Mensah. Look out for the excellent compilation of his 1950s' hits released under the title *All For You*.

A superb compilation to look out for of 1950s' and early 1960s' highlife hits is *Akomko* — it features tracks from such greats as The Black Beats, Stargazers Dance Band and Red Spot. For a taste of more recent music from Ghana, the *Guitar And The Gun* compilations are also worth a listen.

Nigeria

As well as having the largest population in Africa, Nigeria also has the most developed music industry. Its best known musical style is 'juju' — typically guitar-based bands, weaving melodies around a core of talking drums. Its best-known exponents are Ebenezer Obey, King Sunny Ade and Segun Adewale. A good introduction is Segun Adewale's *Ojo Je*.

No account of Nigerian music would be complete without reference to Fela Kuti, whose politically charged 'Afro-beat' music has made sure he has often been in conflict with the authorities —

he was even jailed for two years from 1984 to 1986. A live concert is a real experience, with as many as 40 musicians on stage putting together complex patterns of cross-rhythms.

Zaïre and Congo

The heart of African music. You will hear the sounds of 'soukous' wherever you go in Africa, with its infectious jangling guitar lines and sweet vocals.

The king of soukous, Franco, sadly died in 1990. For a taste of him at his best listen to the 1985 release *Mario* and the compilation of his 1950s' classics *Originalité*. Franco's band, OK Jazz, was for many years effectively a training school for all of the greats of Zaïre music. Thankfully, they continued after their leader's death, immediately recording the impeccable *Champions Du Zaïre* (they were rejoined for this album by former member Ndombe Opetum, whose solo albums are a delight).

One former member of OK Jazz who warrants special mention is Papa Noel — if only because he rarely receives the praise he so richly deserves. Two albums, *Nono* and *Ya Nono*, are among the most prized records in our collection. Pass them by at your peril.

Franco's great rival over many years was Tabu Ley, who has a similarly large catalogue of releases. Check also on his protégés Sam Mangwana and top female vocalist Mbilia Bel.

The 1980s saw a shift in the music of Zaïre, with the rise of a new generation of younger stars preferring to leap straight into the faster dance sections of the soukous style and dropping the traditional ballad sections. Top of this group of musicians is Kanda Bongo Man, possibly the most commonly played throughout Africa. Many of his albums are available but try *Non Stop Non Stop*. Other bands at the forefront of this new wave are Pepe Kalle's Empire Bakuba, Zaiko Langa Langa and Papa Wemba.

Gabon

An honourable mention should go to the Gabonese soukous band Les Diablotins. Their best known albums are a whole series recorded in Paris in 1983 — the best is *Les Diablotins À Paris Volume 7*.

Kenya and Tanzania

East African music is dominated by three main styles — a local version of the soukous of Zaïre, the unique sound of Swahili Taarab music and the big band sound of Tanzania. For soukous try Orchestra Virunga or Orchestra Maquis Original. For the Swahili sound, try *Black Lady and Lucky Star Musical Clubs' Nyota: Classic Taraab From Tanga*. Of the Tanzanian big bands, the all time great was Mbaraka Mwinshehe. By the time of his death in 1979 he had recorded dozens of albums. Look out particularly for the *Ukumbusho* series.

Zimbabwe

The modern music of Zimbabwe has been popularised in the West by the music of The Bhundu Boys and The Four Brothers. Albums by both are readily available. But also try to listen to Oliver Mtukutzi and Thomas Mapfumo, Zimbabwe's number one singers and band leaders. A classic collection of Mapfumo's earlier work is *The Chimurenga Singles*. For Mtukutzi try *Shoko*. A great introduction to the dance music of Zimbabwe is provided in the compilation of various artists on *Viva Zimbabwe*.

The live music scene in Harare is one of the best in the world. All the top names play most nights of the week in the various hotels, beer gardens and clubs. Make sure you build in enough time for the music when you hit town.

South Africa

Paul Simon may have popularised the music of Southern Africa with his *Graceland* album but if you enjoyed the singing featured by Ladysmith Black Mambazo, far better to check out the records from their own large output. The music of South Africa is incredibly varied with everything from traditional music to township jive and some of the best jazz in the world. There are a number of very good compilation albums of various artists — in particular *Zulu Jive* and *The Indestructible Beat of Soweto*.

LITERATURE

The best of modern African literature has brought together the oral traditions of the past with alien Western traditions of the novel and theatre. A good starting point for anyone interested in the whole range of contemporary African writing is the anthology *Voices From Twentieth-Century Africa — Griots And Towncriers* (Faber and Faber). It is a collection that will lead you towards the strongest writers of the continent. *The Traveller's Literary Companion to Africa* by Oona Strathem (In Print Publishing) takes readers on a country by country literary tour. The following is a guide to a handful of the most important writers to look at.

Chinua Achebe

Nigeria's great man of letters. The two novels that are most highly recommended were written some 30 years apart and reflect themes of very different periods in the country's history. The effect on African society of the arrival of Europeans is the subject of his first novel, *Things Fall Apart* (Heinemann), published in 1958. His subject matter moves on to the problems of corruption and governing modern Africa in his 1987 novel *Anthills Of The Savannah*.

Ayi Kwei Armah

Ghanaian novelist, much influenced by black American writers. Novels include *The Beautyful Ones Are Not Yet Born, Why Are We So Blest* and *Two Thousand Seasons*.

Sembene Ousmane

The Senegalese writer and film director is best-known for his masterpiece novel *God's Bits Of Wood* (Heinemann), which vividly tells the story of the great strike on the Bamako to Dakar railway. It is particularly recommended reading if you plan to take that route.

Stanlake Samkane

Zimbabwe's best know novelist and historian. His classic novel *On Trial for my Country* puts both Cecil Rhodes and the Matabele King Lobengula on trial to discover the truth behind the 1890 invasion of what became Rhodesia.

Wole Soyinka

This prolific Nigerian playwright and poet was awarded the Nobel prize for literature in 1986. *The Man Died* (Arrow) is a vivid account of the two and a half years he spent in prison at the time of the Nigerian civil war in the late 1960s. *A Dance In The Forests* is one of his most ambitious and powerful plays, steeped in the beliefs and background of a Yoruba heritage.

Ngugi Wa Thiong'o

Kenya's greatest writer has been highly critical of his homeland and has had many conflicts with the authorities as a result, including time in jail and in exile. Earlier books concentrated on the struggle against colonialism but he then moved on to criticise post-colonial Kenya as well — most forcefully in the classic *Devil On The Cross* (Heinemann).

Literary criticism

The South African critic, novelist and short story writer Es'kia Mphahlele is reckoned to be the father of serious study of African literature. His book *The African Image* was the first comprehensive work of African literary criticism.

One other particularly interesting work we can recommend is *Land, Freedom And Fiction* by David Maughn-Brown (Zed). This successfully weaves together the history, literature and politics of Kenya by discussing the distortions and reworking of history by writers about the Mau Mau struggle that led to independence.

SCULPTURE

Sculpture is one of Africa's greatest art forms. Wherever you travel, you are sure to come across wonderful carvings of one kind or another — each of them distinctive to their own particular region. Of course, the main tourist areas are swamped with souvenir reproductions of little merit at all. But take the trouble to visit the many national museums in Africa and you will discover a treasure trove of astounding proportions.

Zimbabwe had gained a particular reputation in the world of sculpture — with some experts claiming the country has no fewer than six of the world's top ten stone sculptors. A visit to the Chapungu Sculpture Park in Harare is an absolute must.

If you would like to get a flavour for African sculpture before you go, there is a great deal of it on display in European museums. A comprehensive guide to African sculpture that can be seen in England and Scotland has been published as *African Assortment* by Michael Pennie (Artworth). It discusses and illustrates works on display in 34 separate museums.

HISTORY AND POLITICS

African And Caribbean Politics by Manning Marable (Verso) provides a good overview to African history and politics, with particular reference to Ghana.

Kwame Nkrumah (Panaf Books). An introduction to the man who led Ghana to freedom in 1956 and also led the Pan African liberation movement.

Sékou Touré (Panaf Books, ISBN 901787-43-4). The story of Guinea's unique road to independence and of its charismatic first leader.

Thomas Sankara Speaks (Pathfinder, ISBN 0-87348-526-2). Key speeches by the inspiring and popular former president of Burkina Faso.

Not Yet Uhuru by Oginga Odinga (Heinemann, ISBN 9966-46-005-5). Autobiography of the man who went from being Kenya's vice-president under Jomo Kenyatta to a leading opposition force in exile.

Tom Mboya: The Man Kenya Wanted To Forget by David Goldsworthy (Heinemann, ISBN 0-535-96275-2). Fascinating book on the former Kenyan trade union leader and politician who was murdered in 1969. Provides an insight to Kenya's history in the 1950s and 1960s.

FURTHER READING - TRAVEL

Africa guide books

Africa On A Shoestring by Geoff Crowther (Lonely Planet, ISBN 0-86442-127-3). The classic budget travellers' guide to Africa. A mine of information, although you do have to remember that with a vast number of contributors its accuracy does vary considerably. Not very helpful on places to stay if you have your own vehicle to worry about.

Transafrique/Durch Afrika (Touring Club Suisse, ISBN 2-291-0083-7). Available in French or German, this book gives details of routes throughout Africa.

Africa Motorrad Reisen by Bernd Tesch (ISBN 3-98000099-2-0). A comprehensive German language guide to motorcycling in Africa by the experienced motorbike traveller who also runs the Globetrott Zentrale equipment shop and mail order business.

The Rough Guide series has expanded its range to cover most parts of the continent. These well researched books are always worth checking for more detailed information on individual countries and are generally also good on history and cultural background.

North Africa

Sahara Handbook by Simon and Jan Glen (Roger Lascelles, ISBN 0-903909-31-6). A wonderful guide to the desert pistes but it only covers Algeria and the northern parts of Niger and Mali - all of which have of late been out of bounds to overlanders because of threats of violence from Touareg separatists.

Desert Biking: A Guide to Independent Motorcycling in the Sahara by Chris Scott (The Travellers' Press, ISBN 1-874472-00-9). A mine of information for those planning a trip by motorbike — although specifically covering the requirements of desert biking rather than for a comprehensive African trip. Lots of advice on bikes and equipment as well as details of a number of North African routes. Available from the Travellers' Bookshop (see section *Sources of maps* on page 13).

North African Handbook (Trade and Travel Handbooks, ISBN 0-900751-58-4). Comprehensive if a little touristy.

West and Central Africa
The Rough Guide To West Africa (ISBN 1-85828-014-1). A substantial and excellent country by country guide to this extraordinary region.

West Africa (Lonely Planet, ISBN 0-86442-137-0). An alternative guide from the publisher of *Africa On A Shoestring*.

Central Africa (Lonely Planet, ISBN 0-86442-138-9). A full guide to the region from the publisher of *Africa On A Shoestring*.

East and Southern Africa
Backpacker's Africa — East and Southern by Hilary Bradt (Bradt, ISBN 0-946983-20-8). A mine of information for anyone planning walking tours in the area. Also a lot of detail on natural history.

East Africa (Lonely Planet, ISBN 0-86442-209-1). A full guide to the region from the publisher of *Africa On A Shoestring*.

East Africa with Zambia and Malawi by JR Yogerst (Roger Lascelles, ISBN 0-903909-28-6). Sympathetic and useful guide to the area.

Details of titles on individual countries are included in the reference sections on each country.

Other useful reading
Half The Earth (Pandora). Excellent collection of guidance and

personal encounters by women travellers, based on their experiences around the world.

Jupiter's Travels by Ted Simon (Penguin, ISBN 0-14-00.5410-3). The classic story of a round-the-world journey by motorbike — includes the trip from Tunis to Cape Town. As this was undertaken in 1974 to 1978, hard information is rather out of date (he rides through Libya). But it is the spirit of the book that makes it unmissable.

Mack's four-wheel drive directory, prepared by and available from Ovex (see *Suppliers*, page 60).

Two Roads To Africa by Humfrey Simons (The Travel Book Club). Rather out of date — our copy was published in 1939! It may be hard to track down but is well worth the effort. The book tells of a series of record-breaking car journeys made by Simons in the 1930s — London to Timbuktu in seven days, London to Kano in ten days, London to Nairobi in 23 days (including a 10 day delay in N'djamena) and finally London to Cape Town in 32 days. Sixty years later Simons is still an inspiration. Now, if only we had taken a Fortnum and Mason hamper and a few bottles of champagne!

Stay Alive In The Desert by K E M Melville (Roger Lascelles). All you need to know about desert survival — but in far more detail than most travellers will ever need.

Traveller's Health Guide by Dr Anthony C Turner (Roger Lascelles, ISBN 0-903909-51-0). This is the best and most comprehensive book on health.

The Traveller's Handbook by Melissa Shales (WEXAS). Packed with information on travel around the world. A bit of a mixed bag.

Senile Safari: A Journey from Durban to Alexandria by Hazel Barker. A retired couple's drive through Africa. Available from the author: 18, Lovisa Road, Birchgrove, Sydney, Australia. Tel/fax: (612) 810 5040.

WHATEVER HAPPENED TO Q 407 CPF?

The vehicle we used for our first 23,000 mile African trip in 1988 was an aging ex-military Land Rover which we bought for £4,000 — inclusive of a complete overhaul, additional fuel tanks and various other overlanding extras. After our normal share of mechanical mishaps we brought our beloved Q 407 CPF back home, using it once again a year later for a three month tour of Eastern Europe.

We then sold it to a group of New Zealanders on their way to Cape Town, who were glad of the opportunity of finding a vehicle that was already fully equipped. That was the last we heard of it until this edition of *Africa By Road* was going to press, when we received a letter from Essex County cricketer Mike Garnham who had just returned from a 22,000 mile trip to South Africa. He drove a Toyota but his brother Clive took good old Q 407 CPF.

After a full military career and three African safaris, it has to be said that the Land Rover was beginning to feel its age. But despite a host of mechanical problems along the way, they made it. 'Out of the 22,000 miles of the trip, Q 407 CPF gave us about 22 miles of trouble free motoring — but I suppose we wouldn't have it any other way,' says Mike.

And there's still life in the old thing yet. Clive sold the vehicle at the end of the trip — at a profit — to the Roman Catholic Bishop of Windhoek!

OTHER AFRICA GUIDES FROM BRADT

Africa Handbooks: Ivory Coast, Senegal, Zaire
Pocket-sized guides to the less-visited countries of Africa.

Backpacker's Africa — East and Southern Hilary Bradt
Hiking and backpacking off the beaten track, with an emphasis on natural history. Covers Eritrea, Ethiopia and Sudan, and countries south.

Guide to Eritrea Edward Paice
"A welcome addition to the bookshelf. Its easy style and beautiful photos will whet the appetite of [readers] who long for a glimpse of Africa's newest state." *Eritrea Profile*

Guide to Ethiopia Philip Briggs
Every corner of this green and fertile land is covered, with historical and cultural background as well as essential information for travellers of all budgets.

Guide to Madagascar Hilary Bradt
"The model of what a good guide book should be ... has the reader reaching for the airline timetable." *Country Life*

Madagascar Wildlife Hilary Bradt and Derek Schuurman
200 superb colour photographs and lively text evoke the unique fauna of Madagascar, the island where evolution took a different path.
(Publication May 1996)

Guide to Malawi Philip Briggs
A well-researched guide introducing Malawi's near-perfect climate, mountains and hiking trails, small game parks and, of course, Lake Malawi.
(Publication June 1996)

Guide to Mozambique Bernhard Skrodzki and others
A new edition of this guide, reflecting the developments in rebuilding the tourist infrastructure while leaving intact the attractions of its beaches and offshore islands.

Guide to Namibia & Botswana Chris McIntyre and Simon Atkins
The second edition of this guide, covering areas both on and off the

beaten track. "A sensible, practical guide to two destinations yet to be touched by mass tourism." *Independent*

Guide to South Africa Philip Briggs
Second edition of this comprehensive guide, fully updated to take into account recent political changes. Budget travel and birdwatching, walks and game parks, beaches and cities, suggested itineraries.

Guide to Tanzania Philip Briggs
A practical guide to the country, introducing many new places as well as favourites such as Kilimanjaro and Serengeti.

Guide to Uganda Philip Briggs
Lush countryside, uncrowded game parks, trekking and climbing, and Africa's most exciting wildlife experience: gorilla viewing.

Guide to Zanzibar David Else
Second edition of this guide to the islands of Zanzibar and Pemba, with expanded sections on history and the natural world.
"Essential reading" *Tanzania Bulletin*

Guide to Zimbabwe & Botswana David Else
A handy guide for budget travellers, full of hard information on where to stay, what to see and how to get around.

And then there's the rest of the world...

Send for a catalogue from Bradt Publications, 41 Nortoft Road, Chalfont St Peter, Bucks SL9 0LA, England. Tel/fax: 01494 873478

MEASUREMENTS AND CONVERSIONS

To convert	Multiply by
Inches to centimetres	2.54
Centimetres to inches	0.3937
Feet to metres	0.3048
Metres to feet	3.281
Yards to metres	0.9144
Metres to yards	1.094
Miles to kilometres	1.609
Kilometres to miles	0.6214
Acres to hectares	0.4047
Hectares to acres	2.471
Imperial gallons to litres	4.546
Litres to imperial gallons	0.22
US gallons to litres	3.785
Litres to US gallons	0.264
Ounces to grams	28.35
Grams to ounces	0.03527
Pounds to grams	453.6
Grams to pounds	0.002205
Pounds to kilograms	0.4536
Kilograms to pounds	2.205
British tons to kilograms	1016.0
Kilograms to British tons	0.0009812
US tons to kilograms	907.0
Kilograms to US tons	0.000907

5 imperial gallons are equal to 6 US gallons
A British ton is 2.240lbs. A US ton is 2,000lbs.

Temperature conversion table

The bold figures in the central columns can be read as either centigrade or fahrenheit.

Centigrade		Fahrenheit	Centigrade		Fahrenheit
-18	**0**	32	10	**50**	122
-15	**5**	41	13	**55**	131
-12	**10**	50	16	**60**	140
- 9	**15**	59	18	**65**	149
- 7	**20**	68	21	**70**	158
- 4	**25**	77	24	**75**	167
- 1	**30**	86	27	**80**	176
2	**35**	95	32	**90**	194
4	**40**	104	38	**100**	212
7	**45**	113	40	**104**	

NOTES

NOTES

NOTES

NOTES

NOTES

NOTES

INDEX